TITANIC
ON TRIAL

This edition published by Bloomsbury Publishing PLC
50 Bedford Square, London WC1B 3DP
www.bloomsbury.com

Front cover photo, top © Bridgeman Art Library and
The Illustrated London News Picture Library
Front cover photo, bottom, and back cover photo © Getty Images

ISBN 978-1-4081-4028-4

A CIP catalogue record for this book is available from the
British Library.

This book is produced using paper that is made from wood
grown in managed, sustainable forests. It is natural, renewable
and recyclable. The logging and manufacturing processes
conform to the environmental regulations of the country of
origin.

Typeset in 10.85pt Sabon
Printed in Great Britain by Clays Ltd, St Ives plc

NIC COMPTON

TITANIC
ON TRIAL

THE NIGHT THE TITANIC SANK
TOLD THROUGH THE TESTIMONIES OF HER PASSENGERS AND CREW

BLOOMSBURY

LONDON · BERLIN · NEW YORK · SYDNEY

To Anna, the unsinkable.

Contents

Timeline   7
Prologue   11
Introduction   13

SEA TRIALS AND THE MAIDEN VOYAGE
2-14 April 1912   25

COLLISION
14-15 April 1912, 11.40pm   85

IN THE BOATS
Monday 15 April 1912   193

RESCUE
Monday 15 April 1912   247

EPILOGUE
Extracts from the inquiry verdicts   273

The biographies   297

1909
31 March | *Titanic*'s keel laid at Harland & Wolff, Belfast

1911
31 May | *Titanic* is launched

1912
2 April | Sea trials; *Titanic* leaves Belfast for Southampton

3 April | *Titanic* arrives in Southampton

10 April | **8.30am** Lifeboat drill, two lifeboats lowered

12 noon *Titanic* leaves Southampton; narrowly avoids collision with *New York*

6.30pm *Titanic* arrives Cherbourg

8pm *Titanic* leaves Cherbourg

11 April | **11.30am** *Titanic* arrives Queenstown*
1.30pm *Titanic* leaves Queenstown

12 April | **12 noon** *Titanic* clocks 464 miles in 22½ hours

13 April | **12am** *Titanic* clocks 519 miles in 24 hours

2 noon Wilde on watch (senior officer)**

4am Pitman and Lowe on watch (junior officers)

6am Lightoller on watch (senior officer)

8am Boxhall and Moody on watch (junior officers)

9am *Titanic* receives ice warning from *La Caronia*

10am Murdoch on watch (senior officer)

12 noon *Titanic* clocks 546 miles in 24 hours
Pitman & Lowe on watch (junior officers)

1.35pm *Titanic* relays ice warning from *Amerika*

1.42pm *Titanic* receives ice warning from *Baltic*

2pm Wilde on watch (senior officer)

4pm Boxhall and Moody on watch (junior officers)

5.50pm *Titanic* turns 'corner' and heads west
to New York

6pm Lightoller on watch (senior officer); Pitman and
Lowe on watch (junior officers)

7.25pm *Titanic* intercepts ice warning from
Californian to *Antillian*

8pm Boxhall and Moody on watch (junior officers)

9.20pm Captain Smith retires to his cabin

9.30pm Warning sent to lookouts to watch
out for ice

9.40pm *Titanic* receives ice warning from *Mesaba*
(never reaches bridge)

10pm Murdoch on watch (senior officer)

10.21pm *Californian* forced to stop due to ice

10.55pm *Titanic* wireless operator rebuffs attempt
by *Californian* to send ice warning

11.40pm *Titanic* collides with iceberg

12 midnight Captain Smith orders wireless
operator to send CQD/SOS

* Queenstown in
Co Cork, Ireland,
is now known
as Cobh.

** Senior and
junior officers
operated an
overlapping system
of watches which
ensured that one
senior and two
junior officers were
on watch at
all times.

Monday 15 April	**12.05am** Order given to uncover lifeboats
	12.20am Order given to board lifeboats
	12.25am *Carpathia* receives CQD/SOS message
	12.45am Lifeboat No 7 launched; first distress rocket fired
	12.55am Lifeboat Nos 5 and 6 launched
	1am Lifeboat Nos 1 and 3 launched
	1.10am Lifeboat No 8 launched
	1.20am Lifeboat Nos 9 and 10 launched
	1.25am Lifeboat No 12 launched
	1.30am Lifeboat Nos 13 and 14 launched
	1.35am Lifeboat Nos 15 and 16 launched
	1.40am Collapsible C launched
	1.45am Lifeboat Nos 2 and 11 launched
	1.55am Lifeboat No 4 launched
	2.05am Collapsible D launched
	2.17am Last CQD/SOS message sent by wireless operator
	2.20am *Titanic* sinks; collapsibles A and B swept into sea
	4.10am *Carpathia* picks up first lifeboat
	5.20am *Californian* heads for *Titanic*
	8am *Californian* arrives at scene of disaster
	8.30am *Carpathia* picks up last lifeboat; service held
	8.50am *Carpathia* heads for New York
18 April	*Carpathia* arrives New York
19 April	US Inquiry begins
2 May	British Inquiry begins

Note: All times are ship's time, ie New York time + 1hr 50mins

PROLOGUE

Frederick Fleet – Lookout

I was on the lookout at the time of the collision. Lee and I relieved Symons and Jewell. They told us to keep a sharp lookout for small ice and growlers. They said they had had orders from the bridge. The sea was calm. The first part of the watch we could see the horizon, then there came a slight haze. It was nothing to talk about; it was only about two points on each side. It did not affect us, the haze; we could see just as well. I daresay it was somewhere near seven bells. The watch was nearly over.

I saw a black object right ahead, high above the water. I struck three bells as soon as I saw it. Then I went straight to the telephone, and rang them up on the bridge. They said, 'What do you see?' I said, 'Iceberg right ahead.' They said, 'Thank you.' I do not know who it was.

After I rang them up, I looked over the nest, and the ship was going to port. The iceberg struck on the starboard bow, just before the foremast, about 20 feet from the stem. The ship did not stop at all; she did not stop until she passed the iceberg. Some ice fell on the forecastle head and some on the well deck, just a little bit higher than the forecastle.

I went back to my own place again. I told Lee I thought it was a narrow shave. That was only my idea; it was such a slight noise, that is why I said it.

INTRODUCTION

The sinking of the *Titanic* was not the worst maritime disaster in history. That dubious honour belongs to the German liner *Wilhelm Gustloff*, which was sunk by a Russian submarine in January 1945, while evacuating civilians and troops from East Prussia. More than 9,000 people are thought to have died in that incident, half of whom were children. The worst peacetime maritime disaster took place as recently as December 1987, when the Philippines ferry *Doña Paz* collided with an oil tanker on her way to Manila, creating a firestorm which enveloped both ships. All but 24 of the estimated 4,000-plus passengers and crew on board both ships perished, including more than 1,000 children.* By comparison, the *Titanic*'s death toll of nearly 1,500, although horrific, seems relatively small. Yet how many people have heard of the *Wilhelm Gustloff* or the *Doña Paz*? And who hasn't heard of the *Titanic*?

One explanation for the phenomenal notoriety of the *Titanic* is purely geographical. At the beginning of the last century, Britain and the United States were the dominant world cultures – albeit one was in decline while the other was in the ascendant. By sinking two-thirds of the way across the Atlantic en route between these two great powers, the *Titanic* ensured it gained maximum media coverage, not just in the immediate aftermath, but for decades to come.

Another factor was its famous cargo. Thanks to the great fanfare that surrounded its launching, the *Titanic* carried

---

* The casualty figures for both these incidents are disputed by some, but seem to be the most accurate based on current information.

more than its fair share of celebrities. There was real estate tycoon John Astor IV, billed as 'the richest man in America', returning from honeymoon with his new wife Madeleine (who would give birth to their child four months after saying goodbye to her husband on the *Titanic*). The great British socialite Lady Lucy Duff Gordon, famed for her Lucile range of boutiques, was travelling to New York with her husband, the Olympic sportsman Sir Cosmo Duff Gordon. Ironically, given the events that would follow, they were travelling incognito as 'Mr & Mrs Morgan', to avoid the attention of the press. There were millionaire industrialist Benjamin Guggenheim and his mistress, and the co-founder of Macy's department store, Isidor Straus, along with his wife Ida, as well as various actors, politicians and titled gentry. Most of them would never be seen again.

But perhaps the main reason the sinking of the *Titanic* has exerted such enduring fascination is because it contains so many of the elements of a classic drama – or even a soap opera. There is action aplenty (a 46,000-ton ship colliding with an iceberg), there is pathos (people separated from their loved ones for ever), there are heroes (the crew staying on the ship to the last), and villains (the wealthy socialites supposedly buying their way to safety). There's courage (the engineers fighting to keep the ship afloat), there's cowardice (men rushing the lifeboats), there's romance (there were thought to be 13 honeymooners on board), and there's class conflict (First and Second Class passengers vs Third Class passengers and the stokers).

And the stories work at every level. There are big themes, such as the arrogance of man brought into check by the elements (technology vs nature), the greed of multinational companies putting corporate profit before human life (was the White Star Line trying to outdo the Cunard Line by setting a new record?), and the failure of public institutions (why did the Board of Trade not specify more lifeboats?). And then there are the minutiae of individual lives, such as the plucky suffragette who not only survived the *Titanic* but went on to witness the Russian Revolution at close quarters; the only black passenger returning with his family to Haiti to escape the racism of pre-war France; the journalist turned military attaché returning from a mission to the Vatican; and of course the numerous emigrant families travelling to America to start new lives. Even before the ship left the dock at Southampton, most of the people on board, it seemed, had a story to tell.

The intrigue surrounding the event started even before the survivors had disembarked in New York. For various reasons, the telegraph operators on the rescue ship, the *Carpathia*, were slow to send the list of survivors to the authorities, leaving anxious relatives and friends in an agony of suspense. They were even slower in releasing details of the disaster, leading to accusations of controlling the news to their own benefit, when it later emerged they had sold their stories to the *New York Times*. Already the conspiracy theorists were having a field day, and the revelations had only just begun.

Not surprisingly, the *Titanic* has been seized upon by filmmakers as ready-made material for the most emotive kind of disaster movie (after all, these are the lives of real people we're talking about, and the last survivor died as recently as 2009). At least eight movies about the *Titanic* have been made since *Saved From the Titanic* was premiered just a month after the sinking, and the ship has featured indirectly in many more – such as *The Unsinkable Molly Brown*, based (very loosely) on the life of *Titanic* survivor Margaret Brown (née Tobin). But of course none came near to achieving the success of James Cameron's 1997 *Titanic*, which for 12 years held the record of highest-grossing movie of all time. Cameron took enormous liberties with the facts, however, including showing First Officer William Murdoch shooting himself in the head – something vehemently denied by the relatives of the unfortunate man.

The United States Senate Inquiry into the sinking of the *Titanic* was set up in response to the rising hysteria that was sweeping the United States as details of the tragedy trickled out to an outraged public. The inquiry was instigated by Senator William Smith on 17 April, the day before the *Carpathia* arrived in New York, and subpoenas for key witnesses were issued the following day. On 19 April, just four days after the *Titanic* sank, the inquiry began. Bruce Ismay, Chairman and Managing Director of the White Star Line, was the first witness to testify. Over the course of 18 days, 86 people were questioned, and more than 1,000 pages of testimony were taken.

The UK soon followed suit with its own British Wreck Commissioner's Inquiry, chaired by John Bingham (aka Lord Mersey), which took place over 36 days, starting on 2 May. 95 people testified, and 1,500 pages of testimony were recorded.

Some of the issues the inquiries were set up to investigate were:

- Why did the *Titanic* ignore ice warnings from nearby ships and continue to steam at full speed into an ice zone?

- Did Ismay exert any pressure on Captain Smith to maintain or even increase the ship's speed in order to gain publicity with an earlier-than-expected arrival in New York? This was particularly important in the light of possible legal claims by victims' families against the White Star Line. According to the Limitation of Shipowners' Liability Act of 1885, the owners of the *Titanic* were only liable for the post-wreck value of the ship and could not be held responsible for any loss of life due to acts of nature or the negligence of the ship's captain and/or crew. The only exception to this rule was if the owners could be proven to have prior knowledge or any involvement in the events that led to the accident. In other words, if it could be proven that Ismay tried to influence either the course or the speed of the *Titanic*, then his company would be liable for the 1,500 lives lost.

  This rule was one of the main reasons the subpoenas were issued so quickly in the US, and why the subsequent inquiry was held so soon. The US Navy had intercepted a message from Ismay, sent while he was recuperating on board the *Carpathia*, that the surviving *Titanic* crew should be sent back to the UK at the 'earliest moment possible' after arrival in New York – possibly the very next day. He may simply have been concerned for his employees' welfare and wanted them to be reunited with their families, but there was a strong suspicion that he was trying to spirit potential witnesses away before anyone had had a chance to question them.

- Did the *Titanic* have enough lifeboats? The ship was carrying 20 lifeboats of various kinds, with a total capacity of 1,176 people. Yet its total complement of passengers and crew when it left Queenstown in Ireland (its last port of call before setting off for New York) was around 2,200. Even if the lifeboats had been fully filled, that would have left more than 1,000 people with only lifejackets to save them. Yet the ship's lifeboats had been passed by the British Board of Trade shortly before she left Southampton. How could that be?

- Were the lifeboats properly equipped?
- Were Third Class passengers unfairly discriminated against? Even before the *Carpathia* docked in New York, the lists of survivors telegraphed ahead of her raised uncomfortable questions. While 60 per cent of First Class passengers had been saved, only 42 per cent of Second Class passengers and a mere 25 per cent of Third Class passengers had escaped. Just 24 per cent of the crew had survived.
- Were the lookouts supplied with binoculars, and if not, why not?
- Were the wireless facilities on board functioning correctly, and were they used as effectively as possible? Wireless communication was then in its infancy, and it was just 13 years since the first ship-to-shore communication had been achieved by Guglielmo Marconi. The *Titanic* was fitted with the latest apparatus from Marconi, but its range was still limited to 400–500 miles by day and 1,000 miles at night. The system depended on the recipient being at a machine to receive the signal, and because the *Titanic* sank late at night, only a few ships received her CQD/SOS. Nevertheless, those lives that were saved can be directly attributed to the use of her wireless. Had the ship struck ice only a few years earlier, the outcome would have been even more horrific.

- Did nearby vessels ignore or respond too late to the *Titanic*'s calls for help? At least two ships were thought to be close to the position where the *Titanic* sank. Why did they not respond immediately to her radio messages and distress signals? In particular, the SS *Californian* was stopped in ice less than 20 (possibly even as little as five) miles away and came under heavy criticism for ignoring the ship's distress flares. The crew's excuse was that they thought they were 'company signals', used by ships to communicate non-emergency messages.

As the inquiries proceeded, the individual behaviour of both passengers and crew came under the spotlight. Predictably, the public wanted not just answers to questions but scapegoats to pin the blame on. In particular, the inquiries had to grapple with two highly contentious questions:

- Did Sir Cosmo bribe the crew of Lifeboat No 1? Sir Cosmo was widely ridiculed by the press on both sides of the Atlantic when it emerged he and his wife had been among 12 people to escape on a boat which had a capacity of 40. During the course of the night, he told the crew he would give them each £5 to cover the loss of their possessions, an act which was widely interpreted as a bribe. The boat was immediately called the 'money boat' by the press, and its passengers and crew were dragged into the media spotlight.
- Did Ismay leave the ship too soon? On his return to New York, Ismay was vilified for leaving the *Titanic* while there were still women and children on board and for not going down with the ship in true heroic fashion.

He was dubbed 'the coward of the *Titanic*' and 'J Brute Ismay', a tradition which was continued in Cameron's 1997 movie, where he is shown sneaking into a lifeboat. In fact, Ismay got away on Collapsible B, which was the 14th out of 19 lifeboats to be successfully launched. It was lowered into the water nearly an hour after the first lifeboat, and 40 minutes before the last. Not the bravest act, but not the most cowardly either.

Inevitably, the scope of both inquiries was limited by the types of witnesses available, as well as the prejudices of the times. While the US inquiry questioned 21 passengers, nearly all of those were from First Class, with just three Third Class passengers being called to give evidence. No Second Class passengers were questioned. The British inquiry fared even worse, seeing fit to question only three passengers out of 95 witnesses, all of them from First Class: Bruce Ismay, Sir Cosmo Duff Gordon and Lady Lucy Duff Gordon. Evidence of discrimination against Third Class passengers was unlikely to come from any of them.

The inquiries were flawed in other ways. The US Inquiry had the advantage of taking place when events were fresh in the witnesses' minds, and the committee went out of its way to allow people to tell their stories in their own words. On the other hand, many survivors were still in shock, and their evidence may not have been completely reliable. By the time the British Inquiry took place, the witnesses had had time to separate fact from imagination, and several used the opportunity to correct statements they had made in the US. But the delay also meant they had had time to settle on their story and to fine-tune their version of events. And, while the

British committee questioned the witnesses more rigorously than their American counterpart did, it was by no means the thorough cross-examination you would expect in a court of law.

There is also evidence that some of the witnesses may have been unduly influenced prior to the British Inquiry. At least two survivors from Lifeboat No 1 admitted to being visited by someone representing Sir Duff Gordon and being asked to sign statements about what had happened that night. One was even paid seven shillings for his troubles. Sir Duff Gordon may have simply been trying to protect his reputation by ensuring the truth was recorded, but to many it looked very much like he was interfering with the witnesses.

Whatever else, the varying accounts of all the people questioned, as well as the differences between the two inquiries themselves, suggested that absolute truth is an elusive thing indeed.

Flawed as they are, the witness testimonies nevertheless provide an extremely vivid account of one of the most dramatic events of the twentieth century. Not only are they unfiltered by any author, but they are absolutely contemporaneous and are imbued with the character of the times – good and bad. There are wonderful turns of phrase which were once the norm but now sound impossibly poetic – such as 'I will take a sky', meaning 'I will take a look'. And there are casual racial biases – such as the repeated references to 'Italians' and 'Japanese/Chinese' for anyone of a Mediterranean or Asian appearance. There is also very real drama in the inquiry itself as new evidence is revealed – most notably when a previously unmentioned message from the *Mesaba*, warning of ice directly in the *Titanic*'s path, is discovered halfway through the British Inquiry.

For many years, the transcripts of these accounts were not available to the general public and were only available to researchers with some difficulty. But recently, both inquiries have been transcribed by a group of enthusiasts and made available on the web (www.titanicinquiry.org). It is these transcripts that this book is based on. Thousands of pages of eyewitness accounts have been sifted through, and the most relevant and interesting passages extracted. These have then been reassembled, more or less chronologically, to tell the story of the *Titanic* using entirely the first-hand accounts – the first time this has been done, as far as we know.

Most of the accounts come from the survivors themselves, but both inquiries also included testimonies from people involved in the ship in other ways – such as the wireless manufacturer Guglielmo Marconi, and representatives from the ship's builders Harland & Wolff – as well as several expert witnesses. The most prominent among these was none other than the explorer Ernest Shackleton, then at the peak of his career, and brought in to advise on the nature of icebergs. Extracts from these non-survivor accounts have been included in this book, set in bold italic to differentiate them. Biographies of all the survivors quoted in this book, as well as several of the expert witnesses, can be found on page 297.

As well as the two official inquiries, a few excerpts have been extracted from the Limitation of Liability Hearings, which are transcripts of a lawsuit against the Oceanic Steam Navigation Company, owners of the White Star Line. Like the evidence given during the official inquiries, these depositions were made under oath, and therefore carry more weight than eyewitness accounts published in other forms. The most dramatic of these are the statements given by Elizabeth Lines and Emily Ryerson, which explicitly challenge Ismay's assertion that they were not trying to make a fast crossing.

Titanic experts will see that some of the accounts have been edited. Mostly, this has consisted of shuffling the order of sentences around to make narrative sense; occasionally it has meant 'reconstructing' sentences which have been broken up in the interviewing process. In all cases, this editing process has been kept to a minimum to ensure that these accounts are, as much as possible, told in the witnesses' own words – grammatical errors and all. Some witnesses were, in any case, not native English speakers, such as Secretary to the Chef, Frenchman Paul Mauge, who came out with the immortal line: 'But the chef was too fat I must say [...] He could not jump.'

For, above all, the sinking of the *Titanic* is a human story. It is a story about ordinary people in an extraordinary situation. How they cope with that experience – be it through bravery, cunning, cowardice or even, in a few cases, humour – is what defines them as human beings. In that sense, it's a story that touches us all.

PART ONE

SEA TRIALS
AND THE MAIDEN
VOYAGE

2-14 April 1912

'The position was taken up that
the ship was looked upon as
practically unsinkable'

Bruce Ismay – Managing Director, International Mercantile Marine

When we built the *Titanic*, we wanted the very best ship the builders could possibly produce. She was the latest thing in the art of shipbuilding; absolutely no money was spared in her construction.

The *Titanic* was built in Belfast by Messrs Harland & Wolff of Belfast. They built practically the whole fleet of the White Star Line – the *Olympic* and the *Baltic* and all those ships. Messrs Harland & Wolff have carte blanche to build the ship and put everything of the very best into her. After they have spent all the money they can on the ship, they add on their commission to the gross cost, which we pay them. We would naturally try to get the best ship we possibly could.

The ship cost $7,500,000. She was insured for $5,000,000.

When you build a ship, you have to start building her probably five or six years before you want her. Messrs Harland & Wolff prepare the plans. They are then submitted to us, to the directors of the White Star Line or to the manager of the White Star Line. They are carefully gone through with the representatives from the shipbuilders. They try to make suggestions to improve those plans. They are taken back and thoroughly thrashed out again, and they are submitted, I should be afraid to say how often.

We were very anxious indeed to have a ship which

would float with her two largest watertight compartments full of water. What we wanted to guard against was any steamer running into the ship and hitting her on a bulkhead, because if the ship ran into her broadside on and happened to hit her right on a bulkhead, that would open up two big compartments, and we were anxious to guard against the possibility of that happening. The *Olympic* and *Titanic* were so constructed that they would float with the two largest compartments full of water. I think I am right in saying that there are very few ships of which the same can be said.

The *Titanic* left Belfast, as far as I remember, on the first of April.* She underwent her trials, which were entirely satisfactory.

Harold Sanderson – Co-director, White Star Line

The Titanic *was built with an unusual number of watertight bulkheads; 15 in all. Those bulkheads were of special construction, carried up as much as possible in one fair line, and they were built in excess of the requirements of Lloyd's. The plating and connections were also of special strength, and in excess, I am told, of what Lloyd's requirements would have been. She had a double bottom, which was carried nine-tenths of the way. That double bottom, instead of terminating at the bottom of the bilge, which is ordinarily the case, was carried up to the top of the bilge. The pumping arrangements were exceptional, each boiler compartment having its own equipment, which is quite an unusual thing of the kind.*

---

* This is the date the *Titanic* was supposed to leave for sea trials. Due to adverse weather, the trials were postponed to the following day.

Charles Lightoller – Second Officer

Sea trials were held on Belfast Lough. The ship was run a certain distance on a comparatively straight course and back again, over approximately four hours – two out and two back. For a ship of that size, she went at a fair speed.

When the ship was built, we only expected her to go 21 knots, therefore all over 21 we thought very good. I do not know what her speed was on the trial trip, but we understood she would eventually go faster when she was tuned up. I dare say we wanted her to go at her maximum speed at some time or other, and naturally we talked; we wondered what her maximum speed would eventually be.

I saw the watertight doors myself tested, and they were all in perfect working order.

Harold Lowe – Fifth Officer

We arrived in Belfast and went around everything, taking stock of everything on board the ship, and also noting the condition of these things. We went around the lifeboats. The odd numbers, Nos 1, 3, 5, 7, 9, 11, 13 and 15, were on the starboard side of the ship, and the even numbers were on the port side.

Mr Moody and myself took the starboard boats, and Mr Pitman and Mr Boxhall took the port boats, and we overhauled them; that is to say, we counted the oars, the rowlocks, or thole pins, and saw there was a mast and sail, rigging, gear, and everything else that fitted in the boats, and also that the biscuit tin was all right, and that there were two water beakers in the boat, two bailers, two plugs and the steering rowlock. There is a compass, a light and oil to burn for eight hours. Everything was absolutely correct with the exception of one dipper. A dipper is a long thin can, an inch and a quarter diameter, which you dip into the water breaker and draw the water. That was the only thing that was short out of our boats.

These are the outside boats, the boats that hang on the ship's side. Then there are two collapsibles on each side, two on port and two starboard, and we examined them.

Everything was absolutely correct; I will swear to that.

Harold Bride – Assistant Telegraphist

I went up to Belfast to join the *Titanic* and test the Marconi apparatus. We had a special sending apparatus which doubled our range; during the daytime, we reckoned to be able to do 400 miles. Coming around from Belfast to Southampton, there were messages transmitted for Mr Ismay regarding the speed of the ship. They were sent to the White Star offices at Liverpool and Southampton, saying generally that the trials of the speed of the ship were very favourable.

Guglielmo Marconi – Chairman, Marconi International

The Titanic *was equipped by my company. The wireless equipment on board was a fairly powerful set, capable, I should say, of communicating 400 or 500 hundred miles during the daytime and much further during the night-time. At night it would very often be capable of communicating 1,000 miles, with accuracy. It was the latest apparatus for that purpose.*

The wireless apparatus was in duplicate, and it had a spare battery by means of which it could be operated in case of the current being cut off from the dynamos of the ship, consequent upon the flooding of the engine room. This was done in consultation with the White Star Line.

Charles Lightoller – Second Officer

Almost immediately after taking on board a few things that had been left behind – requisites down in the galley, cooking apparatus, a few chairs, and such things as that – we proceeded toward Southampton. From Belfast round to Southampton, we averaged about 18 knots. Her greatest speed was perhaps 18½ knots; I do not think she got much higher than that.

There, the ship was heeled for stability. The builders knowing the exact weights on board, additional weights are placed on each side of the ship. A pendulum is suspended in the most convenient place in the ship with a plumb on the end of it, and a method of registering the difference with the plumb line. A number of men then transfer the weights from one side of the ship to the other, bringing all the weight on one side and transferring the whole of it back again; and with this, I believe, the builders are able to draw up a stability scale.

The Southampton Board of Trade officer, Captain Maurice Clarke, carried out the requisite tests. We call him a nuisance because he is so strict, because he makes us fork out every detail. He would insist upon everything that contributes to the ship's life-saving equipment being absolutely brought out on deck every time. Life-preservers throughout the ship, all the boats turned out, uncovered, all the tanks examined, all the breakers examined, oars counted, rudders tried, all the davits tried. The boats lowered, put in the water, and pulled out, and brought back again, and if he was not satisfied, sent back again. Lifebelts in every room, in every compartment, where, as we say, there was habitation, where a man could live – including steerage and the crew's quarters. There was innumerable detail work.

Harold Lowe – Fifth Officer

After the general muster at 8.30, Mr Moody, the sixth officer, and myself manned two boats. We were lowered down on the starboard side with a boat's crew. The boats were manned, and we rowed around a couple of turns, and then came back and were hoisted up and had breakfast, and then we went about our duties. I should say it would take 20 minutes to half an hour. There is not only practice in the rowing of the boats, but there is also practice in the lowering away and clearing. It would take about half an hour, hoisting and lowering.

No boat drill took place from the time of departure. A fire drill did take place, and it always does take place. There are so many hoses on each deck, and the water service is on, and the hoses are manned by the men, and the commander sends word along, 'That will do for fire exercise', and then we switch off the water.

Alexander Carlisle – Former Managing Director, Harland & Wolff

Personally I consider there were not enough boats. I have said so over and over again. I have said it in the works. I said it at the Merchant Shipping Advisory committee, before either of the ships went to sea. I said it to the entire meeting; whoever was present heard me say it. I said I thought there ought to be a very much larger number. I

*thought there ought to be three on each set of davits. 48
boats, instead of 16.*

When working out the designs of the Olympic *and the*
Titanic *I put my ideas before the davit constructors, and got
them to design me davits which would allow me to place,
if necessary, four lifeboats on each pair of davits. They all
will carry four. I see no difficulty. One would be hanging
outboard by the spars, the same as the P&O Company
generally carry their boats.*

*When I pointed out that I expected the Board of Trade
and the Government would require much larger boat
accommodation on these large ships, I was authorised then
to go ahead and get out full plans and designs, so that if the
Board of Trade did call upon us to fit anything more, we
would have no extra trouble or extra expense.*

*I came over from Belfast in October 1909, with these
plans that were worked out, and also the decorations, and
Mr Ismay and Mr Sanderson and Lord Pirrie and myself
spent about four hours together. That was over the whole
of the decorations; the lifeboat part I suppose took five
or ten minutes. I showed them the advantage, and that
it would put them to no expense or trouble in case the
Board of Trade called upon them to do something at the
last minute.*

*Mr Ismay quite agreed that it would be a good thing
to make preparations for supplying the larger number of
boats. How many boats would ultimately be fitted in the
ship before she left Liverpool, Belfast, or Southampton was
not settled when I was present, nor did I hear it. I merely
ordered the davits after that. I would say they were entirely
waiting to see what the Board of Trade would require.*

I showed them the plans of my proposals; I could not do any more.

The White Star and other friends give us a great deal of liberty, but at the same time we cannot build a ship any bigger than they order, or put anything in her more than they are prepared to pay for. We have a very free hand, and always have had; but I do not think that we could possibly have supplied any more boats to the ship without getting the sanction and the order of the White Star Line.

Bruce Ismay – Managing Director, IMM

The *Titanic* conformed to the Board of Trade requirements; in fact she was largely in excess of the requirements. If she had not been fully equipped, she could not have sailed. The ship receives a Board of Trade passenger certificate; otherwise she would not be allowed to carry passengers. You could not sail your ship without it.

The lifeboat requirements are based on the tonnage of the ship. The *Titanic* had more boats than were necessary by the Board of Trade regulations.

The design for lifeboats would be submitted to us by the shipbuilders. I never saw any design which showed the *Titanic* fitted up for forty boats, and I do not know that anybody connected with the White Star Line saw such a design. I have no recollection of seeing any such design.

The position was taken up that the ship was looked upon as practically unsinkable; she was looked upon as being a lifeboat in herself. This was due to the bulkheads and the power of flotation she had in case of accident. We carried lifeboats because we might have to use them to pick up a crew from another ship. Or landing passengers, in the case of the ship going ashore. Or if the passengers had to leave the ship on account of fire.

Alfred Young – Professional Member, Board of Trade
It occurred to me that it is manifestly impracticable to provide boats sufficient in number and capacity to accommodate the entire number of passengers and crew that the modern large liner can carry. What avail would a large number of boats be if there were not enough deckhands to properly tend them when launched in an emergency? Taking it for granted that a considerable number of persons must be excluded from the boats under any circumstances, what we have to do apparently is to seek for a number of boats which will afford an assurance of safety to the travelling public.

'The weather was very pleasant.
There was very little wind'

Arthur Peuchen – First Class Passenger

The day was fine. Shortly after leaving our pier, our wash or suction caused some trouble at the head of the pier that we were going around, at which there were two or three boats of the same company as ours. There was excitement on the wharves when the larger ship commenced to snap one or two of her moorings. But I do not think there was any accident.

The smaller boat, I think, was the *New York*. She drifted away, not being under steam and having no control of herself. The result was that she was helpless. At first she drifted to our stern, and then afterwards she drifted along and got very near our bows. I think we stopped our boat and we were simply standing still. They got a tug or two to take hold of the *New York* and they moved her out of harm's way. I should think we were delayed probably three-quarters of an hour by this trouble. Then we moved out of the harbour.

The weather up to the time of Sunday was pleasant. There was very little wind; it was quite calm. Everything seemed to be running very smoothly on the steamer, and there was nothing that occurred. In fact, it was a very pleasant voyage up to Sunday evening. We were all pleased with the way the new steamer was progressing and we had hopes of arriving in New York quite early on Wednesday morning.

Bruce Ismay – Managing Director, IMM

The *Titanic* left Southampton at 12 o'clock on Wednesday the tenth of April. She arrived in Cherbourg that evening, having run over at 68 revolutions. We left Cherbourg and proceeded to Queenstown. We arrived there, I think, about midday on Thursday. We ran from Cherbourg to Queenstown at 70 revolutions. After embarking the mails and passengers, we proceeded at 70 revolutions. I am not absolutely clear what the first day's run was, whether it was 464 miles or 484 miles.

The second day the number of revolutions was increased. I think the number of revolutions on the second day was about 72, and I think we ran 519 miles. The third day the revolutions were increased to 75, and I think we ran 546 or 549 miles. The weather during this time was absolutely fine, with the exception, I think, of about ten minutes' fog one evening.

Harold Lowe – Fifth Officer

The service of the junior officers was pretty well general; to do anything we were told to do. We worked out things; worked out the odds and ends, and then submitted them to the senior officer. We are there to do the navigating part so the senior officer can be and shall be in full charge of the bridge and have nothing to worry his head about. We have all that, the junior officers; there are four of us. The three senior officers are in absolute charge of the boat. They simply have to walk backward and forward and look after the ship, and we do all the figuring and all that sort of thing in our chart room. They have nothing to worry themselves about.

We have the log every two hours, and we are all the time navigating. We do not take observations once a day; we perhaps take 25 or 30 observations a day. The quartermaster takes the log. We ring him up, and we see how she is doing with the revolutions, whether she is going faster or going slower; and you will find a corresponding difference in the log. You send it in with the chit.*

We were working out a slip table, to see how many turns of the engine it would require to do so many knots. It is a table based upon so many revolutions of engines and so much per cent slip; and you work that out, and that gives you so many miles per hour. This table extended from the rate of 30 revolutions a minute to the rate of 85 and from a percentage of 10 to 40 per cent slip; that is, minus.

I was told that Mr Ismay was on board, and two or three more, but I do not know who they were; and some of Messrs Harland & Wolff's people. I would not know them if I did see them, because I am a stranger in this part. You must remember this is my first voyage across here, and I do not know.

Bruce Ismay – Managing Director, IMM

I had no business to bring me to New York at all. I simply came in the natural course of events, as one is apt to in the case of a new ship, to see how she works, and with the idea of seeing how we could improve on her for the next ship which we are building in Belfast. I was there to inspect the ship and see if there were any defects in her, with the idea of not repeating them in the other ship. And to observe the ship.

My quarters were on B deck, just aft of the main companionway. The sun deck is the upper deck of all. Then we have what we call the A deck, which is the next deck, and

---

*A 'chit' was simply a written report for the ship's log – literally a chit of paper.

then the B deck. I was never outside the First Class passenger accommodations on board the ship. I never went in any part of that ship that any other First Class passenger had not a perfect right to go to. I intended to go around the ship before we arrived at New York.

The only time the captain dined with me was on Friday night. He left us immediately after dinner. I went into my own room with the people who were dining with me, and we sat in my room and played bridge. But I never saw the captain after we left the restaurant. He never came near my room.

So far as the navigation of the ship was concerned, I looked upon myself simply as an ordinary passenger. I did not pay my fare. But I think if I had crossed on any other ship going across the Atlantic, I should have travelled exactly on the same terms.

'You could smell the ice'

George Turnbull – Deputy Manager, Marconi International
Message sent by La Caronia *on 14 April at 7.10am [9am ship's time]:*

'*Captain,* Titanic. *West-bound steamers report bergs, growlers, and field ice in 42° N, from 49° to 51° W. April 12. Compliments. Barr.*'

Message sent by Titanic *on 14 April at 1.26pm:*

'*Captain,* Caronia. *Thanks for message and information. Have had variable weather throughout. Smith.*'

Harold Bride – Assistant Telegraphist
On Sunday, Mr Phillips and myself had had a deal of trouble, owing to the leads from the secondary of the transformers having burnt through inside the casing and made contact with certain iron bolts holding the woodwork and frame together, thereby earthing the power to a great extent. After binding these leads with rubber tape, we once more had the apparatus in perfect working order, but not before we had put in nearly six hours' work.

Owing to this trouble, I had promised to relieve Mr Phillips on the following night at midnight instead of the usual time, two o'clock, as he seemed very tired. Usually Mr Phillips started the watch at eight o'clock at night, and he remained on watch until two o'clock in the morning. I kept the watch from two o'clock to eight o'clock in the morning. During the day, we relieved each other to suit each other's convenience, but a constant watch was kept.

There may be messages from passengers on other ships,

there may be master's service messages, or there may be franked messages from the office, or from the captain of another ship to our captain. Master's service messages deal with the navigation of the ship, and anything relating to the shipping company. They are free between ship and ship. If Captain Smith was sending a message to a passenger it would go free of charge, because the Marconi Company allow the captain and the officers of the ship a grant of so many words free of charge.

To send a message, the passenger goes to the purser's office, is handed a form, and writes down his telegram. The purser charges him for it, and, incidentally, it works back to the Marconi Company. The money is paid to the purser on the majority of ships. In the case of the *Titanic*, the message was sent up by a pneumatic tube to our office.

A message to the captain is written on a piece of paper and enclosed in an envelope. We are close to the captain on the *Titanic*. It is our duty to ascertain, somehow or other, that the message is delivered to the captain; to give it to a responsible man, such as the captain's steward, or take it ourselves.

I am paid by the Marconi Company. I am paid a fixed salary of £4 a month by Marconi and £2 2s 6d a month by the White Star Line.

Charles Lightoller – Second Officer

Captain Smith came on the bridge during the time that I was relieving First Officer Mr Murdoch. In his hands he had a wireless message, a Marconigram. He came across the bridge, and holding it in his hands told me to read it. It was about 12.45 as near as I can remember. The actual wording of the message I do not remember, and I cannot remember the ship it came from.* But it had reference to ice.

That is the first information about ice I have any recollection of.

I particularly made a mental note of the meridians: 49 to 51 W. I did not calculate exactly how far from the ice we were at that time. I ran it roughly off in my mind – the degrees of longitude. We take very little notice of the latitude because it conveys very little with regard to ice; ice tends to set north and south, so you cannot rely on latitude. I roughly figured out we would be there at about half past nine. I knew that we should not be in the vicinity of the ice before I came on deck again.

When Mr Murdoch came back from lunch, I mentioned the ice to him. I really could not say whether it was fresh news to him or not; I should judge that it would have been, but I really could not say from his expression – not from what I remember.

The weather was perfectly clear and fine, the sea comparatively smooth. There was not a cloud in the sky. No moon. I cannot remember the compass course, but I know from calculations made afterwards that we were making S 86 W true.**

As far as I could tell, her speed was normal. Full speed. We were steaming, as near as I can tell from what I remember of the revolutions – I believe they were 75 – and I think that works out at about 21½ knots. As a rule, at the end of the watch, the junior officer rings up the engine room and

---

* This was the message from *La Caronia*, received several hours earlier.
** In modern parlance, this equates to 266°.

obtains the average revolutions for the preceding watch. It is entered up in the log book, and anyone who wishes to know can merely ask and the information is given him. I could not say where I got that from, but it is in my mind that it was about 75 revolutions. On one occasion I have a recollection of one side turning 76, not necessarily both sides though.

Frederick Barrett – Leading Fireman
The first two days when she left Southampton, there were nine boilers out. The next two days, there were eight not lit. On Sunday, there were five not lit.

75 revolutions was my order. I got the order on Saturday. The second engineer gives orders to me of the revolutions he wants, and I pass the word to all my other men. They ring through on the telephone. I could not tell you whether we reached 75 because it is a long way to walk – I never used the passage to the engine room. But I heard no complaints.

There were two or three main boilers lit up on the Sunday morning, but I could not tell you whether they were connected with the others or not. When you light a boiler up, it will take 12 hours before you can connect it with the others to get steam on. Those two or three were lit up in No 2 section on the Sunday morning, as near as I could say, eight o'clock in the morning. My other leading hand, Ferris, is in charge of that section and he told me this when he came by.

Henry Stengel – First Class Passenger
As is usual in these voyages, there were pools made to bet on the speed that the boat would make. On Sunday, after the whistle blew, the people who had bet went to the smoking

room, and came out and reported she had made 546 miles. I figured then that, at 24 hours a day, we had made 22¾ knots. But I was told I was mistaken; that I should have figured 25 hours, on account of the elapsed time, which made it almost 22 knots. At the same time a report came from the engine room that the engines were turning three revolutions faster than at any time on the voyage.

Charles Hendrickson – Leading Fireman
The ship was travelling at 21 knots. I know because of the revolutions she was turning; they were 76 revolutions. The second engineer told me. I made it my business to find out.

Bruce Ismay – Managing Director, IMM
I understand it has been stated that the ship was going at full speed. The ship never had been at full speed. The full speed of the ship is 78 revolutions. So far as I am aware, she never exceeded 75 revolutions. She had not all her boilers on. None of the single-ended boilers were on. It was our intention, if we had fine weather on Monday afternoon or Tuesday, to drive the ship at full speed.

I heard one gentleman say that he expected the ship to go 25 knots. All that we expected the *Titanic* to do was to have the same speed as the *Olympic*. I should call the *Olympic* a good 22-knot ship. She can do better under very favourable circumstances. I think she can work up to 22½ or perhaps 22¾ as a maximum. We did not expect the *Titanic* to make any better speed than that.

I had no conversation with the captain with regard to speed or any point of navigation whatever. Or as to the time of landing. I was never in the captain's room the whole voyage over, and the captain was never in my room. I never had any conversation with the captain except casual conversation on the deck.

The only man I spoke to in regard to it was the chief engineer, Mr Bell, when the ship was at anchor in Queenstown Harbour. The reason we discussed it at Queenstown was this, that Mr Bell came into my room; I wanted to know how much coal we had on board the ship, because the ship left after the coal strike was on, and he told me. We only had 6,000 tons of coal leaving Southampton; sufficient to enable her to reach New York, with about two days' spare consumption. The ship's consumption was 820 tons on the day, depending on whether you were going east or west. If you are going west, your day is 24 hours, and if you are going east, your day is 23 hours and some minutes.

I then spoke to him about the ship and I said it is not possible for the ship to arrive in New York on Tuesday. Therefore there is no object in pushing her. We will arrive there at five o'clock on Wednesday morning, and it will be good landing for the passengers in New York, and we shall also be able to economise our coal. We did not want to burn any more coal than we needed. I said to him then, we may have an opportunity of driving her at full speed on Monday or Tuesday if the weather is entirely suitable. I knew if the weather was suitable either on the Monday or the Tuesday the vessel would go at full speed for a few hours. I presume the boilers would have been put on.

The *Titanic* being a new ship, we were gradually working her up. When you bring out a new ship you naturally do not start her running at full speed until you get everything working smoothly and satisfactorily down below. She was going 75 revolutions on Saturday. That, of course, is nothing near her full speed.

Herbert Pitman – Third Officer
I understood we had not quite sufficient coal; there was not sufficient there on board to drive her on at full speed. I had that from one of the engineers. I knew we had not. We were intending to arrive in New York Wednesday morning, from the beginning of the trip. That was the general impression throughout the ship.

George Turnbull – Deputy Manager, Marconi International
Message sent by Amerika *on 14 April at 11.45am [1.35pm ship's time]:*

'To the steamer Titanic *MSG via Cape Race to the Hydrographic Office, Washington. "D. S. Amerika passed two large icebergs in 41° 27' N, 50° 8' W on 14th April. Knuth."'*

The position of the Amerika *was such that she was not at that moment within range of a coast station, but she was in communication with another ship, which happened to be the* Titanic, *which would very shortly be within range of that coast station. Therefore, she asked the* Titanic *to relay the message to the Hydrographic Office in Washington, via the Cape Race wireless station. The message was received the same day by Cape Race.*

Elizabeth Lines – First Class Passenger
On Saturday afternoon, after the midday meal, I went into the lounge to have my coffee. Captain Smith and Mr Ismay came in after I was seated, and went to a table near me. They

had coffee and liqueurs and cigars. Mr Ismay lived in New York a number of years ago, and I had seen him there. I knew him by sight, but I did not know him personally. Captain Smith was in uniform, and Mr Ismay was in ordinary clothes. They stayed and conversed for at least two hours.

At first I did not pay any attention to what they were saying, they were simply talking and I was occupied. Then my attention was arrested by hearing the day's run discussed, which I already knew had been a very good one in the preceding 24 hours. I heard Mr Ismay – it was Mr Ismay who did the talking – I heard him give the length of the run, and I heard him say, 'We made a better run today than we did yesterday, we will make a better run tomorrow. Things are working smoothly, the machinery is bearing the test, the boilers are working well, they are standing the pressure.' They went on discussing it. Mr Ismay gave the runs made on certain days by the *Olympic* on its maiden voyage and compared them with the runs made by the *Titanic* on the first days. Then I heard him make the statement: 'We will beat the *Olympic*, and get in to New York on Tuesday.'

Mr Ismay was very positive, one might almost say dictatorial. He asked no questions. I did not hear the captain say anything; I saw him nod his head a few times in assent. Then Mr Ismay said, 'Come on, Captain, we will get somebody and go down to the squash courts.'

Bruce Ismay – Managing Director, IMM
We have a mail contract for carrying the mails from Southampton to New York, for which we receive a lump-sum payment of £70,000 a year; $350,000 a year. We carry the mails from Southampton. We pick up the mails at

Southampton, and then we go on to Queenstown and pick up any mails that are there, and land them in New York. We are supposed to use the fastest ships we have in our fleet for the conveyance of the mails. I think there is a minimum; or we are not allowed to put the mails into ships that will go less than 16 knots, or something like that. It must have done so; because, naturally, they would not give a contract to any ships which were slow ships.

It all helps, but I do not think that £70,000 a year would induce anybody to build big ships.

George Turnbull – Deputy Manager, Marconi International
Message sent by the Baltic *on 14 April at 11.52am [1.42pm ship's time]:*

'*Captain Smith,* Titanic. *Have had moderate variable winds and clear fine weather since leaving. Greek steamer* Athenai *reports passing icebergs and large quantities of field ice today in lat. 41° 51' N, long. 49° 52' W. Last night we spoke German oil-tank steamer* Deutschland, *Stettin to Philadelphia, not under control, short of coal, lat. 40° 42' N long. 55° 11' W. Wishes to be reported to* New York *and other steamers. Wish you and* Titanic *all success. Commander.*'

Message sent by the Titanic *on 14 April at 12.55pm:*

'*Commander,* Baltic. *Thanks for your message and good wishes; had fine weather since leaving. Smith.*'

Bruce Ismay – Managing Director, IMM
Just before lunch on the Sunday, the captain handed me a Marconi message which he had received from the *Baltic*. It was a report of ice and this steamer being short of coal. I

think he handed it to me simply as a matter of information, a matter of interest. He said not a word. I glanced at it very casually – I was on A deck talking to some passengers – and I put it in my pocket. I have crossed with Captain Smith before, and he has handed me messages which have been of no importance at all.

The lunch bugle went almost immediately, and I went down to lunch alone. In the afternoon, I spoke to Mrs Thayer and Mrs Ryerson. I cannot recollect what I said. I think I read part of the message to them about the ice and the steamer that was broken down; short of coal she was. I did not think it was of special importance at all.

The only conversation I had with Captain Smith was in the smoking room that night. As he walked out of the smoking room he asked me if I had the Marconi message, and I said, yes, I had, and I gave it to him. I think it was ten minutes or a quarter past seven. I had never been on the bridge during the whole trip. He said he wished to put it up in the officers' chart room. I presume he put it up for the officers' information. We had no further conversation at all.

Emily Ryerson – First Class Passenger

I was down in my cabin until quite late, and then I went on deck; it was the first time I had been on deck in the daytime. I went up and walked up and down with a friend, Mrs John Thayer, and then went and sat down by the companionway. It was around six o'clock, and the sky was quite pink. The weather was perfectly beautiful; it was very clear, and there was no wind – but it was very cold.

My husband went to have a talk and walk with Mr Thayer, and Mr Ismay came up and spoke to me. We had met before, and I knew him perfectly by sight. He was in a dark blue coat, and had no hat on. I think he asked if our staterooms were comfortable, and if we had everything we wanted. My husband had told me when we came on at Cherbourg that Mr Ismay had been very kind and had offered us an extra stateroom, which we had, and an extra steward who waited on us.

He produced from his pocket a telegram blank on which some words were written in typewriting, and he said that we were in among the icebergs. He said, as he held the telegram out in front of me, 'We are in among the icebergs.' I don't remember what the telegram said; it had the word '*Deutschland*'.

Something was said about speed, whether I said it I don't know, but he said, 'We are not going very fast, 20 or 21 knots, but we are going to start up some extra boilers this evening.' How many there were I don't know, it was two or three. I know the fact of the extra boilers because I didn't know what it meant except going faster.

I said, 'What is the rest of the telegram?' He said, 'It is the *Deutschland*, wanting a tow, not under control,' or something of that sort. I remember saying, 'What are you going to do about that?' and he said they weren't going to do anything about it.

I can't remember his exact words; the impression left on my mind was that: 'We are going to get in and surprise everybody.' I don't know whether he used the word 'record', but it was left on my mind that we had no time to delay aiding other steamers. I wouldn't say he said those words, but his attitude, or his language, assumed that we were trying to make a record.

There was some discussion about when we would arrive, and my impression was it would be very late Tuesday night, or early Wednesday morning, because I discussed it with my husband after I went downstairs and the question was what we would do if we got in so very late. But at the time the conversation had no importance to me; I was very much over-burdened with other things that were on my mind. I carried on the conversation merely to keep the ball going, and the words have faded from my mind.

He sat down beside us, and he talked about one or two other things I don't remember. He was not a friend of mine, and I didn't want to talk to him. He was talking to Mrs Thayer and me, and presently Mr Ryerson and Mr Thayer came up, and he stood up and went downstairs. He wasn't talking to us over ten minutes. As we went down, he was at the foot of that first flight, near the restaurant.

Harold Bride – Assistant Telegraphist

Communication had been established with the *Baltic* on Sunday afternoon, and compliments were exchanged between the two commanders, and the state of the weather. I have no knowledge of a wireless message received from the *Amerika* regarding any iceberg. There may have been, received by Mr Phillips, but I did not see one myself.

The first and last message about ice I recollect on the fourteenth of April was from the *Californian*. It is the only one I recollect. The time was between five and half past in the afternoon, ship's time. It stated that the *Californian* was passing close to large icebergs and gave the latitude and longitude.

The *Californian* had called me, with an ice report. I was

rather busy just for the minute, writing up an abstract of all the telegrams sent the day before, and I did not take it. She did not call again. About half an hour later, she transmitted the ice report to the *Baltic*,* and as she was transmitting it to the *Baltic*, I took it down. I made it on a slip of paper, and delivered it to the officer on the bridge.

It was the only ice message, but it was not the only message for Captain Smith. There were messages coming through for Captain Smith all the time, but they did not affect the navigation of the ship. They were invariably delivered to the captain.

As to what Mr Phillips received, I cannot say.

Cyril Evans – Marconi Officer, SS *Californian*

*It was a message reporting ice. 'To Captain, Antillian, 6.30pm apparent ship's time**; latitude, 42° 3' N; longitude, 49° 9' W. Three large bergs 5 miles to southward of us. Regards. Lord.' I was sending to the Antillian and the Titanic called me up and we exchanged signals, we exchanged an official TR [time rush]. We call it a TR when a ship gets in communication with another. I said, 'Here is a message; an ice report.' He said, 'It's all right, old man. I heard you send to the Antillian.' He said, 'Bi.' That is an expression used among ourselves. It means to say 'enough' or 'finished'. It does not mean goodbye.*

---

*Bride is mistaken. The message was actually being transmitted to the *Antillian*.

** This message was sent at 5.35pm NY time, i.e. 7.25pm ship's time.

'In the event of meeting ice, there are many things we look for'

Frederick Fleet – Lookout
We had no glasses this time. We had nothing at all, only our own eyes, to look out. We asked them in Southampton, and they said there was none intended for us. We had a pair from Belfast to Southampton, but none from Southampton to New York. We do not know why. We only know we never got a pair.

George Symons – Lookout
After we left Southampton and got clear of the Nab Lightship, I went up to the officers' mess room and asked for glasses. I asked Mr Lightoller, and he went into another officers' room, which I presume was Mr Murdoch's, and he came out and said, 'Symons, there are none.' With that I went back and told my mates.

It is always customary to have glasses in the crow's nest. I served three years and five months on the *Oceanic*, and they had glasses all the time. As far as I have heard from other people, they have glasses in all the other ships.

George Hogg – Lookout
The idea of the glasses is that if you happen to see something on the horizon you can pick your ship out, if it is a ship, for instance. You would still strike the bell, but you would make sure, if you had the glasses, that it was a vessel and not a piece of cloud on the horizon.

I have always had night glasses in the White Star boats. I asked for the glasses, and I did not see why I should not have them. I had them from Belfast to Southampton; but from Southampton we never had them. I asked for the glasses several times. We never had night glasses; just the naked eye.

Bruce Ismay – Managing Director, IMM
I believe up to the year 1895 we used to supply lookout glasses to the lookout men, and since that date I think it has been left to the discretion of the commander whether he gives them lookout glasses or not. We certainly would if they are asked for.

Bertram Hayes – Captain, White Star Line
Glasses are a source of danger. They spoil the lookout. The lookout man when he sees a light if he has glasses is more liable to look at it and see what kind of a ship it is. That is the officer's business. The lookout man's business is to look out for other lights. It is the officer's business to find out what kind of a light it is, what way it is going, and so on.

Charles Lightoller – Second Officer
We place no reliance on the lookouts. They are there to assist you, but, speaking personally, I never rely on them. I keep a lookout myself, and so does every other officer. Occasionally a man will see a light or a vessel first, particularly in daytime, when naturally we trust to them seeing. Then, they will report a steamer long before she is in sight, apparently, by her smoke. In night-time, particularly in channels where there are a great many lights, we may be watching one light, and there may be another light in our

course, and the man in the crow's nest will strike, say, one bell. That signifies something on the port bow, and calls our attention to it.

Speaking for myself, I always select old lookout men that I know. As a rule, the lookout men run perhaps a year in the crow's nest in one ship. For instance, the men I had with me on the *Titanic* had been with me on the *Oceanic* for years, doing nothing but keeping a lookout. They are very smart at it, indeed. There is one man here who is the smartest man I know at it. Symons.

The White Star Company, I may say incidentally, is the only company in the world, so far as I know, that carries six lookout men. We carry men who do nothing else, night and day, from the commencement to the finish of the voyage, except keep a lookout. They are two hours on and four off.

Arthur Rostron – Captain, SS *Carpathia*
About 75 per cent of the objects that are seen at sea every day or night are picked up from the bridge first. Naturally, the officer will take more interest in these things than a lookout man. It does not necessarily say we shall pick them up quicker from the bridge, but naturally an officer is more on the qui vive; *he is keener on his work than a man would be, and he knows what to look for. He is more intelligent than a sailor. I always trust to the bridge preferably to the men.*

Frederick Fleet – Lookout
We are supposed to have our eyes examined every year, or every two years, by the Board of Trade. As to colour, and looking at a distance. My eyes were tested about a year ago, at Southampton. I had a certificate, but I lost it in the *Titanic*.

Reginald Lee – Lookout
I was examined by the Board of Trade doctor at Southampton, but not specially for eyesight. We were falling in on the lounge deck, and the doctor came and examined us all. I do not know that he particularly asked me anything. It was a casual kind of examination – not a test to get a certificate so that I can prove it.

I suppose he pleased himself. A medical man generally does, does not he?

Bruce Ismay – Managing Director, IMM
We follow the track which was agreed to by all the various steamship companies in 1895. It is absolutely laid down. They have a northern track which they use in the winter months, and during the summer months they use the southern route. The track was originally agreed to by all the steamship companies in conference. If the commander in his discretion thought that it was advisable to depart from the track, there would be no reason why he should not do so. It is a matter entirely in his hands.

I think on two occasions, when ice has been reported on the southern track, we have adopted a more southern route, and gone further south. I think it has been done on two occasions. That would be done by mutual consent of all the steamship companies interested in the tracks. If there was a small quantity of ice reported on the track, we certainly would not do it. If there was an abnormal quantity of ice reported on the track, then we probably would, in conjunction with the other steamship companies, agree to follow a more southern route.

When the captain left Liverpool or Southampton, he

would know that he had to follow either the southern or the northern route. Our instructions to the commanders are that they are not to do anything which will in any way imperil the ships or the lives that are on the ship. Our instructions in regard to that matter are very clear, and I think they are already on the record.

Joseph Boxhall – Fourth Officer

The night order book was written out and there was an order for the course to be altered at 5.50. I saw it, and I remarked to the chief officer between four o'clock and six o'clock that I considered the course ought to have been altered some considerable time before 5.50 – that is, if the course was meant to be altered at the 'corner',* 42 N, 47 W. Whether we spoke to the captain about it or not I do not know. I just remarked that to the chief officer, and the course was altered at 5.50. I consider that the ship was away to the southward and to the westward of the 'corner' when the course was altered.

Herbert Pitman – Third Officer

I considered we went at least ten miles further south than was necessary. We had a certain distance to run to the 'corner', and we did not alter the course so early as I anticipated. Therefore we must have gone much further south.

The commander gave the order to alter course to the officer of the watch, Mr Wilde. He did not mention whether

---

*The 'corner' is the point at which the ship stopped heading south-west to avoid the ice, and turned west towards New York.

he had deviated to avoid the ice. Captain Smith gives the orders to alter the course at the time he thinks fit.

Harold Lowe – Fifth Officer

I was on duty on Sunday evening, from 6pm to 8pm. From six to eight, I was busy working out this slip table, and doing various odds and ends and working a dead-reckoning position for 8pm to hand in to the captain. That was to indicate the position of the ship at that time, eight o'clock.

I suppose it must have been shortly after six, when I saw the chit. It was a square chit of paper on our chart room table about three inches by three inches. It was stuck in the frame above the table. It had the word 'ice', and then a position underneath the word 'ice'. That means to say a latitude and a longitude. I suppose I only looked at it casually. I worked it out mentally, and I found that we should not come to that position during my watch from six to eight.

I do not remember having heard of any other ice reports, and that is the only one that I saw. They may have been on the notice board, and I may not have looked at it. I do not remember looking at the notice board, and that is the only paper or note that I saw referring to ice. There was nothing particular about it; there was no signature or anything.

I handed the captain the slip report, on his chart room table. We simply put the slip on the table, and put a paper weight or something on it, and he comes in and sees it. It is nothing of any great importance. It has always been done, so that the position of the ship might be filled in the night order book.

I got her position by the chronometer. We have a fair idea of what she is doing. Her speed from noon until we turned the corner was just a fraction under 21 knots. If the speed had been increased or reduced during the interval when I was off duty, I would have been informed of it. We are informed of all. Wherever there is an altering of the course, we say, 'She is doing so and so, and so and so.' 'All right.' Then you are relieved.

It is the White Star routine. The White Star Company have regulations, just the same, in fact, as the Navy, and we all know exactly what to do, how to do it, when to do it, and where to do it. Everybody knows his business, and they do it. There is no hitch in anything.

Charles Lightoller – Second Officer
There were two junior officers on watch at all times, a quartermaster at the wheel and a stand-by quartermaster. We had two lookout men in the crow's nest at all times. In anything but clear weather, we carry extra lookouts. If the weather is fine, that is to say if the sea allows it, we place them near the stem head; when the weather does not allow us to place them at the stem head, then we probably place them on the bridge.

Joseph Boxhall – Fourth Officer
The lookout may have been increased; I cannot say. I was busy most of the watch in the chart room, making calculations. I did not hear any extra lookouts reported as being put on.

Sir Ernest Shackleton – Explorer
When navigating in an ice zone, I would put a lookout man in the bow or as near to the waterline as possible, even on

a clear night, but I would only have one man in the crow's nest. My main reason for saying one man in the crow's nest is that I think one man gives more attention to the work in hand than two men.

Joseph Boxhall – Fourth Officer

His duty is assigned to a man when he is assigned to his ship, and he grows up with it. He learns the different duties he has to perform in whatever rank he is on board ship.

The senior officer always takes the observations; he simply takes the observations with his sextant. The junior officer takes the time with the chronometer, and then is told to work them out. If the senior officer does not think these things are correct, he tells you to work them over, and you have to do it again.

When you take stars you always endeavour, as we did that night, to take a set of stars. One position checks another. You take two stars for latitude, and two for longitude; one star north and one star south, one star east and one star west. If you find a big difference between eastern and western stars, you know there is a mistake somewhere. But, as it happened, I think I worked out three stars for latitude and I think I worked out three stars for longitude. They all agreed.

After I had worked these observations of Mr Lightoller's, I was taking star bearings for compass error for myself, and was working those out. That is what kept me in the chart room most of the time. I was making computations most of the time.

Samuel Hemming – Lamp-trimmer

Mr Murdoch told me about the ice when I put the lights

out that night. At about 7.15, I was walking off the bridge, and he called me back. He said, 'Hemming, when you go forward, get the fore-scuttle hatch closed. There is a glow left from that and, as we are in the vicinity of ice, I want everything dark before the bridge.' It was the hatch on the forecastle head. I closed it myself.

Charles Lightoller – Second Officer

In the event of meeting ice, there are many things we look for. In the first place, a slight breeze. Of course, the stronger the breeze the more visible will the ice be, or rather the breakers on the ice. Therefore at any time when there is a slight breeze you will always see at night-time a phosphorescent line round a berg, growler, or whatever it may be. The slight swell which we invariably look for in the North Atlantic causes the same effect; the break on the base of the berg, so showing a phosphorescent glow. All bergs – all ice – more or less have a crystallised side. This side has been crystallised through exposure, and in all cases will reflect a certain amount of light – what is termed 'ice-blink'. You will frequently see ice-blink from a fairly large berg before the berg comes above the horizon.

You can see a big iceberg at least a mile and a half or two miles off – that is more or less the minimum. You could very probably see it a far greater distance than that. If it were a very white berg, flat topped or the flat side towards you, under normal conditions you would probably see that berg three or four miles away.

I judged I should see any ice that was large enough to damage the ship with sufficient distinctness to define it.

As far as we could see from the bridge, the sea was

comparatively smooth. Not that we expected it to actually be smooth, because looking from the ship's bridge very frequently with quite a swell on, the sea will appear just as smooth as a billiard table, perfectly smooth; you cannot detect the swell. The higher you are the more difficult it is to detect a slight swell. We generally assume that, though the sea may appear smooth, we pretty well know that there is a swell, though it may not be visible to the eye, nor yet have any effect on the ship. A flat calm is a most rare occurrence.

As far as icebergs were concerned, it would be more difficult to spot them in a flat sea. Naturally you would not see the water breaking on it if there were no wind; and so you would not have that to look for.

Sir Ernest Shackleton – Explorer

It entirely depends on the height of the iceberg. Take an iceberg of about 80 feet high, and the ordinary type of iceberg that has not turned over, you could see that in daytime in clear weather about 10 to 12 miles. Or, providing it was an ordinary berg, about five miles on a clear night.

There are many bergs I have seen that appear to be black, due to the construction of the berg itself, and also due to the earthy matter and rocks that are in all bergs. In fact, in the south many of these so-called islands, and charted as islands, must have been big bergs with earthy matter on them. After a berg has capsized, if it is not of close construction, it is more porous and, taking up the water, does not reflect light in any way. Its visibility might be only three miles, depending on the night and depending almost entirely on the condition of the sea at the time.

If the berg is capsized, it may extend underwater perhaps 200 yards or more, depending on the size of the berg. Some bergs that are five miles long may extend 200 or 300 yards – what we call a spur. I have seen spurs 200 yards away, but I think a couple of hundred feet would be about the average. A lot depends upon the sort of ice – what sort of mountain it came off, and how it was formed, and what its specific gravity is, whether it is worn down in the current by the temperature of the water.

'The dinner was an exceptionally good dinner'

Arthur Peuchen – First Class Passenger
Sunday evening I dined with my friends, Markleham Molson, Mr Allison, and Mrs Allison; and their daughter Helen was there for a short time. The dinner was an exceptionally good dinner. It seemed to be a better bill of fare than usual, although they are all good. After dinner my friends and I went to the sitting-out room and had some coffee. I left the friends I had dined with about nine o'clock, I think, or a little later. I then went up to the smoking room and joined Mr Beatty, Mr McCaffry, and another English gentleman who was going to Canada. We sat chatting and smoking there until probably 20 minutes after 11, or it may have been a little later than that. I then bid them good night and went to my room.

Bruce Ismay – Managing Director, IMM
I was all alone, so I asked Dr O'Loughlin to come and dine with me, and he dined with me in the restaurant at half past seven. No other persons were present excepting the doctor and myself.

The captain dined in the same restaurant, but I do not know at what time. I believe he dined with Mr and Mrs Widener, and I think Mr and Mrs Carter were there, and Mr and Mrs Thayer. I did not see Major Butt, but I could not see the whole of the table. They were dining at the forward end of the restaurant, on the starboard side. Part of their table was in an alcove. I was dining in the middle of the room on the same side of the ship, but I could see only part of their table. In fact, I was sitting with my back toward them.

I should think they were there half or three-quarters of an hour. They were sitting at the table when I went out of the room.

I had known Captain Smith a great many years. He had been commander of a great many of our ships, and was looked upon as our senior commander. The first time I remember Captain Smith being commander of one of our ships was when he was in command of one of our cargo boats called the *Cufic*, a great many years ago. He was in command of the *Olympic*, he was in the *Adriatic*, the *Baltic*, and the old *Britannic*. I cannot remember them all, but we have a record in the office of every ship he has commanded. I think he was about 62.

Captain Smith was a man who had a very, very clear record. I should think very few commanders crossing the Atlantic have as good a record as Captain Smith had, until he had the unfortunate collision with the *Hawke*. It was in the Solent in either August or September of last year. The *Olympic* was run into by the cruiser *Hawke* and very seriously damaged. She had to go back to Belfast to be repaired. The outside of her hull was very badly damaged and the shafting was bent. She was in the hands of a compulsory pilot.

Mary Smith – First Class Passenger
At 7.30pm, as usual, my husband and I went to dinner in the café. There was a dinner party going on, given by Mr Ismay to the captain and various other people on board ship. This was a usual occurrence of the evening, so we paid no

attention to it. The dinner did not seem to be particularly gay; while they had various wines to drink, I am positive none were intoxicated at a quarter of nine o'clock, when we left the dining room. There was a coffee room directly outside of the café, in which people sat and listened to the music and drank coffee and cordials after dinner. My husband was with some friends just outside of what I know as the Parisian Café. I stayed up until 10.30, and then went to bed. I passed through the coffee room, and Mr Ismay and his party were still there. The reason I am positive about the time is because I asked my husband at the three intervals what time it was. I went to bed, and my husband joined his friends.

Henry Stengel – First Class Passenger
I have a distinct recollection of Mrs Thorne stating, while talking about the captain being to dinner, that she was in that party, and she said, 'I was in that party, and the captain did not drink a drop.' He smoked two cigars, that was all, and left the dining room about ten o'clock.

William Ward – Saloon Steward
There was no drinking whatever. Had there been extra dinners or banquets, or the like of that, I certainly should have known it, working in the saloon. There was nothing in the way of banquets since we left Southampton, barring ordinary dinners. If there had been any banquet at all, some of us would certainly have been working for that purpose. I do not know of anything in the captain's room at all. There was no room in his room for any banquet. It would be impossible.

Harold Lowe – Fifth Officer
I never touched alcohol in my life. I am an abstainer. I say it without fear of contradiction. Water is the strongest drink I ever take.

Joseph Boxhall – Fourth Officer
I was inside the chart room working up stellar observations from eight o'clock. It was perfectly clear. There was no haze whatever. Whenever I was on the deck or at the compass I never saw any haze whatever.

I had seen reports of ice and put them on the chart. All the ice marked on the captain's chart I put down myself. There were icebergs reported from the captain of the *Touraine* some time previously; it might have been a couple of days before. I put their position on the chart, and found that those positions were considerably north of the track. In fact, they were between the northern track and the southern track.

I remarked to Captain Smith, that those positions were of no use to us because they were absolutely north of our track. You will understand these French boats do not keep the recognised tracks we do. French boats are always to be found to the northward. Therefore I plotted all these positions out. He had given us the position of a derelict, and when I plotted this derelict and these various icebergs he had seen, I could almost form an opinion of this track he had taken. He had gone considerably north, right across the Banks. And I said, 'They are out of our way.'

It was put down just as carefully as I should have put it down if it had been on our course. The captain saw me, and he was there alongside of me where I was putting the positions down, or shortly after I put them down, anyhow.

He read the telegram and looked at it, and these positions satisfied him.

Later, more positions came. I put those on the chart. All the ice I remember plotting out was to the northward of the track. If it had been on the track or to the southward I should have seen fit then to call the captain's special attention to it at the time I put it on. But I just merely remarked to him that I had put down the ice we had had reported; whenever I did put it on the chart, I remarked to him that I had done so.

I did not look at the chart when I came on at eight o'clock. I do not recollect any message about ice. I do not think there were any received at all of ice on our track, or the word would have been passed around right away; everybody would have known it.

From all the positions of icebergs that I had, of course I knew that we should be getting close up to those positions in the early hours of the middle watch. I did not think we should be up to any of those positions before midnight that night.

George Turnbull – Deputy Manager, Marconi International Message sent by *Mesaba* on 14 April at 7.50pm [9.40pm ship's time]

'*From* Mesaba *to* Titanic *and all east-bound ships. Ice report in latitude 42° N to 41° 25' N, longitude 49° W to longitude 50° 30' W. Saw much heavy pack ice, and great number large icebergs. Also field ice. Weather good, clear.*'

At the bottom of the form there appears this entry by the operator: 'Reply received. Thanks. Sent this to about ten other ships as well; names in PV', meaning his procès-verbal. It is initialled SHA. His name is Adams, the operator of the Mesaba.

Stanley Adams – Marconi Officer, SS *Mesaba*
It was an ice report from the captain. He said that it should be transmitted to all east-bound ships. It was with reference to the ice we had seen in the morning and the ice we had seen in the afternoon. It ran something like this: 'Latitude so and so, and longitude so and so, passed so many bergs,' and giving the time.

I sent this message, and the Titanic *sent: 'Received, thanks.' As soon as I received the official received signal I timed it, dated it, put the office sent to, and initialled it. I was waiting for a probable reply from the captain of the* Titanic *to the captain of the* Mesaba; *I thought that he would have some news to communicate to us. But the answer never came.*

Joseph Boxhall – Fourth Officer
I do not think for a moment that we had those messages.

Herbert Pitman – Third Officer
I heard something about a wireless message from some ship. Mr Boxhall put on the chart the position of the iceberg. I saw the mark there. He would just simply make a cross and write 'ice' in front of it.

I understand that Mr Lightoller warned Mr Murdoch. We had mentioned it before. We spoke of it amongst ourselves on Sunday. We were remarking that we should be in the vicinity of ice in Mr Murdoch's watch [starting at 10pm], and that we might see it. I had nothing to say in the matter. I was not interested in it. I cannot remember when the conversation occurred, and I have not the slightest idea who was there. I just heard the remark passed; that was all.

It was not my place to talk with the captain about such things. He used to pay periodical visits to the bridge. He may have been up there a half a dozen times in a watch.

Charles Lightoller – Second Officer

The temperature had fallen considerably. I know exactly how much because when I relieved Mr Murdoch after my dinner he made the remark to me that the temperature had dropped four degrees whilst I was away. It had fallen from 43 degrees to 39, which was a pretty sharp drop. It had been going down previously to that before I left the deck. Later on in the watch, the quartermaster two or three times told me what the temperature was in order that I might know when it got near to freezing point to send word to the engine room and the carpenter.

At about nine o'clock, it was 33 degrees, one degree above freezing. I sent word to the carpenter to look after his fresh water – to drain it off to prevent the pipes freezing – and to the engine room for them to take the necessary precautions for the winches.

A change of temperature indicates nothing whatever with regards to ice; you may have it any time in the year, summer and winter, going across the Atlantic. It is not quite so noticeable in winter because the air generally is cold. Though it may seem strange, it is quite possible for the temperature to go up if the ice happens to be floating in slightly warmer water, or if the wind were to come round from the southward. It is absolutely no indication whatever.

At five minutes to nine, when the commander came on the bridge he remarked that it was cold, and I said, 'Yes, it is very cold, sir. In fact,' I said, 'it is only one degree above freezing. I have sent word down to the carpenter and rung up the engine room and told them that it is freezing or will be during the night.' It was merely to indicate that the necessary duty had been done.

We then commenced to speak about the weather. He said, 'There is not much wind.' I said, 'No, it is a flat calm, as a matter of fact.' He repeated it; he said, 'A flat calm.' I said, 'Yes, quite flat, there is no wind.' I said something about it was rather a pity the breeze had not kept up whilst we were going through the ice region. Of course, my reason was obvious; he knew I meant the water ripples breaking on the base of the berg.

Sir Ernest Shackleton – Explorer
With a dead calm sea there is no sign at all to give you any indication that there is anything there. If you first see the breaking sea, then you look for the rest and you generally see it. You detect it better the nearer you are to the waterline, because from a height it is not so easily seen; it blends with the ocean if you are looking down at an angle like that. If you are on the sea level it may loom up. You suffered from a disadvantage, certainly, in the Titanic, *by not being able to get as near to the waterline.*

Charles Lightoller – Second Officer
It was a beautiful night, there was not a cloud in the sky. The sea was apparently smooth, and there was no wind, but at that time you could see the stars rising and setting on the horizon.

We then discussed the indications of ice. I remember saying, 'In any case there will be a certain amount of reflected lights from the bergs.' The captain said, 'Oh, yes, there will be a certain amount of reflected light.' I said, or he said, that even though the dark side of the berg was towards us, probably the outline, the white outline would give us sufficient warning, that we should be able to see it at a good distance, and, as far as we could see, we should be able to see it. Of course it was just with regard to that possibility of the blue side being towards us, and that if it did happen to be turned with the purely blue side towards us, there would still be the white outline.

We knew we were in the vicinity of ice, and though you cross the Atlantic for years and have ice reported and never see it, and at other times it is not reported and you do see it, you nevertheless do take necessary precautions, all you can, to make perfectly sure that the weather is clear and that the officers understand the indications of ice and all that sort of thing.

Edwin Cannons – Captain, Atlantic Transport Line

In the day, they appear as a white glistening mass, irregular in shape, white. At night they throw off an effulgence that can be seen. I have seen the outlines of an iceberg by taking a bearing over seven miles. Ice-blink is an effulgence thrown off the berg or ice because the ice absorbs the light by day, and throws it off at night. It would look like a large mass of luminous paint. That is the description one might venture upon.

I have seen them much darker. When I was chief officer of our Michigan, I saw an iceberg capsize in the daytime. What appeared prior to the iceberg capsizing as a white glistening mass, after the sea had subsided and the water

*run off the portion that was then exposed, was apparently
dark blue. It was different in outline and different in colour.*

Herbert Pitman – Third Officer

A change in the temperature would not denote anything at
all, because in this country [USA] and our own country [UK]
we will probably want no clothes on at all, and the next day
we will want overcoats, winter clothes, and that is not due
to ice.

I do not think there are any signs at all. As regards the
temperature of the water, it is absolutely useless. I have
proven it. I saw one about 18 months ago – there were three,
as a matter of fact – off the Falkland Islands. One was about
700 feet long and 600 feet wide and fully 500 feet high.
When the sun was shining on it, it was a perfect white. In the
morning, about eight o'clock, when the sun was not shining
on it, it looked like a perfectly black berg, like a huge island.
That is where I proved that the temperature of the water
is absolutely no indication of icebergs. It did not affect the
temperature in the slightest.

Taking the temperature of the water is a custom in
the ships, and it is for meteorological observation. The
quartermaster does that every two hours. I have seen the
men going to do it. We usually have a canvas bucket which
they lower into the water. We did not have time to make
one, so they were using a tin attached to a piece of rope long
enough to reach the water.

Sir Ernest Shackleton – Explorer

*If there was no wind and the temperature fell abnormally
for the time of the year, I would consider I was approaching*

*an area that might have ice in it. But, unless the wind is
blowing from a large field of ice to windward, the change
of sea temperature is a very poor thing to go upon. The film
of fresh water that covers the sea is so thin that by dipping
in a bucket you do not pick up that thin cold water; and if
the temperature of the air is approximately the temperature
of the sea, there is practically no haze; it is only when the
water is warmer or the air is warmer that the haze occurs.
There are no methods that I have heard of before this that
can really give you an indication of approaching ice by
ordinary temperature methods.*

Bruce Ismay – Managing Director, IMM

There is always danger with ice – more or less danger with
ice. I knew we were approaching the region of ice, by this
Marconi message. Because I presumed the man would not
send the Marconi message to us unless the ice was there and
that we were approaching it, or it must have been very close
to the track.

I could not say exactly where the ice was. I do not
understand latitude and longitude. The Marconi message
did not convey any meaning to me as to the exact position
of that ice. That is for the captain of the ship. He was
responsible for the navigation of the ship. I had nothing to
do with the navigation. I was simply a passenger on board
the ship. I had never seen an iceberg in my life before.

The other information I got was from Dr O'Loughlin,
who said we had 'turned the corner'. He had been in the
service over 40 years. He made the remark at dinner, 'We
have turned the corner.' Crossing the Atlantic, you come
down to a point and then you go up; it is what is always

known as 'turning the corner'. I knew, when we had turned the corner, we must be getting towards the ice region.

Ella White – First Class Passenger

Everybody knew we were in the vicinity of icebergs. Even in our staterooms it was so cold that we could not leave the porthole open. It was terribly cold. It was unusually cold. I made the remark to Miss Young, on Sunday morning: 'We must be very near icebergs to have such cold weather as this.'

Charles Lightoller – Second Officer

The captain said, 'If it becomes at all doubtful' – I think those were his words – 'If it becomes at all doubtful, let me know at once; I will be just inside.' He meant to say, if I had any doubt at all in my mind about the weather, about the distance I could see. If there were the slightest degree of haze to arise, the slightest haze whatever, if that were to any degree noticeable, to immediately notify him.

If we were coming on a large berg there might be a haze, as there frequently is in that position, where warm and cold streams are intermixing. You will very frequently get a little low-lying haze, smoke we call it, lying on the water perhaps a couple of feet. The slightest haze would render the situation far more difficult, and far more dangerous if there were ice.

Shortly afterwards, I sent a message to the crow's nest to keep a sharp lookout for ice, particularly small ice and growlers. And I think I told them to pass that word on until daylight – to keep a sharp lookout till daylight. That is a message I always send along when approaching the vicinity of ice or a derelict, as the case may be. If I know we are approaching the vicinity of a derelict, I send the word along to let them know what to look out for. It is just the same with regard to a lightship, say the Nantucket Lightship; I tell them to keep a sharp lookout for the Nantucket Lightship to give them an idea what they are looking for.

George Symons – Lookout

We had special orders about 9.30 from some officer on the bridge. 'Keep a sharp lookout for small ice and bergs till daylight, and pass the word along.' That was the order received by Jewell and me; we both heard it through the 'phone.

Charles Lightoller – Second Officer

At 9.30 or about 9.30 I took up a position on the bridge where I could see distinctly right ahead – a view which cleared the back stays and stays and so on – and there I remained during the remainder of my watch. Keeping a sharp lookout, as sharp as was possible. Looking out for ice and watching the weather; watching the conditions generally to see there was no haze which would rise that I should not notice, and, of course, keeping a sharp lookout for ice as well.

The next hour it went colder by one degree. That was exactly freezing. I probably noticed at about ten minutes to ten, when the quartermaster took the temperature of the air and the water by thermometer.

Mr Murdoch came on deck in his overcoat and said, 'It is pretty cold.' I said, 'Yes, it is freezing.' I said something about we might be up around the ice any time now. I cannot remember the exact words. I gave him to understand that we were within the region where ice had been reported. I told Mr Murdoch I had already sent to the crow's nest, the carpenter and the engine room as to the temperature, and such things as that – naturally, in the ordinary course in handing over the ship everything I could think of.

No orders were passed on about speed. I have never known speed to be reduced in any ship I have ever been in the north Atlantic in clear weather, not on account of ice.

We were making for a vicinity where ice had been reported year after year, and time and again. I do not think for the last two or three years I have seen an iceberg, although ships ahead of us have reported ice time and time again. There was no absolute certainty that we were running into an ice-field or running amongst icebergs or anything else, and it might have been, as it has been in years before, ice reported inside a certain longitude.

So it is hardly correct to say we knew we were in the presence of ice. We did not; we only had reports to go on. On the contrary, we had reason to disbelieve those reports, having so many years gone across and never seen ice, though it is repeatedly reported. In the view of the reports we have had in other voyages, if I say in the light of good seamanship or extra good seamanship, we should have stopped, the thousands of ships that have crossed the Atlantic would likewise have stopped, and then you come to the end of your tether.

In the view of after-events, of course, we form a totally different opinion. It would naturally have been safer, we can see now, not to have gone ahead at all.

Bertram Hayes – Captain, White Star Line
Ice does not make any difference to speed in clear weather. We proceed at the same rate of speed. No alteration. It is the practice all over the world so far as I know – every ship that crosses the Atlantic. You can always see ice in clear weather.

You can see it from six or seven miles away – I have seen it ten miles. You see a light there; the ice is light. It is like looking at that piece of paper on the wall; you can see the brightness. That is the way you distinguish it any time; you see the colour of it. It is differentiated from land in the daytime.

I have steamed in between icebergs at night-time. They have been scattered all over about the course on either bow, and I have gone on my course steering between them. That was at night-time, approaching Belle Isle on the north track. We were doing 18 knots, full speed, on the Laurentic, *of the White Star Line.*

Charles Lightoller – Second Officer

I have never known the route to be changed by the commander. When we have the absolute position of anything that is reliable, when the latitude and longitude is given by a ship immediately ahead of an iceberg or a derelict, some commanders will alter their course a few miles just to avoid it, particularly if it is in the night-time. You have the position of that one derelict and if you cross there at night-time you might haul a little to the southward or northward.

Every man has a different idea with regard to navigation. Each man has his own individual idea with regard to the safety of which he exercises to the utmost to keep the ship from danger in its various forms.

Bruce Ismay – Managing Director, IMM

I am not a navigator, but I should say if a man can see far enough to clear ice, he is perfectly justified in going full speed. I presume that the man would be anxious to get through the ice region. He would not want to slow down upon the chance of a fog coming on. I presume that if a man on a perfectly clear night could see far enough to clear an iceberg he would be perfectly justified in getting through the ice region as quickly as he possibly could.

Assuming the weather was perfectly fine, I should say the captain was perfectly justified in going full speed.

Sir Ernest Shackleton – Explorer

A certain state of things has evolved in the last few years by public desire and competition. There is a general feeling amongst people at sea that you have to make your passage; if you do not make your passage it is not so good for you. But the possibility of accident is greatly enhanced by the speed the ship goes.

When navigating in an ice zone, I would take the ordinary precaution of slowing down, whether I was in a ship equipped for ice or any other, compatible with keeping steerage way for the size of the ship. I have been in a ship which was specially built for ice, but I took the precaution to slow down because you can only tell the condition of any ice you see; there may be projecting spurs and you may suddenly come across them. She was only six knots at full speed. She was 40 years old.

As soon as they know they are in an absolute ice locality, a liner should slow down sufficiently to give her steering way; I should say ten knots. You have no right to go at 21 knots in an ice zone.

George Rheims – First Class Passenger

I was in the smoking room with my brother-in-law, Joseph Loring, and we were trying to figure on the speed of the boat to see what the run would be the next day. Then the steward, whom I think they called the commodore steward, because I think he is the oldest steward, came up to us and said we might figure on a bigger run. We said, 'Why?' He answered, 'Because we are making faster speed than we were yesterday.' My brother-in-law said, 'What do you know about it?' He said, 'I got it from the engine room.' My brother-in-law said, 'That don't mean anything.' He said, 'Gentlemen, come out and see for yourself.

We went out in the passage hallway right outside of the smoking room and we stood there, and he said, 'You notice that the vibration of the boat is much greater tonight than it has ever been.' And we did notice the vibration, which was very strong that night, and my brother-in-law, whose stateroom was right underneath the passage, said, 'I never noticed this vibration before; we are evidently making very good speed.'

Henry Stengel – First Class Passenger

When I retired at about ten o'clock, I could hear the engines, and I noticed that they were running fast. I called my wife's attention to the fact that the engines were running faster than at any other time during the trip. I noticed just through being familiar with engines in the manufacturing business. We have bought a great many engines in 28 or 29 years, and we generally take the speed of the engine. We want to buy an engine that will run a certain speed to do a certain amount of work. It was just natural instinct, that was all.

Harold Bride – Assistant Telegraphist

Just before I turned in, I heard Mr Phillips sending the

preliminaries to Cape Race.* I was reading what Mr Phillips was sending from his apparatus. I could hear the make and break of his key. It was just before I went to bed; I was not asleep, I had nothing else to do but lie and listen.

We had a very large accumulation of messages waiting to be sent to America. At the same time, Cape Race would have a number of telegrams to transmit to him. I should estimate he could not have finished before nine from the batch he had. I am judging by the amount of work that was got through. From leaving Southampton to the time we had finished with Cape Race, we had transmitted 250 telegrams.

Cyril Evans – Marconi Officer, SS *Californian*

On the same evening, we were stopped, and I went to the captain and I asked him if there was anything the matter. He told me he had stopped because of the ice, and he asked me if I had any boats. I said the Titanic. *He said, 'Better advise him we are surrounded by ice and stopped.' So I went to my cabin, and at 9.05pm New York time [10.55pm ship's time] I called him up. I said, 'Say, old man, we are stopped and surrounded by ice.' The operator on the* Titanic *turned around and said, 'Shut up, shut up, I am busy; I am working Cape Race,' and at that I jammed him.*

It meant he did not want me to interfere; you do not take it as an insult or anything like that. By jamming we mean when somebody is sending a message to somebody else and you start to send at the same time, you jam him. He does not get his message. I was nearer than Cape Race station,

---

*Cape Race was the Marconi wireless station in Newfoundland which was used to relay messages from ship to shore.

therefore my signals came in with a bang, and he could read me and he could not read Cape Race. He must have heard the message, but I do not know whether he took it down.

Directly afterwards, he called up Cape Race and said, 'Sorry, please repeat, jammed.' He continued to send messages right up till I turned in. I had the phone on my ear, and heard him sending, but I did not take them down. They were all private messages; you can tell by the prefix. At 11.35, ship's time, I put the phones down and took off my clothes and turned in.

Stanley Lord – Captain, SS *Californian*
We were surrounded by a lot of loose ice, and we were about a quarter of a mile off the edge of the field. We stopped altogether, so we would not run over the top of the ice. The field was about 26 miles long and from one to two miles wide.

I sent the message just as a matter of courtesy. We always pass the news around when we get hold of anything like that. I thought he would be a long way from where we were. I did not think he was anywhere near the ice. By rights, he ought to have been 18 or 19 miles to the southward of where I was. I never thought the ice was stretching that far down.

Robert Hichens – Quartermaster
At a quarter to ten, I called the first officer, Mr Murdoch, to let him know it was one bell, which is part of our duty. It is the duty of the quartermaster to strike the bell every half hour. I also took the thermometer and barometer, the temperature of the water, and the log. We had to do this duty every two hours. We write it down in the log book for

the junior officer, and it is copied off in the quartermaster's log book. After that we don't take no notice of it.

We have a small bucket, leaded at the bottom, attached to a piece of line about 20 fathoms long, which we put over the lee side of the ship, and draw just sufficient water to put the instrument in to cover the mercury to make its temperature rise. It was an old paint tin the quartermaster got for the occasion, because we had nothing else. It would hold about a quart, if it was full up. The proper thing they use is a long piece of leather, leaded.

It began to get very, very cold; exceedingly cold. So cold, we could hardly suffer the cold. I thought there was ice about, somewhere. It did not concern me. It had nothing to do with me at all. The officers had to do with it. I am only a junior officer.

Reginald Lee – Lookout
There was a sudden change in the temperature. You could smell the ice.

PART TWO

COLLISION
14-15 April 1912

'I saw a black object right
ahead, high above the water.
I said, "Iceberg right ahead"'

Frederick Fleet – Lookout

I was on the lookout at the time of the collision. Lee and I relieved Symons and Jewell. They told us to keep a sharp lookout for small ice and growlers. They said they had had orders from the bridge. The sea was calm. The first part of the watch we could see the horizon, then there came a slight haze. It was nothing to talk about; it was only about two points on each side. It did not affect us, the haze; we could see just as well. I daresay it was somewhere near seven bells. The watch was nearly over.

I saw a black object right ahead, high above the water. I struck three bells as soon as I saw it. Then I went straight to the telephone, and rang them up on the bridge. They said, 'What do you see?' I said, 'Iceberg right ahead.' They said, 'Thank you.' I do not know who it was.

After I rang them up I looked over the nest, and the ship was going to port. The iceberg struck on the starboard bow, just before the foremast, about 20 feet from the stem. The ship did not stop at all; she did not stop until she passed the iceberg. Some ice fell on the forecastle head and some on the well deck, just a little bit higher than the forecastle.

I went back to my own place again. I told Lee I thought it was a narrow shave. That was only my idea; it was such a slight noise, that is why I said it.

Reginald Lee – Lookout
It was a dark mass that came through that haze, and there was no white appearing until it was just close alongside the ship, and that was just a fringe at the top. That was the only white about it, until she passed by, and then you could see she was white; one side of it seemed to be black, and the other side seemed to be white. When I had a look at it going astern, it appeared to be white.

As soon as the reply came back 'Thank you,' the helm must have been put either hard a-starboard or very close to it, because she veered to port, and it seemed almost as if she might clear it. But I suppose there was ice under water.

Just at that time I happened to be right in front of the nest, because the nest is semi-circular, and the telephone is in the corner of the nest on the starboard side. My mate was telephoning from there, and I was standing in the front of the nest watching the boat. The iceberg was just about amidships, in front of the nest. It was higher than the forecastle; but I could not say what height was clear of the water.

The ship seemed to heel slightly over to port as she struck the berg along the starboard side. There was a rending of metal – you could hear that from where we were. It seemed to be running right along the starboard side.

Bertram Hayes – Captain, White Star Line
There must have been some abnormal conditions which misled them. I do not think there was a bad lookout. I have known the two men, and there is no carelessness.

Joseph Scarrott – Able Seaman
The shock caused everybody to turn out, and we came on

deck to see what was the cause of the vibration. We saw a large quantity of ice on the starboard side on the fore-well deck. I went and looked over the rail there, and I saw an iceberg that I took it we had struck. It would be abaft the starboard beam then, not a ship's length away. It seemed the ship was acting on her helm, and we had swung clear of the iceberg. Her starboard quarter was going off the iceberg, and the starboard bow was going as if to make a circle round it.

The iceberg was about as high as the boat deck; it appeared to be that from the position of it. It struck me at the time that it resembled the Rock of Gibraltar looking at it from Europa Point. It looked very much the same shape as that, only much smaller. The highest point would be on my right, as it appeared to me.

Robert Hichens – Quartermaster
At the time of the collision I was at the wheel, steering the ship. At 20 minutes to 12, three gongs came from the lookout, and immediately afterwards a report on the telephone, 'Iceberg right ahead.' The chief officer rushed from the wing to the bridge. I was enclosed in the wheelhouse, and I could not see – I could only see my compass. Mr Murdoch rushed to the engines. I heard the telegraph bell ring; and he gave the order 'Hard a-starboard.'* The sixth officer was standing by me to see the duty carried out, and the other quartermaster was standing by my left side. The sixth officer repeated the order, 'Hard a-starboard. The helm is hard over, sir.'

---

*The order 'hard a-starboard' was a hangover from the days when ships were steered by a tiller, which had to be pushed to starboard to turn the ship to port (and vice versa).

But, during the time, she was crushing the ice. We could hear the grinding noise along the ship's bottom. I heard the telegraph ring. The captain came rushing out of his cabin and asked, 'What is that?' Mr Murdoch said, 'An iceberg.' The captain said, 'Close the emergency doors.' Mr Murdoch replied, 'The doors are already closed.'

The captain sent then for the carpenter to sound the ship. He also came back to the wheelhouse and looked at the commutator in front of the compass, which is a little instrument like a clock to tell you how the ship is listing. The ship had a list of five degrees to starboard.

Joseph Boxhall – Fourth Officer

I was just coming along the deck and almost abreast of the captain's quarters, and I heard the report of three bells from the crow's nest. That signifies something has been seen ahead. Almost at the same time I heard the first officer give the order 'Hard a-starboard', and the engine telegraph rang 'Full speed astern'.

I was almost on the bridge when the iceberg struck. It seemed to strike the bluff of the bow – the forward part of the ship, but almost on the side. It is just where the ship begins to widen out on the starboard side. It was a glancing blow; a slight impact. It did not seem to me to be very serious. I did not take it seriously.

I saw Mr Murdoch pulling the lever and closing the watertight doors then. The captain was alongside of me when I turned round. He said, 'What have we struck?' The first officer said, 'An iceberg, sir. I hard-a-starboarded and reversed the engines, and I was going to hard-a-port round it but she was too close. I could not do any more. I have closed the watertight doors.' The captain asked him if he had rung the warning bell. He said, 'Yes, sir.'

We all walked out to the corner of the bridge then, to look at the iceberg, the captain, the first officer and myself. I was not very sure of seeing it. I had just come out of the light, and my eyes were not accustomed to the darkness. It seemed to me to be just a small black mass not rising very high out of the water, just a little on the starboard quarter. The ship was past it then. I could not judge the size of it, but it seemed to me to be very, very low-lying. In my own opinion I do not think the thing extended above the ship's rail. Probably about 30 feet – no, hardly 30 feet.

I do not know what was done, because I left the bridge then. I went right down below, in the lowest steerage, as far as I could possibly get without going into the cargo portion of the ship, and inspected all the decks as I came up, in the vicinity of where I thought she had struck. I found no indications to show that the ship had damaged herself. Then I went on the bridge and reported to the captain that I could not see any damage.

He said, 'Go down and find the carpenter and get him to sound the ship.' I was proceeding down, but I met the carpenter on the way. I said, 'The captain wants you to sound the ship.' He said, 'The ship is making water,' and he went on the bridge to the captain. I thought I would go down forward again and investigate; and then I met a mail clerk, a man named Smith, and he asked where the captain was. I said, 'He is on the bridge.' He said, 'The mail hold is filling rapidly.' I said, 'Well, you go and report it to the captain and I will go down and see,' and I proceeded right down into the mail room.

I went down as far as the sorting room deck and found mail clerks down there working. Taking letters out of the racks, they seemed to me to be doing. I could not see what they were putting them in. I looked through an open door and saw these men working at the racks, and directly beneath me was the mail hold, and the water seemed to be then within two feet of the deck we were standing on. There were bags of mail floating about.

I met the second steward, Mr Dodd, on my way to the bridge, and he asked me about sending men down below for those mails. I said, 'You had better wait till I go to the bridge and find what we can do.' I went to the bridge and reported to the captain what I had seen. He said all right, and then the order came out for the boats.

George Rowe – Quartermaster
I had charge of the taffrail log. As soon as the berg was gone, I looked at the log and it read 260 miles. It had been reset at noon.*

Alfred Olliver – Quartermaster
I happened to be looking at the lights in the standing compass when I heard three bells rung up in the crow's nest. That was my duty, to look at the lights in the standing compass, and I was trimming them so that they would burn properly. When I heard the report, I knew that it was something ahead. I looked, but could not see anything. I left that and was just entering on the bridge as the shock came.

---

*If correct, this suggests the ship had averaged over 21.3 knots in the previous 12 hours, on corrected time.

I knew we had touched something.

I saw the captain on the bridge. He gave me orders to tell the carpenter to go and take the draught of the water. I went down and I saw the carpenter taking the draught. He says, 'All right, I am doing it.'

As soon as I got on the bridge, I had another message to take, this time to the chief engineer. I cannot say what was in the message, as it was on a piece of paper and the paper was closed. I delivered the message to the chief engineer, and I waited for an answer. I waited for two or three minutes. Then he saw me standing, and he asked me what I wanted. I said I was waiting for an answer to the message I took him. He told me to tell the captain that he would get it done as soon as possible.

As soon as I came on the bridge, I delivered back the message that the chief engineer told me he would get it done as soon as possible. After I delivered that message, the chief officer sent me to the boatswain of the ship and told me to tell the boatswain to get the oar lines and to uncover the boats and get them ready for lowering. I done so, and came back on the bridge. No sooner did I get on the bridge, than the sixth officer told me to go and get the boat's list, so that he could muster the men at the boats. I went and got the sailors' boat list and took it to him. Then I went to my boat to muster the men.

I did not run any more messages.

Annie Robinson – First Class Stewardess
The mail man passed along first and he returned with Mr McElroy and the captain and they went in the direction of the mail room. I followed after they had come back. I saw

two mail bags and a man's Gladstone bag, and on looking down the staircase I saw water within six steps of coming on to E deck.

The carpenter was the next man I saw. He came along when I was looking down at the water, and he had the lead line in his hand. I could not tell you why. The man looked absolutely bewildered, distracted. He did not speak.

George Cavell – Trimmer

I felt a shock, and with that all the coal round me fell around me. I had a job to get out myself. It did not have time to knock me over. The coal surrounded me before I knew where I was. After that I came up right up to the bunker door, and then came down the ladder and into the stokehold. As soon as I got into the stokehold, the lights went out. I heard the bell go and I knew in a minute what it was for. I went on deck to see what it was, and I saw people running along wet through with lifebelts in their hands. They were going towards after-way. I should think they were the Third Class passengers. My mate said we had struck an iceberg.

The lights were on by the time I got back. The water had started coming up over her stokehold plates. It came gradually. We stopped as long as we could. And then I thought to myself, it was time, and I went for the escape ladder. By then, I was standing in about a foot of water.

Thomas Dillon – Trimmer

It was my first trip down below, to the engine room where the main engines are. I belonged to the upper section, but the upper section of boilers was not lit up, and they sent us to the engine room to assist in cleaning the gear.

The telegraph rang two seconds before she struck. About a minute and a half later, the engines stopped. About half a minute after that, they went slow astern for about two minutes. Then they went ahead again for about two minutes. Then they stopped.

There were a number of engineers there – I did not know their names. They rushed to their stations to work the pumps and valves. In the meantime, the watertight compartments were closed. That was three minutes after the ship struck.

The next order we got was to get out of the engine room and into the stokehold and open the watertight doors. The one leading from the engine room to the first boiler room was lifted up by hand high enough to let us get underneath. We then opened the watertight doors from the engine room to the second, third and fourth boiler room, and left them open. We were ordered to by the chief engineer, to allow the engineers to get forward to their duties with the valves and the pumps.

We did not open the door into No 5 boiler room because there was too much water in No 5.

Then we got the order, 'All hands on deck; put your life-preservers on.' That was an hour and 40 minutes after the ship struck. There was water coming in forward, coming from underneath.

Frederick Barrett – Leading Fireman

I was in a stokehold on the starboard side in No 6 section talking to the second engineer, Mr Hesketh. There is like a clock rigged up in the stokehold, and a red light goes up when the ship is supposed to stop; a white light for full speed, and I think it is a blue light for slow. A bell rings when the signal appears. This red light came up. It says 'Stop'. I called out, 'Shut all dampers,' to shut the wind off the fires.

The crash came before we had them all shut. Water came pouring in from the ship's side two feet abaft the watertight bulkhead. The ship's side was torn from the third stokehold to the forward end, about two feet from where I was standing. The watertight bulkhead was not damaged. I could not estimate exactly how large the hole was but a large volume of water came through.

Me and Mr Hesketh jumped into the next section, just before the watertight compartment closed up. Mr Hesketh shouted out, 'All hands stand by your stations.' That is the order for the men to stand by the fires. My station was in the next boiler room, so the engineer Mr Shepherd and I went up an escape ladder and down to the boiler room. We could not get in, because there were eight feet of water in it.

We came back to No 5 section, where the second assistant engineers, Mr Harvey and Mr Wilson, were attending to the pumps. The hole was not so big in that section as it was in No 6 section. The lights went out, and Mr Harvey sent me up for some lamps. I went to the top of the escape ladder and sent two firemen into the engine room for them. They fetched 12 to 15 lamps back, but by the time I went down with them the electric lights were burning again.

I looked at the boilers and there was no water in them. So I ran to the engineer, and he told me to get some firemen down to draw the fires.* I got 15 men down below. There were 30 furnaces to pull.* It would take them 20 minutes.

---

*To 'draw the fires' and 'pull the furnaces' means to smother the fires and reduce heat in the boilers.

Mr Harvey asked me to lift the manhole plate off on the starboard side of No 5 section to get at the valves. But all the water which had been thrown on the furnaces when they were pulled out was making the stokehold thick with steam. Mr Shepherd was walking across in a hurry to do something when he fell down the hole and broke his leg. We lifted him up and carried him into the pump room.

Up until then, the water had never come above the floor plates. Then, all at once, I saw a wave of green foam come tearing through between the boilers and I jumped for the escape ladder.

Charles Hendrickson – Leading Fireman
I saw the water rushing in from the starboard side at the bottom of the spiral stairway leading from our quarters to the stokehold. There was a lot of water there and from the way it was rushing in you could not exactly tell how it was coming.

I met Mr Hesketh, the second engineer, and reported to him. He told me to get some men and get some lamps and take them down below. I went right through by the engine room and got all the lamps I could get that were ready. I got five, and left four or five men there to get more if they could. Then I came back by the engine room, went along and down the escape to go to No 6 section. When I got down there I found I could not get any further, the water was up too high; so I came back by the escape again and went to No 5 section.

When I got down there, I met Mr Shepherd. He said to me, 'You have got the lamps, have not you?' and I said, 'Yes, sir.' He said, 'That is right, light them, and put them up by the water-gauges of the boilers.' So I lit them up and took them up and came down below again, and Mr Shepherd said to me, 'Start drawing fires.' I said, 'Yes.' I went to get the rake to start pulling some of the fires out, when Mr Harvey came to me and asked me to get some men down to get the fires out. I went up top and saw a few belonging to the eight-to-twelve watch, and asked them if they would come, and some went down. The ship was going down a little by the head then.

Frederick Scott – Greaser

They rang down 'Stop', and two greasers on the bottom rang the telegraph back to answer it. Then they rang down 'Slow ahead'. For ten minutes she was going ahead. Then they rang down 'Stop', and then 'Astern'. She went astern for five minutes. Then they rang down 'Stop'.

They cannot stop the engines at once; they are bound to let the steam get out of the cylinder first, otherwise they would blow the cylinder covers off if they tried to stop them at once.

Charles Lightoller – Second Officer

My light was out but I was still awake. The impact is best described as a jar and a grinding sound. There was a slight jar followed by this grinding sound. It struck me we had struck something and then, thinking it over, it was a feeling as if she may have hit something with her propellers, and I thought perhaps she had struck some obstruction with her propeller and stripped the blades off. It flashed through my mind that possibly it was a piece of wreckage, or something – a piece of ice had been struck by a propeller blade, which might have given a similar feeling to the ship.

I lay there for a few moments, it might have been a few

minutes, and then, feeling the engines had stopped, I got up. I went out on deck, on to the boat deck on the port side. First of all, I looked forward to the bridge and everything seemed quiet there. Everything seemed normal. I could see the first officer standing on the footbridge keeping the lookout. I then walked across to the side, and I saw the ship had slowed down and was proceeding slowly through the water, at a matter of perhaps six knots or something like that. I did not stay there long.

After looking over the side and seeing the bridge, I went back to the quarters and crossed over to the starboard side. I looked out of the starboard door and I could see the commander standing on the bridge in just the same manner as I had seen Mr Murdoch, just the outline. I could not see which was which in the dark. It was pretty cold and I went back to my bunk and turned in. I did not think it was anything serious. I thought she had either bumped something or fouled something. If it was sufficiently serious, I knew I should be called.

It is very difficult to say how long I was in my bunk after that. I should say roughly about half an hour perhaps – it might have been longer, it might have been less. There were no noises. I turned in my bunk, covered myself up and waited for somebody to come along and tell me if they wanted me. I knew that if they wanted us, it was a moment's work for the quartermaster to come along and tell us.

After some time, Mr Boxhall just came in and quietly remarked, 'You know we have struck an iceberg.' I said, 'I know we have struck something.' He then said, 'The water is up to F deck in the mail room.' He had no need to say anything further then.

Herbert Pitman – Third Officer

I saw a little ice on the well deck. I went further, to the forecastle head, to see if there was any damage. I could not see any at all. On my return, before emerging from under the forecastle head, I saw a crowd of firemen coming out with their bags of clothing. I said, 'What is the matter?' They said, 'The water is coming in our place.' I said, 'That is funny.' I looked down No 1 hatch, then, and saw the water flowing over the hatch.

Bruce Ismay – Managing Director, IMM

I presume the impact awakened me. I lay in bed for a moment or two afterwards, not realising, probably, what had happened. I really thought we had lost a blade off the propeller. Eventually I got up and walked along the passageway and met one of the stewards, and said, 'What has happened?' He said, 'I do not know, sir.'

I then went back into my room, put my coat on, and went up on the bridge, where I found Captain Smith. I asked him what had happened, and he said, 'We have struck ice.' I said, 'Do you think the ship is seriously damaged?' He said, 'I am afraid she is.'

I then went down below, where I met Mr Bell, the chief engineer, who was in the main companionway. I asked if he thought the ship was seriously damaged, and he said he thought she was, but was quite satisfied the pumps would keep her afloat.

I went back on to the bridge, where I heard Captain Smith give the order to get the boats out. It is difficult to remember exactly what was said. I know I heard him give the order to lower the boats. I think that is all he said. I think he simply turned around and gave the order. As soon as I heard him give the order to lower the boats, I left the bridge. I walked along to the starboard side of the ship, where I met one of the officers. I told him to get the boats out. I then assisted, as best I could, getting the boats out and putting the women and children into the boats.

Frederick Clench – Able Seaman
I was awakened by the crunching and jarring, as if the ship was hitting up against something. Of course I put on my trousers and I went on deck on the starboard side of the well deck and I saw a lot of ice on the deck. With that, I went in the alleyway again under the forecastle head to come down and put on my shoes. Someone said to me, 'Did you hear the rush of water?' I said, 'No.' They said, 'Look down under the hatchway.' I looked down under the hatchway and I saw the tarpaulin belly out as if there was a lot of wind under it, and I heard the rush of water coming through.

I went down below and put my guernsey on, my round hat on, and after that I sat down on a stool having a smoke, down in the forecastle. I seen the water coming in, and I thought it was all right. I thought she would not sink then.

Edward Wilding – Naval Architect, Harland & Wolff
Assuming the forepeak and Nos 1, 2 and 3 holds and No 6 boiler room flooded, and that the water has risen to a certain level, it would mean that about 16,000 tons of water had found their way into the vessel. That is the volume of the water which would have to come in. As far as I can follow from the evidence, the water was up to that

level in about forty minutes. It may be a few minutes more or less, but that is the best estimate I can make.

My estimate for the size of the hole required (and making some allowance for the obstruction due to the presence of decks and other things), is that the total area through which water was entering the ship, was somewhere about 12 square feet. The extent of the damage fore and aft, that is from the foremost puncture to the aftermost puncture in the cross bunker at the forward end of No 5 boiler room, is about 500 feet, and the average width of the hole extending the whole way is only about three-quarters of an inch. That is my reason for stating that I believe it must have been in several places – that is, not a continuous rip. A hole three-quarters of an inch wide and 200 feet long does not seem to describe to me the probable damage, but it must have averaged about that amount.

It can only have been a comparatively short length, and the aggregate of the holes must have been somewhere about 12 square feet. One cannot put it any better than that.

Norman Chambers – First Class Passenger

At the time of the collision I was in bed, and I noticed no very great shock, the loudest noise by far being that of jangling chains whipping along the side of the ship. This passed so quickly that I assumed something had gone wrong with the engines on the starboard side.

At the request of my wife, I prepared to investigate what had happened, leaving her dressing. I threw on sufficient clothes, including my overcoat. I went up, in a leisurely manner, as far as the A deck on the starboard side. There I noted only an unusual coldness of the air. Looking over the side I was unable to see anything in any direction.

I returned below, where I was joined by my wife, and we came up again to investigate, still finding nothing. However, there was then a noticeable list to starboard, with probably a few degrees of pitch; and as the ship had a list to port nearly all afternoon, I decided to remain up, in spite of a feeling of perfect safety.

Upon returning to the stateroom for the purpose of completing dressing, I looked at the starboard end of our passage, where there was the companion leading to the quarters of the mail clerks and farther on to the baggage room and, I believe, the mail-sorting room. At the top of these stairs I found a couple of mail clerks wet to their knees, who had just come up from below, bringing their registered mail bags. As the door in the bulkhead in the next deck was open, I was able to look directly into the trunk room, which was then filled with water, and was within 18 inches or two feet of the deck above.

We were standing there joking about our baggage being completely soaked, and about the correspondence which was seen floating about on the top of the water. I personally felt no sense of danger, as this water was forward of the bulkhead.

While we were standing there, three of the ship's officers – I did not notice their rank or department – descended the first companion and looked into the baggage room, coming back up immediately, saying that we were not making any more water. This was not an announcement, but merely a remark passed from one to the other. Then my wife and myself returned in the direction of our stateroom, a matter of a few yards away only, and as we were going down our own alleyway to the stateroom door our steward came by and told us that we could go back to bed again; that there was no danger. In this I agreed with him, personally.

However, I finished dressing, my wife being already fully and warmly clothed, and she, in the meanwhile having gone out into the passage to note any later developments, came rushing back to me, saying that she had seen another passenger who informed her that the call had been given out for lifebelts and to go on the boat deck. I went out myself, and found my room steward passing down the alleyway, and had the order verified.

As I was at the time fully dressed and wore my heavy overcoat, in the pockets of which I had already placed certain necessities, we started up. My wife had presence of mind enough to take a lifebelt. I opened my steamer trunk and took out a small pocket compass, and, sending my wife on ahead, opened my bag and removed my automatic pistol. We then proceeded immediately upward, my wife being rather alarmed, as she had also been at the time of the collision.

But for her I should have remained in bed, reading.

Henry Etches – Bedroom Steward
At that minute I heard a loud shout, 'Close watertight bulkheads.' I recognised it as our boatswain's voice; it was extra loud. I looked out and he was running from fore to aft. The one shout, 'Close watertight bulkhead doors.'

I partly dressed and looked out of the door, and I saw the Third Class passengers coming along from forward with their portmanteaus. I had gotten about 30 yards, when I met a passenger with a piece of ice, and he said, 'Will you believe it now?' And threw it down on the deck. With that, I went back and finished dressing, and then went up on deck. As I was going through the door I met a bedroom steward named Stone. I said, 'What is the time?' He said, 'Never mind about that; there is something else for you to do. I saw them pull up bags of mail, and the water running out of the bottom of them.'

When I got on A deck, the bedroom steward was assisting passengers then, and most of the doors were open. I said, 'Have you called all of your people?' He said, 'Yes, but I can't get them to dress.' They were standing in the corridors partly dressed. I said, 'I will go down on my deck,' and with that I went down to B deck, arousing my passengers.

I aroused the passengers in my stateroom. The first cabin I went to was at the foot of the pantry stairs. I pulled the bottom drawer out there and stood on it, and got out lifebelts. As a gentleman was passing there, I gave him one of those. He was a stout gentleman; he appeared to be an Englishman. He said, 'Show me how to put this on,' and I showed him how. Then he said, 'Tie it for me.' I said, 'Pull the strings around to the front and tie it,' and as he was doing it I ran outside and opened other doors.

Mr Guggenheim and his secretary were in their room. He apparently had only just gone to his room, for he answered the first knock. The lifebelts in this cabin were in the wardrobe, in a small rack. There were three lifebelts there, and I took them out and put one on Mr Guggenheim. He said, 'This will hurt.' I said, 'You have plenty of time, put on some clothes, and I will be back in a few minutes.'

I then found No 78 cabin door shut, and I banged with both hands on the door loudly, and a voice answered,

'What is it?' Then a lady's voice said, 'Tell me what the trouble is.' I said, 'It is necessary that you should open the door, and I will explain everything, but please put the lifebelts on or bring them in the corridor.' They said, 'I want to know what is the matter.' I said, 'Kindly open the door,' and I still kept banging.

I passed along, and I found one cabin was empty, and then I came to another cabin, and a lady and a gentleman stood at the door. They were swinging a lifebelt in their hands. I don't know the name. It was a shortish name, and I fancy it began with S. They were a stiff-built gentleman and a rather short, thin lady. They were undoubtedly Americans.

I went along to the purser's place. He said, 'It is necessary to go up on the boat deck.' And he said, 'Tell all the other bedroom stewards to assemble their passengers on the boat deck and stand by.'

Charles Lightoller – Second Officer
The lifebelt consists of a series of pieces of cork. A hole is cut for the head to go through, the flaps fall over front and back, and there are tapes from the back then tied around the front. It is tied to the body. It is a new idea and very effective, because no one can make a mistake in putting it on.

Joseph Wheat – Assistant Second Steward
I saw the mail men dragging bags of mail up, which I took to be the registered mail. The water was already on G deck when I got on it, and rising rapidly. I went upstairs to E deck again, and down to F deck to close the bulkhead doors by the Turkish baths. There are two bulkhead doors there. I closed the inside one myself, and then to close the other we

had to go on top and turn that one with a key. Mr Dodd and Crosby, the Turkish bath attendant, helped me.

I went and saw if all the people were out of the Turkish bath attendants' quarters. As I was coming up, there was water running off E deck, down the stairway on to F deck. It was more than trickling, but it was not exactly a stream.

I thought the water had come up the stairway leading down to the Post Office, and then ran along E deck, and then down on to F. There is no bulkhead between the stairway and those stairs on E deck. The watertight doors are further aft. There is nothing to stop the water from coming up to F deck.

Francis Carruthers – Board of Trade Surveyor
As these bulkheads were built I followed their construction. When they were riveted I inspected them to see how they were riveted and if they were well riveted; and when they were finished I went round and tested the caulking of the bulkheads and at the end of the survey, a few days before she was finished, I went round the bulkheads to see that all the small holes that are drilled for carrying through the heating pipes and the electric light wires were all properly made fast. I went over the bulkheads with a feeler, a small-bladed knife, round the caulking, and saw there were no rivet holes left unfilled.

I found them all very good indeed. I think if I had found any of the bulkheads not watertight I would have submitted the question to London.

John Binns – Former Marconi Operator, SS *Republic*
From the plans of the Titanic, *the vessel has been built*

to meet every possible accident, with the exception of a glancing blow. The ship has a certain number of watertight compartments and also a double bottom; but according to the plans the sides of the ship are just a single shell under the waterline. In the event of a glancing blow extending from one end of the ship to the other the watertight compartments would be rendered absolutely useless, owing to the fact that there is no side protection.

Helen Bishop – First Class Passenger

My husband awakened me at about a quarter of 12 and told me that the boat had struck something. We both dressed and went up on the deck, looked around, and could find nothing. We noticed the intense cold; in fact, we had noticed that about 11 o'clock that night. It was uncomfortably cold in the lounge. We looked all over the deck; walked up and down a couple of times, and one of the stewards met us and laughed at us. He said, 'You go back downstairs. There is nothing to be afraid of. We have only struck a little piece of ice and passed it.' So we returned to our stateroom and retired.

About 15 minutes later we were awakened by a man who had a room near us. He told us to come upstairs. So we dressed again thoroughly, looked over all our belongings and went upstairs. After being there about five or ten minutes, Mr Astor, one of the men we were with, ran up and spoke to the captain, who was just then coming down the stairs. The captain told him something in an undertone. He came back and told six of us, who were standing with his wife, that we had better put on our lifebelts. I had gotten down two flights of stairs to tell my husband, who had returned to the stateroom for a moment, before I heard the captain announce that the lifebelts should be put on. That was about three or four minutes later.

We came back upstairs and found very few people up. There was very little confusion; only the older women were a little frightened. They were up, partially dressed. So I sent a number of them back and saw that they were thoroughly dressed before they came up again. Then we went up on to the boat deck on the starboard side. We looked around, and there were so very few people up there that my husband and I went to the port side to see if there was anyone there. There were only two people, a young French bride and groom, on that side of the boat, and they followed us immediately to the starboard side. By that time an old man had come upstairs and found Mr and Mrs Harder, of New York. He brought us all together and told us to be sure and stay together; that he would be back in a moment. We never saw him again. About five minutes later the boats were lowered, and we were pushed in. At the time our lifeboat was lowered I had no idea that it was time to get off.

We thought of nothing at all except the luxury of the ship, and how wonderful it was.

George Harder – First Class Passenger
When we came out of our stateroom and took our lifebelts and coats, I noticed about four or five men on this E deck. One of them had one of those T-handled wrenches, used to turn some kind of a nut or bolt, and two or three of the other men had wrenches with them. I did not take any particular notice, but I did notice this one man trying to turn this thing in the floor. There was a circular brass plate about

ten inches or a foot wide; it was marked 'WTC' or 'WTD' or something like that. A few days before, I noticed that brass plate and, naturally, seeing the initials 'WT' I thought it meant watertight doors, or compartments. It was between the stairs and the elevators on the starboard side of the boat.

We heard one of these men with the wrenches say: 'Well, it's no use. This one won't work. Let's try another one.' They did not seem to be nervous at all; so I thought at the time there was no danger; that they were just doing that for the sake of precaution.

Norman Chambers – First Class Passenger

I was rather surprised at the time when she struck to hear no particular orders or signals for closing the watertight doors. While I did not make a careful examination of the mechanism of the doors, I, at the same time, had looked them over rather more than casually, on my way to and from the swimming pool in the mornings. I remember being somewhat surprised that these doors were not nowadays operated by electricity, this being only a landsman's point of view.

The cover plates to the mechanism of the watertight doors, as far as I am able to state, were not removed before our final departure for the upper decks. I saw no attempt being made to remove them. I have no reason to believe that any attempt was made by the stewards, on whom I have always understood this duty devolved, to close these doors, particularly as a large percentage of the steward part of the crew were new. Seeing these door plates undisturbed just before our final departure to the upper decks, I reached the conclusion that the doors had not been closed.

Charles Lightoller – Second Officer
I am given to understand from passengers that every discipline was shown amongst the stewards. They all went to their watertight doors and closed them.

Herbert Pitman – Third Officer
The electric watertight doors are operated from the bridge by a lever close to the wheel. There is a lever seven or eight inches long on the bridge, close to the man at the wheel. All you have to do is to just pull it over, and they come right down. There is an electrical bell beside them, which you ring a few minutes before closing, so as to give anyone who might be standing underneath a chance to get out of the way.

Of course, they are not all operated by electricity. It is only those in the bottom of the ship that are operated from the bridge. The others are operated by hand, using a handle and a spindle, which are kept in a rack close alongside. It was our business to see that all the gear was there. The watertight doors worked all right, because I have seen them working at Belfast before we sailed.

Anyhow, the watertight doors were of very little assistance this time, because the ice had ripped the side of the ship out.

'The word came down, "Pass your women up on the boat deck"'

Charles Joughin – Chief Baker

'Provision boats,' or put any spare provisions you have in the boats, that was the order. Any surplus stuff we had around that was handy we would put into the boats. I sent 13 men up with four loaves apiece, 40 pounds of bread each as near as I could guess. That about a quarter past 12.

After I had passed the first lot of bread up, I went down to my room for a drink, and as I was coming back I followed up my men on to the deck. I saw the interpreter passing the people along towards the boats, but there was a difficulty in getting them along because some of the foreign Third Class passengers were bringing their baggage and their children along.

James Johnson – First Saloon Night Watchman

I called all our boys. I told them I thought it was a bit serious. Some of them did come up and some did not, till Mr Dodd came, and he chased everyone out of every glory hole. That is where we all live; it is called 'glory hole' in all ships. We told everyone to get their life-preservers and go to their boats. The bedroom stewards were all told to go to every room and put life-preservers on the passengers and get them out of their cabins. There must have been I think something like 470 stewards altogether. I saw them all bunched together. Everyone was bunched together at first; but after that I only saw one, and he saved himself.

They were told to go to the boats, but they did not think the ship would go down, and they were laughing when the passengers were carrying their baggage about. I am certain if you had got our boys up to the boat stations, they would have been saved. But you could not drive the women – because I tried it, for our boat. I saw the bedroom stewards driving, and I saw Mr Ismay try to drive a few. He had a pair of slippers on and his dust coat, and he was trying to get the women into our boat, and they would not go in for him.

I trampled over a loaf of bread, a big pan loaf. There were biscuits carried up, but nobody seemed to care to put them in. Billy Williams had one box, and there might have been four or five boxes carried up through the companionway. They were shoving each other on, bringing the stores up.

I had no lifebelt then, so I went down for it after. I thought I might have made a mistake in the boat station list, and I went to look at it again. I said, 'I will have a sky again.' I had seen it on Thursday afternoon in the pantry on the port side, right opposite the chief steward's office. It was there from Thursday afternoon. I did see it because I went and looked for my name, and I knew where my boat was. But I went again to make sure I had not made a mistake.

John Hart – Third Class Steward
The chief Third Class steward was there, and he said, 'Get your people roused up and get lifebelts placed upon them; see that they have lifebelts on them.' The majority had retired. I went to each Third Class room and roused them. I saw the lifebelts placed on them that were willing to have them put on them. Some refused to put them on. They said they saw no occasion for putting them on; they did not believe the ship was hurt in any way.

Right from the very first we were trying to convince the

people that she was not hurt. It was not on my own authority at all. The other Third Class steward told me to get my people about as quietly as possible. It was my instructions to do so – in order to keep them quiet; it is quite obvious.

After some little while the word came down, 'Pass your women up on the boat deck.' Those that were willing to go to the boat deck were shown the way. Some were not willing to go to the boat deck, and stayed behind. Some of them went to the boat deck, and found it rather cold, and saw the boats being lowered away, and thought themselves more secure on the ship, and consequently returned to their cabin. I heard two or three say they preferred to remain on the ship than be tossed about on the water like a cockleshell.

I took them up into the after well to the C deck, to the First Class main companion, up to the boat deck. There were barriers that at ordinary times are closed, but they were open. I met several crew on the deck directing them the way to the boat deck. There was one man at the foot of the companion leading from the sleeping accommodation to the after well deck; there was one man at the end of the companion leading from the well deck to the E deck, and there were others along the saloon and second cabin deck showing them the way to the boat deck. So that there was no difficulty for anybody who wanted to get to the boats to find their way there.

There were some that would not come to the deck. They would not leave their apartments; they would not be convinced. Everybody did their best.

Henry Stengel – First Class Passenger

My judgement about the officers is that, when they were

loading, they were cool. They showed very good judgement. They calmed the passengers by making them believe it was not a serious accident. I heard that explained afterwards by an officer of the ship, when he said, 'Suppose we had reported the damage that was done to that vessel; there would not be one of you aboard. The stokers would have come up and taken every boat, and no one would have had a chance of getting aboard of those boats.'

Archibald Gracie – First Class Passenger
The sound was so slight I could not be positive of it. All through the voyage the machinery did not manifest itself at all from my position in my stateroom, so perfect was the boat. I looked out of the door of my stateroom, glanced up and down the passageway to see if there was any commotion, and I did not see anybody nor hear anybody moving at all; but I did not like the sound of it, so I thought I would partially dress myself, which I did, and went on deck.

I went on what they call the A deck. Presently some passengers gathered around. We looked over the sides of the ship to see whether there was any indication of what had caused this noise. I soon learned from friends around that an iceberg had struck us.

Presently along came a gentleman who had ice in his hands. Some of this ice was handed to us with the statement that we had better take this home for souvenirs. Nobody had any fear at that time at all. I looked on deck outside to see if there was any indication of a list. I could not distinguish any. At that time I joined my friend, Mr Clint Smith, and he and I in the cabin did notice a list, but thought it best not to say anything about it for fear of creating some commotion.

Then we agreed to stick by each other through thick and thin if anything occurred, and to meet later on. He went to his cabin and I went to mine. In my cabin I packed my three bags very hurriedly. I thought if we were going to be removed to some other ship it would be easy for the steward to get my luggage out.

As I went up on deck the next time, I saw Mr Ismay with one of the officers. He looked very self-contained, as though he was not fearful of anything, and that gave encouragement to my thought that perhaps the disaster was not anything particularly serious.

Presently I noticed that women and men had life-preservers on, and under protest, as I thought it was rather previous, my steward put a life-preserver around myself and I went up on deck, on the A deck. Here I saw a number of people, among others some ladies whom I had told when I first came on the ship at Southampton that I hoped they would let me do anything I could for them during the voyage. These ladies were Mrs E.D. Appleton, Mrs Cornell, and Mrs Browne, the publisher's wife, of Boston, and Miss Evans. They were somewhat disturbed, of course. I reassured them and pointed out to them the lights of what I thought was a ship or steamer in the distance.

Mr Astor came up and he leaned over the side of the deck, which was an enclosed deck, and there were windows and the glass could be let down. I pointed toward the bow, and there were distinctly seen these lights – or a light, rather one single light. It did not seem to be a star, and that is what we all thought it was, the light of some steamer.

I could not judge how far away, only by what they told me. I should say it could not have been more than six miles away. Ahead toward the bow, because I had to lean over, and here was this lifeboat down by the side at that time, and I pointed right ahead and showed Mr Astor so he could see, and he had to lean away over.

Arthur Peuchen – First Class Passenger

I had only reached my room and was starting to undress when I felt as though a heavy wave had struck our ship. She quivered under it somewhat. If there had been a sea running I would simply have thought it was an unusual wave which had struck the boat; but knowing that it was a calm night and that it was an unusual thing to occur on a calm night, I immediately put my overcoat on and went up on deck. As I started to go through the grand stairway I met a friend, who said, 'Why, we have struck an iceberg.'

I cannot remember his name. He was simply a casual acquaintance I had met. He said, 'If you will go up on the upper deck, you will see the ice on the fore part of the ship.' So I did so. I went up there. I suppose the ice had fallen inside the rail, probably four to four and a half feet. It looked like shell ice, soft ice. But you could see it quite plainly along the bow of the boat. I stood on deck for a few minutes, talking to other friends, and then I went to see my friend, Mr Hugo Ross, to tell him that it was not serious; that we had only struck an iceberg. I suppose fifteen minutes after that I met Mr Hays, his son-in-law, and I said to him, 'Mr Hays, have you seen the ice?' He said, 'No.' I said, 'If you care to see it I will take you up on the deck and show it to you.' So we proceeded from probably C deck to A deck and along forward, and I showed Mr Hays the ice forward.

I know a great many of the passengers were made afraid

by this iceberg passing their portholes. The ship shoved past this ice, and a great many of them told me afterwards they could not understand this thing moving past them – those that were awakened at the time. In fact, it left ice on some of the portholes, they told me.

I happened to look and noticed the boat was listing, probably half an hour after my first visit to the upper deck. I said to Mr Hays, 'Why, she is listing; she should not do that, the water is perfectly calm, and the boat has stopped.' I felt that looked rather serious. He said, 'Oh, I don't know; you cannot sink this boat.' He had a good deal of confidence. He said, 'No matter what we have struck, she is good for eight or ten hours.'

I hardly got back in the grand staircase – I probably waited around there ten minutes more – when I saw the ladies and gentlemen all coming in off of the deck looking very serious, and I caught up to Mr Beatty, and I said, 'What is the matter?' He said, 'Why, the order is for lifebelts and boats.' I could not believe it at first, it seemed so sudden. I said, 'Will you tell Mr Ross?' He said, 'Yes; I will go and see Mr Ross.' I then went to my cabin and changed as quickly as I could from evening dress to heavy clothes. As soon as I got my overcoat on I got my life-preserver and I came out of my cabin.

In the hallway I met a great many people, ladies and gentlemen, with their lifebelts on, and the ladies were crying, principally, most of them. It was a very serious sight, and I commenced to realise how serious matters were.

There was no alarm sounded whatever. In fact, I talked with two young ladies who said their stateroom was right near the Astors', I think almost next to it, and they were not awakened. They slept through this crash, and they were awakened by Mrs Astor. She was in rather an excited state, and their door being open, they think that was the reason they were alerted.

Charles Lightoller – Second Officer

After dressing, I went on deck. At this time the steam was roaring off, and it was very difficult to hear. I met the chief officer almost immediately after coming out of the door of the quarters. First of all he told me to commence to get the covers off the boats. I asked him then if all hands had been called, and he said, 'Yes.'

None of the covers had been stripped, with the exception of the emergency boats. I began on the port side with the port forward boat, that would be No 4, and commenced it stripping off. Then two or three men turned up. I told them off* to No 4 boat and stood off then myself and directed the men as they came up on deck, passing around the boat deck, round the various boats, and seeing that the men were evenly distributed around both the port and starboard.

I did not think it advisable, taking into consideration the row going on with the steam, to make any inquiries about their stations. I could only direct them by motions of the hand. They could not hear what I said.

About the time I had finished seeing the men distributed round the deck, and the boat covers well under way and everything going smoothly, I then enquired of the chief officer whether we should carry on and swing out. Mr Wilde said 'No' or 'Wait', something to that effect, and meeting

---

*To 'tell someone off' meant to assign someone to a post or job.

the commander, I asked him, and he said, 'Yes, swing out.'

From the time we commenced to strip No 4 boat cover until the time when we swung them out, I should judge would be probably at most fifteen or twenty minutes.

Hugh Woolner – First Class Passenger

People were guessing what it might be, and one man called out, 'An iceberg has passed astern,' but who it was I do not know. I then went to look for Mrs Candee, because she was the lady in whom I was most interested, and I met her outside her stateroom. I said: 'Some accident has happened, but I do not think it is anything serious. Let us go for a walk.' We walked the afterdeck for quite a considerable time. As we passed one of the entrances to the corridor, I saw people coming up with lifebelts; so I went inside and asked the steward, 'Is this orders?' and he said, 'Orders.'

I went back to Mrs Candee and took her to her stateroom, and we got her lifebelt down from the top of the wardrobe, and tied hers on to her. Then she chose one or two things out of her baggage, little things she could put into her pocket, or something of that sort, and I said, 'We will now go up on deck and see what has really happened.'

Charles Lightoller – Second Officer

After I had swung out No 4 boat, I asked the chief officer should we put the women and children in, and he said, 'No.' I left the men to go ahead with their work and found the commander, or I met him and I asked him should we put the women and children in, and the commander said, 'Yes, put the women and children in and lower away.' Those were the last orders he gave.

I swung out No 4 with the intention of loading all the boats from A deck, the next deck below the boat deck. I lowered No 4 down to A deck, and gave orders for the women and children to go down to A deck to be loaded through the windows. My reason for loading the boats through the windows from A deck was that there was a coaling wire, a very strong wire running along A deck, and I thought it would be very useful to trice the boat to in case the ship got a slight list or anything. But as I was going down the ladder after giving the order, someone sung out and said the windows were up. I countermanded the order and told the people to come back on the boat deck and instructed two or three, I think they were stewards, to find the handles and lower the windows. That left No 4 boat hanging at A deck, so then I went on to No 6.

Hugh Woolner – First Class Passenger

The captain was there when I came up on to the boat deck. He was between the two lifeboats that were farthest astern on the port side, giving orders. I did not look at my watch, but I should think it was half an hour after the collision. He said: 'I want all the passengers to go down on A deck, because I intend they shall go into the boats from A deck.' I remembered noticing as I came up that all those glass windows were raised to the very top. I went up to the captain and saluted him and said: 'Haven't you forgotten, that all those glass windows are closed?' He said: 'By God, you are right. Call those people back.' Very few people had moved, but the few that had gone down the companionway came up again, and everything went on all right.

Norman Chambers – First Class Passenger

We then proceeded to the boat deck on the starboard side. I gave my wife a drink from my flask, filled my pipe, put on my lifebelt at her urgent request, she having hers already on, and we stood at the rail for a few moments. All this time I considered that the lifeboats were merely a precaution and, upon my wife's suggestion, we moved up forward of the entry from the deck house.

From the moment the engines were stopped, steam was of course blown out from the boilers. This, coming through one single steam pipe on the starboard side of the forward funnel, made a terrific loud noise; so loud, indeed, that persons on the boat deck could only communicate by getting as close as possible and speaking loudly. As a matter of fact, I shouted in my wife's ear.

There were still quite a number of passengers coming out, the stewards standing there directing them to the boats aft. We waited until people had apparently ceased coming and the steward was no longer there, then we started forward again, and stopped at the last one of the forward starboard group of lifeboats. This was already swung out level with the deck, and to my eyes, appeared sufficiently loaded.

However, my wife said that she was going in that boat, and proceeded to jump in, calling me to come. As I knew she would get out again had I not come, I finally jumped into the boat, although I did not consider it, from the looks of things, safe to put very many more people in that boat. As I remember it, there were two more men, both called by their wives, who jumped in after I did.

By the time we were settled and I began to take note of the things on the ship, I noticed a tall young officer clad in a long overcoat giving orders to another officer to go into our boat and take charge of the boats on our side. As a parting injunction he gave our officer instructions to hold on to his painter and pull up alongside the gangway after the boat had reached the water. Preliminary to this, and before lowering, I heard someone in authority say, 'That is enough before lowering. We can get more in after she is in the water.'

I remember these conversations particularly, as at the time I was wondering at the source of the order, being morally certain, myself, that no doors in the ship's side had been opened.

We were then lowered away in a manner which I would consider very satisfactory, taking into account the apparent absolute lack of training of the rank and file of the crew.

Shortly before we reached the water, our officer called and finally blew his whistle for them to stop lowering, that he might find out if the plug was in or not. The inquiry was called in a loud tone of voice, to which one of the crew in our boat replied that it was, that he himself had put it in. Meanwhile a voice from above called down, as nearly as I can recollect it, 'It is your own blooming business to see that the plug is in, anyhow.'

Herbert Pitman – Third Officer

I immediately went to the boat deck, and assisted in getting boats uncovered and ready for swinging out. In the act of clearing away No 5 boat, a man said to me – he was dressed in a dressing gown, with slippers on – he said to me very quietly, 'There is no time to waste.' I thought he did not know anything about it at all. So I said, 'I await the commander's orders,' to which he replied, 'Very well.' It then dawned on me that it might be Mr Ismay, judging by the description I had had given me.

So I went along to the bridge and saw Captain Smith, and I told him that I thought it was Mr Ismay that wished me to get the boat away, with women and children in it. He said, 'Go ahead. Carry on.' I came along and brought in my boat. I stood on it and said, 'Come along, ladies.' There was a big crowd. Mr Ismay helped to get them along; assisted in every way. We got the boat nearly full, and I shouted out for any more ladies. None were to be seen, so I allowed a few men to get into it.

Then I jumped on the ship again. Murdoch said, 'You go in charge of this boat, old man, and hang around the after gangway.' I did not like the idea of going away at all, because I thought I was better off on the ship. He shook hands with me and said, 'Goodbye. Good luck to you,' and I said, 'Lower away.'

I did not think the ship was doomed then, but I thought he must have thought so.

Harold Lowe – Fifth Officer

I first of all went and got my revolver; you never know when you will need it. Then I went and helped everybody all around. The first boat I helped to lower was No 5, starboard boat. I lowered that boat away under the orders of Mr Murdoch. He was the senior officer. He was superintending that deck; he was in charge of everything there.

There was a man at the ship's side, hanging on the davit, and I was slacking away just at his feet. He was trying all in his power to help the work, and he was getting a little bit excited. He said, 'Lower away, lower away, lower away.' I said, 'Do you want me to lower away quickly? You will have me drown the whole lot of them.' I told him, 'If you will get to hell out of that, I shall be able to do something.' Because he was, in a way, interfering with my duties.

He did not make any reply. He walked away and then he went to No 3 boat, the next boat forward of mine, on the same side. He went ahead there on his own hook, getting things ready there, to the best of his ability. I afterwards learned it was Mr Bruce Ismay.

Archibald Gracie – First Class Passenger
Some time elapsed, I should say from three-quarters of an hour to an hour, before we were ordered to the boats. Then a young English officer of the ship, a tall thin chap, Moody was his name, he said, 'No man beyond this line.' Then the women went beyond that line. I saw that these four ladies, with whose safety I considered myself entrusted, went beyond that line to get amidships on this deck, which was A deck. Then I saw Mr Straus and Mrs Straus, of whom I had seen a great deal during the voyage. I had heard them discussing that if they were going to die they would die together. We tried to persuade Mrs Straus to go alone, without her husband, and she said no. Then we wanted to make an exception of the husband, too, because he was an elderly man, and he said no, he would share his fate with the rest of the men, and that he would not go beyond. So I left them there.

Just prior to this time I had passed through A deck, going from the stern toward the bow. I saw four gentlemen all alone in the smoking room, whom I recognised as Mr Millet, Mr Moore and Mr Butt, and who I afterwards ascertained to have been Mr Ryerson. They seemed to be absolutely intent upon what they were doing, and disregarding anything about what was going on on the decks outside.

Then I found my friend Smith, and we worked together under the second officer in loading and helping the women and babies and children aboard the different boats. I think we loaded about two boats there. There were no men allowed in the boats, not one, except the crews necessary to man the boats.

The only incident I remember in particular at this point is when Mrs Astor was put in the boat. She was lifted up through the window, and her husband helped her on the other side, and when she got in, her husband was on one side of this window and I was on the other side, at the next window. I heard Mr Astor ask the second officer whether he would not be allowed to go aboard this boat to protect his wife. He said, 'No, sir; no man is allowed on this boat or any of the boats until the ladies are off.' Mr Astor then said, 'Well, tell me what is the number of this boat so I may find her afterwards,' or words to that effect. The answer came back, 'No 4.'

I think it was on account of the condition of his wife. If it had been explained to the second officer that Mr Astor's wife was with child, possibly he might have been allowed to get in that boat.

I want to say that there was nothing but the most heroic conduct on the part of all men and women at that time, where I was at the bow on the port side. There was no man who asked to get in a boat, with the single exception that I have already mentioned. No woman even sobbed or wrung her hands, and everything appeared perfectly orderly. Lightoller was splendid in his conduct with the crew, and the crew did their duty. It seemed to me it was rather a little bit more difficult than it should have been to launch the boats alongside the ship. I do not know the cause of that. I do not know whether it was on account of the newness of it all, the painting, or something of that sort. I know I had to use my muscle as best I could in trying to push those boats so as to get them over the gunwale.

The crew seemed to resent my working with them, but they were very glad when I worked with them later on. Every opportunity I got to help, I helped.

Emily Ryerson – First Class Passenger

I waked up all the children and my husband, and Miss Bowen and my daughter next door were awake, and we went up on A deck, the enclosed deck. Later, we were ordered to go up to the boat deck by Stout [sic], the second steward in the dining room, whom I knew. I had my meals in my room, I didn't know my way about the ship at all. I hadn't been on deck except that one time in the daytime.

My husband said, 'When they say women and children, you must go.' I said, 'Why do I have to go on that boat?' and he said, 'You must obey the captain's orders, and I will get in somehow.'

Stout, the second steward in the dining room, was at the foot of the stairs as we came from the boat deck, and he put his hand in front of my little boy, who is 13, and said, 'He can't go.' My husband said, 'Of course that boy goes with his mother.' The man said, 'Very well, sir, but no more boys.' And some woman rushed forward and took her hat off and put it on her little boy's head, so he could go as a little girl. That was Mrs Carter, I think.

I remember seeing Mr Astor leaning out, and a man said, 'You can't go.' He said, 'I don't want to go. I was looking to see if my wife was all right,' and he dropped his gloves over to her.

The captain called, 'How many women have you?' Someone said, 'Twenty-four,' and he said, 'That is enough.' The lifeboat seemed to stick, and somebody said we were going to upset, and I thought we had a tremendous drop, but we were so near the water, and finally the davits got loose and we dropped a short distance. After we stuck, someone said something about a knife, but we never used it, and during that wait some men got into the boat. I don't know who they were. I never saw them afterwards – they seemed to disappear. They weren't First Class passengers.

Olaus Abelseth – Third Class Passenger

There was quite a lot of ice on the starboard part of the ship. They wanted us to go down again, and I saw one of the officers, and I said to him: 'Is there any danger?' He said, 'No.' I was not satisfied with that, however, so I went down and told my brother-in-law and my cousin, who were in the same compartment there. They were not in the same room, but they were just a little ways from where I was. I told them about what was happening, and I said they had better get up. Both of them got up and dressed, and we took our overcoats and put them on. We did not take any lifebelts with us. There was no water on the deck at that time.

We walked to the hind part of the ship and got two Norwegian girls up. One was in my charge and one was in the charge of the man who was in the same room with me. He was from the same town that I came from. The other one was just 16 years old, and her father told me to take care of her until we got to Minneapolis. The two girls were in a room in the hind part of the ship, in the steerage.

We all went up on deck and stayed there. We walked over to the port side of the ship, and there were five of us standing, looking, and we thought we saw a light. It was up on the boat deck, the place for the steerage passengers on the deck. We were then on the port side there, and we looked out at this light. I said to my brother-in-law, 'I can see it plain, now. It must be a light.'

I could not say how far it was, but it did not seem to be so very far. I thought I could see this mast light, the front mast light. That is what I thought I could see. A little while later there was one of the officers who came and said to be quiet, that there was a ship coming. That is all he said. He did not say what time, or anything. That is all he said. So I said to them, we had better go and get the lifebelts, as we had not brought them with us. So my cousin and I went down to get the them for all of us. When we came up again we carried the lifebelts on our arms for a while.

There were a lot of steerage people there that were getting on one of these cranes that they had on deck, that they used to lift things with. They can lift about two and a half tons, I believe. These steerage passengers were crawling along on this, over the railing, and away up to the boat deck. A lot of them were doing that. This gate was shut. I do not know whether it was locked, but it was shut so that they could not go that way.

That was in order to get up on this boat deck. But down where we were, in the rooms, I think the steerage passengers had an opportunity to get up. I do not think there was anybody that held anybody back. I could not say that for sure; but I think the most of them got out.

A while later these girls were standing there, and one of the officers came and hollered for all of the ladies to come up on the boat deck. The gate was opened and these two girls went up.

Daniel Buckley – Third Class Passenger
They tried to keep us down at first on our steerage deck. They did not want us to go up to the First Class place at all. I cannot say who they were; I think they were sailors.

The First Class deck was higher up than the steerage deck, and there were some steps leading up to it: nine or ten steps, and a gate just at the top of the steps. There was one steerage passenger, and he was getting up the steps. Just as he was going in the little gate, a fellow came along and chucked him down; threw him down into the steerage place. This fellow got excited, and he ran after him, and he could not find him. He said if he could get hold of him, he would throw him into the ocean.

The gate was not locked at the time we made the attempt to get up there, but the sailor, or whoever he was, locked it. So this fellow that went up after him broke the lock on it. All the steerage passengers went up on the First Class deck then, when the gate was broken. They all got up there. They could not keep them down.

Joseph Scarrott – Able Seaman
It is difficult for Third Class passengers to gain access to the boat deck. There is only one ladder. You have to go inside one part and up another ladder. There are other ladders on

the after part of the deck house, but they are only rungs on the side of a house, hardly ladders. They are straight up and down, and anybody outside seafaring men would find it a difficult job.

First and Second Class passengers had a better chance of getting to the boats, on account of their being allowed on that deck.

Harold Sanderson – Co-director, White Star Line
I think the means of access are as near perfection as they can be on the Titanic. *I do not admit that there was any intricate maze of passages, and I do not think the position of the Third Class passengers had anything to do with their not going away in the same number. I think that the position in which the boats are placed on the ship necessarily being the position which is the best for launching them, happens to be abreast of that portion of the ship in which the First and Second Class passengers are carried. Therefore, when the call for women and children came, the women and children who were handiest came to the boats first.*

The Third Class well deck would be a very inconvenient place to carry a boat and almost an impossible place to launch a boat from, because of the overhang. To launch a boat would be a most dangerous thing to attempt in that portion of the ship.

Edward Wilding – Naval Architect, Harland & Wolff
The Board of Trade insists on a ladder being provided up to the level from each compartment. On this ladderway at the after end of B deck, there is a hinged gate which anyone can lift and walk through – on the port and starboard sides.

That is the only thing preventing Third Class passengers in the ordinary course getting up to the boat deck. There is no lock on it, and no means of locking it provided.

I went at a slow walking pace, from the very lowest part of the Third Class accommodation on to the boat deck. On one occasion one of the assessors accompanied me; on one occasion one of the Board of Trade Counsel, and on one occasion the Counsel for the Third Class passengers. The times varied a little, but they were always between three and three and a half minutes. That is right down from the lowest Third Class cabin that was occupied.

Harold Lowe – Fifth Officer

They did not know how to man or care for lifeboats. They were the same men as you get in every mercantile marine, not the British alone. You will find the best sailors going in the British marine; but that does not matter. It is the same in the American, and just the same everywhere.

A sailor is not necessarily a boatman; neither is a boatman a sailor, because they are two very different callings. I might pride myself that I am both – both a sailor and a boatman. A sailor may go to sea for quite a number of years and never go into a boat, never touch an oar, whereas you put a boatman in a ship and put him to do a job, and he is useless. He does not know anything about it. That is trying to convert a boatman into a sailor. They are both very different callings. That is the reason why many of the sailors could not row.

That is about all I have to say about the sailors not being boatmen.

'Come at once. It is a CQD, old man'

Joseph Boxhall – Fourth Officer

After seeing all the men were well established with their work, I went to the chart room and worked out the ship's position. I worked it out for 11.46. I computed it by star observations that had been taken by Mr Lightoller that same evening; and they were beautiful observations. I have the position in my head: forty-one, forty-six, north; fifty, fourteen west [41° 46' N, 50° 14' W]. That is the position I worked out; that was the position at the time she struck.

I submitted the position to the captain, and he said, 'Take it to the Marconi room.' I found the two operators there, Phillips and Bride. There was too much noise of the steam escaping, so I wrote the position down for them and left it on his table there. He [Phillips] saw it. He made a call, and he was listening, and I did not interrupt him.

Then I heard someone report a light ahead. I went on the bridge and had a look to see what the light was. It was two masthead lights of a steamer. I could see the light with the naked eye, but I could not define what it was. By the aid of a pair of glasses, I found it was the two masthead lights of a vessel, probably about half a point on the port bow, and in the position she would be showing her red if it were visible, but she was too far off then.

Then I saw her sidelights; I saw her green light and the red. She was end-on to us. Later I saw her red light. This is all with the aid of a pair of glasses. Afterwards, I saw the ship's red light with my naked eye, and the two masthead lights. The only description of the ship that I could give is that she was, or I judged her to be, a four-masted steamer, judging by the position of her masthead lights. A sailing vessel does not show steaming lights, or white lights.

Captain Smith was standing by my side, and we both came to the conclusion that she was close enough to be signalled by the Morse lamp. So I signalled to her. The captain said, 'Tell him to come at once, we are sinking.' So I sent that signal out, 'Come at once, we are sinking.'

There were a lot of stewards and men standing around the bridge and around the boat deck. Of course, there were quite a lot of them quite interested in this ship, looking from the bridge, and some said she had shown a light in reply, but I never saw it. I even got the quartermaster to fire off the distress signal and to signal with the Morse lamp, while I watched with a pair of glasses to see if I could see signs of any answer. But I could not see any. Captain Smith also looked, and he could not see any answer.

After I first saw the masthead lights, she must have been still steaming, but by the time I saw her red light with my naked eye she was not steaming very much. So she had probably gotten into the ice, and turned around. I judged her to be about five miles away, and I arrived at it in this way. The masthead lights of a steamer are required by the board of trade regulations to show for five miles, and the signals are required to show for two miles. I could see her lights quite clearly: I think we could see her lights more than the regulation distance, but I do not think we could see them 14 miles. Whatever ship she was had beautiful lights.

And then she turned round. She was turning very, very slowly, until at last I only saw her stern light.

Harold Bride – Assistant Telegraphist

I woke up of my own accord at about a quarter to 12. I had promised to relieve Mr Phillips earlier than usual. He had a big batch of telegrams from Cape Race that he had just finished. He told me that he thought the ship had got damaged in some way, and that he expected that we should have to go back to Harland & Wolff's.

Mr Phillips was going to retire, when the captain came in. He said, 'You had better get assistance.' When Mr Phillips heard him, he came out and asked him if he wanted him to use a distress call. He said, 'Yes. At once.' Mr Phillips immediately sent CQD MGY about half a dozen times – CQD is a recognised distress call, and MGY is the code call of the *Titanic*.

The first answer was from the *Frankfurt*, 'OK. Stand by.' That meant he had got our message and would let us hear from him in a minute or so. Mr Phillips told me to go to the captain and report that he was in communication with the *Frankfurt*.

I went to report to the captain. He was on the boat deck, the starboard side, if I remember. He was superintending the loading of the lifeboats. He wanted to know where the *Frankfurt* was. I told him we would get that as soon as we could.

Next was the *Carpathia*. She sent her latitude and longitude and told us she had turned around and was steaming full speed. I took the message to the captain. He was in the wheelhouse, and came back with me to the cabin. He asked Mr Phillips what other ships he was in communication with. He interrupted Mr Phillips while he was establishing communication with the *Olympic*, so he was told the *Olympic* was there.

Harold Cottam – Marconi Officer, SS *Carpathia*

The receiver was on my head. I was waiting for a confirmation of a previous communication I had had with the Parisian. *I had taken my coat off and should have finished for the night. I would have, if I had ever caught the* Parisian, *but I did not catch him; apparently he had gone to bed. The hour was about eleven o'clock, New York time.*

The first message from the Titanic *was, 'Come at once. It is a CQD, old man.' 'CQD' is the distress call. 'Old man' is simply a complimentary remark that is passed in wireless-telegraph service. Then he sent his position.*

I confirmed it before reporting it to the bridge. I asked him if he intended me to go straight away to the bridge and get the ship turned round immediately, and he said, 'Yes, quick.' I reported it to the officer on watch first, and, from him, to the captain. The ship was turned round immediately, and headed for the position.

The captain told me to tell the Titanic *that all our boats were ready and we were coming as hard as we could come, with a double watch on in the engine room, and to be prepared, when we got there, with lifeboats. The captain gave me our position, and I went straight away back to the cabin and sent it. I got no acknowledgement of that message.*

I kept in touch with the Titanic *the whole time, and helped him to communicate. After I had sent our position, he said he could not read signals because of the escape of steam and the air through the expansion joint; the water rushing into the hollow of the ship was driving the air through the joint, right across the deck just outside the cabin. It would not only be the noise; it would also be the trembling of the ship. He said he could not read them well, so I simply stood by and helped him with the communications.*

Arthur Rostron – Captain, SS *Carpathia*
At 12:35am on Monday, I was informed of the urgent distress signal from the Titanic. *The wireless operator had taken the message and run with it up to the bridge, and gave it to the first officer who was in charge, with a junior officer with him, and both ran down the ladder to my door and called me. I had only just turned in. It was an urgent distress signal from the* Titanic, *requiring immediate assistance and giving me his position. I cannot say whether it was CQD or SOS. The position of the* Titanic *at the time was 41° 46' N, 50° 14' W. We were only 58 miles away from them.*

Immediately on getting the message, I gave the order to turn the ship around, and immediately I had given that order I asked the operator if he was absolutely sure it was a distress signal from the Titanic. *I asked him twice. He simply told me that he had received a distress signal from the* Titanic, *requiring immediate assistance, and gave me his position; and he assured me he was absolutely certain of the message.*

I picked up our position on my chart, and set a course to pick up the Titanic. *The course was north 52° west true, 58 miles from my position. I then sent for the chief engineer. In the meantime, I was dressing and seeing the ship put on her course. The chief engineer came up, and I told him to call another watch of stokers and make all possible speed to the* Titanic, *as she was in trouble. Our speed ordinarily is about*

14 knots, but we worked up to about 17½ knots that night. That was about the highest speed we made.

As soon as I put her on the course for the Titanic's *position, I doubled the lookouts, and took all the precautions I possibly could. I knew there was ice about, because the* Titanic *told me he had struck ice. Therefore, I was prepared to be in the vicinity of ice when I was getting near him, because if he had struck a berg and I was going to his position I knew very well that there must be ice about.*

Although I was running a risk with my own ship and my own passengers, I also had to consider what I was going for; I had to consider the lives of others. Of course there was a chance we would encounter ice, but at the same time I knew quite what I was doing. I considered that I was perfectly free, and that I was doing perfectly right in what I did.

I went full speed, all we could – I did, and doubled my lookouts, and took extra precautions and exerted extra vigilance. Every possible care was taken. We were all on the qui vive.

Harold Bride – Assistant Telegraphist

After the *Olympic*, we did not get any replies. We had transmitted to the *Frankfurt* our position, but we had received nothing from him in return. He had told us to stand by. I believe she was bound east, but I cannot say for certain. I do not think there was any communication established with the *Frankfurt* before we sent the distress signal.

Mr Phillips told me that, judging by the strength of the signals received from the two ships, the *Frankfurt* was the nearer. He was under the impression that when the

Frankfurt had heard the CQD and got our position, he would immediately make it known to his commander and take further steps. Apparently he did not. The captain asked us where the *Frankfurt* was, but we told him we could not tell him.

The *Frankfurt* called us up at a considerably long period afterwards, I should say over twenty minutes afterwards, and merely asked us what was the matter. It struck me he did not seem to be able to realise the position we were in. We made it very clear to him. If you call CQD and give your position, then there is no necessity for another ship to inquire further into the matter, because you could not call CQD unless you were in need of assistance. Any operator hearing a CQD, giving a ship's position, when on the job would immediately, without inquiring further into the matter, go to his captain and inform him. It would be a waste of time asking anything about it. The less time spent in talking, the more time can be spent in getting to the ship. We could not send anything more than CQD. CQD is the whole thing in a nutshell.

Mr Phillips responded rather hurriedly and told him he was a fool. He told him to keep out and not interfere with our communication, because we were in communication with the *Carpathia*, and we knew that the *Carpathia* was the best thing doing.

We received several messages from the *Olympic* from time to time, but to the best of my recollection they were not delivered because Captain Smith was busy and we presumed he would be worried, and we let them go. One message I remember was that the commander of the *Olympic* told Captain Smith to have his lifeboats ready. Captain Haddock [of the *Olympic*] was sending us communications until the time we left the cabin for good.

Harold Cottam – Marconi Officer, SS *Carpathia*
When I came back from the bridge and sent my position he was in communication with the Frankfurt. *After the* Titanic *first sent her position, the* Frankfurt *operator got up apparently, and he came back in twenty minutes and asked what was the matter. I did not hear it all because I was running backwards and forwards from the bridge reporting the whole time.*

There used to be a certain amount of rivalry, before the Marconi company amalgamated with the Telefunken. But the CQD call ought to be quite sufficient for any man who understands the English language, or the German language, for that matter. When a man sends his position and CQD, the first thing to do is to turn right around and steer for that position. The position of the Frankfurt *to the* Titanic *did not matter at all. He ought not to have hesitated a minute.*

He told him to 'keep out' because if he had not done it he would have been a nuisance, as we were in good, satisfactory communication. When a man takes twenty minutes to answer in a case like that, when two hours is between life and death, a fool is about the only fit thing you can call him. I should have told him the same. I should not give up a certainty for an uncertainty, when I was working the certainty.

After that the communications ceased from what I could hear. That was about 10.45pm New York time [12.35am ship's time].

Guglielmo Marconi – Chairman, Marconi International
The call of the Berlin convention, which has only been recently introduced, is this SOS call, but the Marconi companies have used and use the CQD call. The Frankfurt was equipped with wireless made in Germany under my patents, and belonged to one of what I may call the Marconi companies. I should state that the international signal is really less known than the Marconi signal.

James Moore – Captain, SS *Mount Temple*
At 12.30am on 15 April I was awakened by the steward with a message from the Marconi operator. The message was: 'Titanic sends CQD. Requires assistance. Position 41° 46' N, 50° 14' W. Come at once. Iceberg.'

I immediately blew the whistle on the bridge. I have a pipe leading down from the bridge to my cabin, and I blew the whistle at once. I told the second officer to turn the ship around at once and put her on north 45° east, and to come down at once. When he came down, we took the chart out and found out where the Titanic *was and steered north 65° east true by the compass in the direction of the* Titanic. *We were about 49 miles away.*

After I was sufficiently dressed, I went down to the chief engineer and I told him that the Titanic *was sending out messages for help, and I said, 'Go down and try to shake up the fireman, and, if necessary, even give him a tot of rum if you think he can do any more.' I believe this was carried out. I also told him to inform the fireman that we wanted to get back as fast as we possibly could.*

'We were saving life'

Hugh Woolner – First Class Passenger

Very shortly afterwards I noticed the ship was down by the head. When I left No 4 and went to No 6, she was distinctly down by the head, and I think it was while working at that boat it was noticed that she had a pretty heavy list to port. My notice was called to this by Mr Wilde calling out, 'All passengers over to the starboard side.' That was an endeavour to give her a righting movement, and it was then I noticed that the ship had a list. But it would have been far more noticeable on the starboard side than on the port.

Charles Lightoller – Second Officer

I then proceeded to put out No 6 and lower away. I put the women and children in myself. There were no orders. I stood with one foot on the seat just inside the gunwale of the boat, and the other foot on the ship's deck, and the women merely held out their wrist, their hand, and I took them by the wrist and hooked their arm underneath my arm.

We were not undertaking a boat drill then; we were saving life, and were using the men to the best of my knowledge and ability. As a rule, I put about two seamen in a boat. There is no use in sending too many men away and then finding yourself short. If I didn't have a seaman there I had to put a steward there. Sometimes there would be three seamen in a boat. As soon as the boats were lowered to the level of the rail, I would detail one man to jump in and ship the rudder, one man to cast adrift the oars, and one man would see that the plugs were in, and it would take three men.

I used my own judgment about the strength of the tackle to decide how many to put in. In the first boat I put about 20 or 25 women and two seamen. Two was quite sufficient under the conditions. We wanted them up on deck, lowering away the boats.

I knew that it was not practicable to lower the boats full of people. I should not think they were capable of being lowered full of people. I have never seen them full of people, but if they are only supposed to carry 65 people afloat, it hardly seems feasible that they would carry 65 people when suspended at each end. It does not seem seamanlike to fill a boat chock full of people when it is only suspended at each end. It is to guard principally against accidents in lowering.

That must be taken into consideration a very great deal – the fact that you have to lower a boat from a great height and get her safely into the water. It is of more importance to get the boat into the water than it is to actually fill her at the boat deck, because it is no use filling her if you are going to lose those people before you get her down; it is far better to save a few and safely.

I did not know it was urgent then. If had known, I would have taken more risks. I should not have considered it wise to put more in, but I might have taken risks.

Edward Wilding – Naval Architect, Harland & Wolff
I do not think there was any doubt the boats were strong enough to be lowered containing the full number of passengers. We design and construct them ourselves for the purpose of carrying that number and of being lowered. Whether they are filled once afloat, of course, is a question

of sea discipline; but we feel that we must provide, at any rate, that the boats can be lowered from the boat deck with their full number, whatever way they are actually used. To the best of our knowledge and belief we did so.

As far as I know there was no special direct intimation given to the officers that they would carry their full number, but I should have thought it was a matter of general knowledge that they were so constructed. If I had thought there was any doubt on the matter in the officers' minds, I would have done my best to remove it. Of course, what the officers thought one really cannot tell. If the officers had asked about it, or had expressed any doubt about it at Belfast, they would have been told, and the test would have been mentioned to them.

Charles Lightoller – Second Officer

I knew there was this light on the port bow about two points. I had already been calling many of the passengers' attention to it, pointing it out to them and saying there was a ship over there, that probably it was a sailing ship, as she did not appear to come any closer, and that at daylight very likely a breeze would spring up and she would come in and pick us up out of the boats, and generally reassuring them by pointing out the light; but whether I told them to pull towards the light I really could not say. I might have done and I might not.

I had already told the boatswain to go down below and take some men with him and open the gangway doors, with the intention of sending the boats to the gangway doors to be filled up, if there were sufficient time. We had what we term a pilot ladder – a rope ladder – which the men would be able to climb down. I had not discussed the matter with the captain, but it came to both our minds. Anyone familiar with the ship would know at once that was the best means of putting the people into the boat, for it is far better to get the boat waterborne before filling her.

I heard the commander two or three times hail through the megaphone to bring the boats alongside, and I presumed he was alluding to the gangway doors, giving orders to the boats to go to the gangway doors.

Whether the doors were opened, I could not say. I do not think it likely, because it is most probable the boats lying off the ship would have noticed the gangway doors, had they succeeded in opening them. Hanging about the ship they could not very well fail to see if the gangway doors were open – the light shining through, the blaze of lights, and they would very soon be hailed by people at the gangway doors.

The boatswain was down there. He has to use a little common sense as well, and when he has opened the gangway door he would naturally hail a boat, and tell them, 'Starboard gangway door open,' 'The port gangway door open,' and so let them know. On a calm night like that, the voice will carry a long way.

But I did not take that into consideration at that time; there was not time to take all these particulars into mind. In the first place, at this time I did not think the ship was going down. I knew it was serious, and yet I did not think at that time that the ship was going down. By the time I came to the third boat I was aware that it was getting serious, and then I started to take chances. I filled her up as full as I could, and lowered her as full as I dared.

Samuel Hemming – Lamp-trimmer

Mr Lightoller called me and said, 'Come with me.' He said, 'Get another good man.' I says, 'Foley is here somewhere.' He says, 'I have no time to stop for Foley.' So he called a man himself, and he said, 'Follow me.' So we followed him, and he said, 'Stand by to lower this boat.' It was No 4 boat. We lowered the boat in line with the A deck, when I had an order come from the captain to see that the boats were properly provided with lights.

We had no handy lamps. Every lamp that we had was supplied for a certain purpose. We had none outside of that. They were all in the lamp room, where there was a special compartment to keep them in.

I called Mr Lightoller and told him that I would have to leave the boat's fall; so he put another man in my place. I went away into the lamp room lighting the lamps, and I brought them up on deck. Fourteen, all full of oil. Then I lit the lamps and brought them up, four at a time, two in each hand. The boats that were already lowered, I put them on the deck, and asked them to pass them down to the end of the boat fall. I do not know whether they got lights or not. As to the boats that were not lowered, I gave them into the boats myself.

It was a square lamp. About ten inches high and six inches square, fuelled by Colza oil.

'There was no such thing as selecting. I simply shouted "women and children first"'

Mary Smith – First Class Passenger

While I dressed, my husband and I talked of landing, not mentioning the iceberg. I started out, putting on my life-preserver, when we met a steward, who was on his way to tell us to come on deck. However, I returned to the room with the intention of bringing my jewellery, but my husband said not to delay with such trifles. However, I picked up two rings and went on deck. After getting to the top deck, the ladies were ordered on deck A without our husbands. I refused to go, but, after being told by three or four officers, my husband insisted, and, along with another lady, we went down. After staying there some time with nothing seemingly going on, someone called saying they could not be lowered from that deck, for the reason it was enclosed in glass. That seemed to be the first time the officers and captain had thought of that, and hastened to order us all on the top deck again.

There was some delay in getting lifeboats down: in fact, we had plenty of time to sit in the gymnasium and chat with another gentleman and his wife. I kept asking my husband if I could remain with him rather than go in a lifeboat. He promised me I could. There was no commotion, no panic, and no one seemed to be particularly frightened; in fact, most of the people seemed interested in the unusual occurrence, many having crossed 50 and 60 times. However, I noticed my husband was busy talking to any officer he came in contact with; still I had not the least suspicion of the scarcity of lifeboats, or I never should have left my husband.

When the first boat was lowered from the left-hand side, I refused to get in, and they did not urge me particularly. In the second boat, they kept calling for one more lady to fill it, and my husband insisted that I get in it, my friend having gotten in. I refused unless he would go with me. In the meantime Captain Smith was standing with a megaphone on deck. I approached him and told him I was alone, and asked if my husband might be allowed to go in the boat with me.

He ignored me personally, but shouted again through his megaphone, 'Women and children first.' My husband said, 'Never mind, captain, about that; I will see that she gets in the boat.' He then said, 'I never expected to ask you to obey, but this is one time you must; it is only a matter of form to have women and children first. The boat is thoroughly equipped, and everyone on her will be saved.' I asked him if that was absolutely honest, and he said, 'Yes.' I felt some better then, because I had absolute confidence in what he said. He kissed me goodbye and placed me in the lifeboat with the assistance of an officer. As the boat was being lowered he yelled from the deck, 'Keep your hands in your pockets; it is very cold weather.'

That was the last I saw of him, and now I remember the many husbands that turned their backs as the small boat was lowered, the women blissfully innocent of their husbands' peril, and said goodbye with the expectation of seeing them within the next hour or two.

Hugh Woolner – First Class Passenger
Then I took Mrs Candee up on to the boat deck, and there we saw preparations for lowering the boats going on. My

great desire was to get her into the first boat, which I did. We had brought up a rug, which we threw in with her, and we waited to see that boat filled. It was not filled, but a great many people got into it, and finally it was quietly and orderly lowered away.

The captain was close by at that time. He sort of ordered the people in. He said, 'Come along, madam,' and that sort of thing. There was a certain amount of reluctance on the part of the women to go in, and then some officer said, 'It is a matter of precaution,' and they came forward rather more freely. It was a very distressing scene – the men parting from their wives.

So far as I could see, all the women were persuaded to go on the boats, with the exception of Mrs Straus. She would not get in. I tried to get her to do so, and she refused altogether to leave Mr Straus. The second time we went up to Mr Straus, I said to him, 'There seems to be room in this boat. I am sure nobody would object to an old gentleman like you getting in.' He said: 'I will not go before the other men.'

Arthur Peuchen – First Class Passenger
When I came on deck first, there were about a hundred stokers up with their dunnage bags, and they seemed to crowd this whole deck in front of the boats. One of the officers – I do not know which one, but a very powerful one – came along and drove these men right off that deck. He drove them, every man, like a lot of sheep, right off the deck, and they disappeared. I do not know where they went, but it was a splendid act. They did not put up any resistance. I admired him for it.

I saw Mr Hays again on the upper deck. I shook hands

with him then and he said, 'Peuchen, this boat is good for eight hours yet. I have just been getting this from one of the best old seamen, Mr Crossley.*' And he said, 'Before that time, we will have assistance.'

I noticed the crew were not at their stations, ready to man the boats. I imagine this crew was what we would call in yachting terms a scratch crew, brought from different vessels. They might be the best, but they had not been accustomed to working together.

I was standing near by the second officer and the captain, and one of them said, 'We will have to get these masts out of these boats, and also the sail.' He said, 'You might give us a hand.' I jumped in the boat, and we got a knife and cut the lashings of the mast, which is a very heavy mast, and also the sail, and moved it out of the boat, saying it would not be required. Then there was a cry, as soon as that part was done, that they were ready to put the women in; so the women came forward one by one. A great many women came with their husbands.

This was the largest lifeboat – the first large lifeboat toward the bow on the port side. They would only allow women in that boat, and the men had to stand back. That was the order. The second officer stood there and he carried out that to the limit. He allowed no men, except the sailors who were manning the boat. There were no male passengers that I saw got into that boat.

After a reasonable complement of ladies had got aboard, she was lowered. The boat was loaded, but I think they could have taken more in this boat. They took, however, all

---

*Peuchen is probably referring to Edward Crosby.

the ladies that offered to get in at that point.

I never saw such order. It was perfect order. The discipline was splendid. The officers were carrying out their duty and I think the passengers behaved splendidly. I did not see a cowardly act by any man.

I only got into the boat to assist in taking out the mast and the sail. Then I got out again, and I assisted the ladies into the boat. We then went to the next boat and we did the same thing – got the mast and the sail out of that. There was a quartermaster in the boat, and one sailor, and we commenced to put the ladies in that boat. After that boat had got a full complement of ladies, the boat was lowered down some distance, I should think about the third deck, when the quartermaster called up to the officer and said, 'I cannot manage this boat with only one seaman.'

The second officer leaned over and saw he was quite right in his statement, that he had only one man in the boat, so they said, 'We will have to have some more seamen here.' I did not think they were just at hand, or they may have been getting the next boat ready. However, I was standing by the officer, and I said, 'Can I be of any assistance? I am a yachtsman, and can handle a boat with an average man.'

He said, 'Why, yes. I will order you to the boat in preference to a sailor.'

The captain was standing still by him at that time, and I think, although the officer ordered me to the boat, the captain said, 'You had better go down below and break a window and get into the boat through a window.' That was his suggestion, and I said I did not think it was feasible. I said I could get in the boat if I could get hold of a rope. So we got hold of a loose rope that was hanging from the davit, and by getting hold of it I swung myself off the ship and lowered myself into the boat.

I never saw the captain after that. He was doing everything in his power to get women in these boats, and to see that they were lowered properly. I thought he was doing his duty in regard to the lowering of the boats.

Harold Lowe – Fifth Officer

Mr Murdoch gave the order that that was enough in the boat. He said, 'Lower away,' and I lowered away. It is a matter of opinion whether that boat was properly filled or not. 65 is the floating capacity – that is when she is at rest in the water. That is not when she is in the air. The dangers are that if you overcrowd the boat, it will buckle up at the two ends, because she is suspended from both ends and there is no support in the middle.

The number you put on a boat depends on the man in charge. One man will say, 'I will take the chance with 50 people in this boat.' Another man will say, 'I am not going to run the risk of 50; I will take 25 or 30.' I should not like to put more than 50 in, but it is purely personal what a man considered safety. I am different from another man. I may take on more risk, we will say, than you; or you may take on more risk than me.

The lowering of that boat was not up to me; I was not the boss there. Mr Murdoch was running the show.

Sir Cosmo Duff Gordon – First Class Passenger

My wife and her secretary Miss Francatelli were standing with me; they had refused to go. My wife had refused to leave me and go in the boats, and consequently we stood against the deck house while the boats were going. They were asked two or three times to go. Some men from No 3 boat got hold of her and tried to pull her away, but she would not go. When the third boat had been lowered, she said to me: 'Ought not we to do something?' I said: 'No, we have got to wait for orders.'

Then an officer – I do not know who he was – said to a number of firemen or crew who were standing there, 'Man the emergency boat.' I then spoke to him and I said, 'May we get into the boat?' and he said, 'Yes, I wish you would,' or 'Very glad if you would,' or some expression like that. There were no passengers at all near us then. He put the ladies in and helped me in myself, and we were joined by two Americans who came running along the deck. He then told two other or three of the firemen that they might just as well get in, and then he put one man in charge of the boat, Symons.

Lady Lucy Duff Gordon – First Class Passenger

The sailors came and tried to drag me away. I was holding my husband's arm. They were very anxious that I should go. I absolutely refused. After the three boats had gone down, my husband, Miss Franks* and myself were left standing on the deck. There were no other people on the deck at all visible, and I had quite made up my mind that I was going to be drowned. Then suddenly we saw this little boat in front of us. We saw some sailors, and an officer apparently giving them orders, and I said to my husband, 'Ought we not to be doing something?' He said, 'Oh, we must wait for orders.'

---

*Miss Laura Mabel Francatelli.

We stood there for quite some time while these men were fixing up things, and then my husband went forward and said, 'Might we get into this boat?' The officer said in a very polite way indeed, 'Oh certainly do, I will be very pleased.' Then somebody hitched me up from the deck and pitched me into the boat, and then I think Miss Franks was pitched in. It was not a case of getting in at all. We could not have got in; it was quite high. They pitched us up into the boat, and after we had been in a little while the boat was started to be lowered, and one American gentleman was pitched in while the boat was being lowered down.

Henry Stengel – First Class Passenger

After the five boats on the starboard side were loaded, I turned toward the bow. I do not know what led me there, but there was a small boat that they called an emergency boat, in which there were three people, Sir Duff Gordon and his wife and Miss Francatelli. I asked the officer if I could not get into that boat. There was no one else around, not a person I could see except the people working at the boats, and he said, 'Jump in.'

The railing was rather high – it was an emergency boat and was always swung over toward the water. I jumped on to the railing and rolled into it. The officer then said, 'That is the funniest sight I have seen tonight,' and he laughed quite heartily. That rather gave me some encouragement. I thought perhaps it was not so dangerous as I imagined. After getting down part of the way there was a painter on the boat, and we were beginning to tip, and somebody hollered to stop lowering. Somebody cut that line and we went on down.

Alfred Crawford – Bedroom Steward

We filled No 8 boat up with women first. Mrs Isidor Straus and her husband were there. Mrs Straus attempted to get into the boat first. She stepped on to the gunwales, but then stepped back and clung to her husband and said, 'We have been together all these years. Where you go, I go.' Their maid got in the boat and was saved.

After that, Captain Smith came to the boat and asked how many men were in the boat. There were two sailors. He told me to get into the boat. Myself and a cook were the last to get in the boat – there were so many ladies that there wasn't room for any more.

Ella White – First Class Passenger

I entered the lifeboat from the top deck, where the boats were. We had to enter the boat there. There was no other open deck to the steamer except the top deck. It was a perfect rat trap. I got in the second boat that was lowered. They handled me very carefully, because I could hardly step. It did not hang far out. My condition was such that I had to be handled rather carefully, and there was no inconvenience at all. We got into it very easily. There was no excitement whatever. Nobody seemed frightened. Nobody was panic-stricken. There was a lot of pathos when husbands and wives kissed each other goodbye, of course.

Harold Lowe – Fifth Officer

It was not the launching of the boats that took the time. We got the whole boat out and in the water in less than ten minutes. It was getting the people together that took the time.

There was no such thing as selecting. I simply shouted, 'Women and children first; men stand back.' It was simply the first woman, whether First Class, Second Class, Third Class, or sixty-seventh class. It was all the same. The first woman was first into the boat, and the second woman was second into the boat, regardless of class, or nationality, or pedigree. She was treated just the same, if she was a woman. There was no distinction whatsoever. Even if we had wished to draw a distinction, we would not know who were the stewardesses and who were not.

During the course of the evening, I distinctly remember saying 'One more woman,' or 'Two more women,' or 'Three more women,' and they would step forward and I would pass them into the boat. Mr Murdoch said, 'That will do,' and it was stopped. Then, 'Lower away.'

Everybody was free to go where they wanted to. There was no restraint. Whether there were women there and they would not get into the boat is a different matter. I do not know. I saw some women there, but I did not have time to go and drive them away. I simply shouted, 'Women and children.'

Everything was quite quiet and calm. The only thing – and of course you would expect that – was that the people were messing up the falls, getting foul of the falls, and I had to halloa a bit to get them off the falls. Everything else went nicely; quietly and orderly. The discipline could not have been better. The thing was done as I do not suppose any other ship could do it. No ship could have done it in better time, and better in all respects – in every respect.

Paul Mauge – Secretary to the Chef, A La Carte Restaurant
Well, I go down again, and I said to the chef, 'There is some

danger happening; we must get up.' He lost his temper – he lost himself. I said to the other cooks to wait for us. After that we had been by the Third Class deck just at the back, and we have been trying to go on the Second Class passenger deck. Two or three stewards were there, and would not let us go. I was dressed and the chef was too. He was not in his working dress; he was just like me. I asked the stewards to pass. I said I was the secretary to the chef, and the stewards said, 'Pass along, get away.'

But the other cooks were obliged to stay on the deck there; they could not go up, because the stewards would not let them pass. I think all the members of the restaurant were there. Perhaps 60 people: 20 cooks and 40 waiters.

That is where they die. It was not possible for them to be saved, because on the Third Class passenger deck there was no lifeboat at all, and it was not possible for them to go on the Second Class passenger deck. Some stewards were keeping them from going there. I cannot say if they tried to pass, but anyway they could not, because I stood on the Second Class passenger deck for half an hour. I did not see them.

'The officers drew their revolvers, and fired shots over our heads'

Olaus Abelseth – Third Class Passenger

We stayed a little while longer, and then they said, 'Everybody.' I do not know who that was, but I think it was some of the officers that said it. I could not say that, but it was somebody that said 'Everybody'. We went up. We went over to the port side of the ship, and there were just one or two boats on the port side that were left. We were standing there looking at them lowering this boat. We could see them, some of the crew helping take the ladies in their arms and throwing them into the lifeboats. We saw them lower this boat, and there were no more boats on the port side.

So we walked over to the starboard side of the ship, and just as we were standing there, one of the officers came up and he said just as he walked by, 'Are there any sailors here?' I did not say anything. I have been a fishing man for six years, and, of course, this officer walked right by me and asked, 'Are there any sailors here?' I would have gone, but my brother-in-law and my cousin said, in the Norwegian language, as we were speaking Norwegian, 'Let us stay here together.'

Then we stayed there, and we were just standing still there. We did not talk very much. Just a little ways from us I saw there was an old couple standing there on the deck, and I heard this man say to the lady, 'Go into the lifeboat and get saved.' He put his hand on her shoulder and I think he said: 'Please get into the lifeboat and get saved.' She replied: 'No, let me stay with you.' I could not say who it was, but I saw that he was an old man. I did not pay much attention to him, because I did not know him.

Samuel Hemming – Lamp-trimmer

The last time I saw the captain was just as I was coming down off the house. He was by himself, and he sung out: 'Everyone over to the starboard side, to keep the ship up as long as possible.' It amounted to just one or two hundred men. There were no women.

Archibald Gracie – First Class Passenger

Next we went to the boat deck, which was the deck above, where we loaded at least two boats. When we were loading the last boat, just a short time before it was fully loaded, a palpable list toward the port side began, and the officer called out, 'All passengers to the starboard side,' and Smith and myself went to the starboard side. When we got there, to my surprise, I found there were ladies still there, and Mrs Browne and Miss Evans particularly, the ones whom I supposed had been loaded into a boat from A deck, below, about three-quarters of an hour before.

Of a sudden, I heard the cry that there was room for more women on the port side; so I grabbed by the arm these two ladies, Miss Evans and Mrs Browne, and conducted them to the port side. But I did not get but half way, when the crew made what you might call a dead line, and said, 'No men are allowed beyond this line.' So I let the ladies go beyond, and then about six ladies followed after the two that I had particular charge of.

Frank Evans – Able Seaman
I then went next to No 10, and I lowered the boat with the assistance of a steward. The chief officer, Mr Murdoch, was standing there, and said, 'What are you, Evans?' I said, 'A seaman, sir.' He said, 'All right; get into that boat with the other seamen.' So I got into the bows of this boat.

A young ship's baker was getting the children and chucking them into the boat, and the women were jumping. Mr Murdoch made them jump across into the boat. It was about two feet and a half from the side of the ship. One or two women hesitated; but he compelled them to jump. He told them that they must. One or two women refused, in the first place, to jump; but after he told them, they finally went.

He was making the women jump across, and the children he was chucking across, along with this baker. He throwed them on to the women, and he was catching the children by their dresses and chucking them in. One woman slipped and fell. Her heel must have caught on the rail of the deck, and she fell down and someone on the deck below caught her and pulled her up. Her heel caught in the rail, I think, as she was jumping, and they pulled her in on to the next deck. She was a woman in a black dress.

Charles Joughin – Chief Baker
We had difficulty in finding them. They ran away from the boats and said they were safer where they were. I myself and three or four other chaps went on the next deck and forcibly brought up women and children from the A deck. We brought them up to the boat deck – there are only about ten stairs to go up. We threw them in. The boat was standing off about a yard and a half from the ship's side, with a slight

list. We could not put them in; we could either hand them in or just drop them in.

I went down below to my room after that, and had a drop of liqueur that I had down there. When I came upstairs again, I saw that all the boats had gone.

James Widgery – Bath Steward
Just then some biscuits came up from the storekeeper. I helped him put one of the boxes into the bottom of the boat, and the purser took hold of my arm and said, 'Get in the boat and help the boatswain's mate pass the ladies in.' So I got in the boat, and stepped on the side, and we passed the ladies in. We thought we had them all in, and the purser called out, 'Are there any more women?' Just then someone said, 'Yes.' This woman came along, rather an oldish lady, and she was frightened, and she gave me her hand. I took one hand, and gave it to the boatswain's mate, and he caught hold of the other hand. Then she pulled her hand away, and went back to the door and would not get in. One of them went after her, but she had gone down the stairs.

Joseph Scarrott – Able Seaman
Directly I got to my boat I jumped in, saw the plug in, and saw my dropping ladder was ready to be worked at a moment's notice. Then Mr Wilde, the chief officer, came along and said, 'All right, take the women and children,' and we started taking the women and children. There would be 20 women got into the boat, I should say, when some men tried to rush the boats – foreigners they were, because they could not understand the order which I gave them, and I had to use a bit of persuasion. The only thing I could use was the

boat's tiller. I prevented five getting in. One man jumped in twice and I had to throw him out the third time.

When Mr Lowe came and took charge he asked me how many were in the boat; I told him as far as I could count there were 54 women and four children, one of those children being a baby in arms. It was a very small baby which came under my notice more than anything because of the way the mother was looking after it, being a very small child. The members of the crew were myself, two firemen, and three or four stewards. We were practically full up.

I told Mr Lowe that I had had a bit of trouble through the rushing business, and he said, 'All right.' He pulled out his revolver and he fired two shots into the water between the ship and the boat's side, and issued a warning to the remainder of the men that were about there. He told them that if there was any more rushing he would use it.

He asked me, 'How many got into the boat?' I told him as near as I could count that that was the number, and he said to me, 'Do you think the boat will stand it?' I said, 'Yes, she is hanging all right.' 'All right,' he said, 'lower away 14.'

The forward fall lowered all right, sufficiently far enough that the forepart of the boat was afloat and the forward fall slack. But her aft part hung up, and the boat was at an angle of pretty well 45 degrees. I called Mr Lowe's attention to it. He said, 'What do you think is best to be done?' I said, 'I can ease it. I will cut one part of the fall, and it will come easy. I have not the least doubt but what she will come away with her releasing gear.' He said, 'Do not you think the distance rather too much?' I said 'No. She might start a plug, but I will look out for that.' We dropped her by the releasing gear, and when she was clear I jumped to the plug to see if the impact of the water had started it, but it remained fast. After that we got clear of the ship.

Harold Lowe – Fifth Officer

I saw five boats go away without an officer, and I told Mr Moody that I had seen five boats go away, and an officer ought to go in one of these boats. I asked him who it was to be – him or I – and he told me, 'You go; I will get in another boat.' So I was lowered in No 14.

As I was going down the decks I knew, or I expected every moment, that my boat would double up under my feet. I was quite scared of it, although of course it would not do for me to mention the fact to anybody else. I had overcrowded her, but I knew that I had to take a certain amount of risk. So I thought, 'Well, I shall have to see that nobody else gets into the boat or else it will be a case.'

I thought if one additional body was to fall into that boat, that slight jerk of the additional weight might part the hooks or carry away something, no one would know what. There were a hundred and one things to carry away. Then, I thought, well, I will keep an eye open. So, as we were coming down the decks, coming down past the open decks, I saw a lot of Italians, Latin people, all along the ship's rails. They were all glaring, more or less like wild beasts, ready to spring. That is why I yelled out to look out, and let go, bang, right along the ship's side.

I shot between the boat and the ship's side, so these people would hear and see the discharge. I fired these shots without the intention of hurting anybody and also with the knowledge that I did not hurt anybody. Because I looked where I fired. A man does not want to shoot over here and look over there; or to shoot there and look here, but to look where he shoots. I am absolutely positive I hit nobody. If you shoot at a man directly, you can only see a round blur of the discharge, but if you shoot across him, you will see the length of it.

I fired three times. I shot so for them to know that I was fully armed. That is the reason. Then I put the pistol in my pocket and put the safety catch on, because it is a Browning automatic. I think it carries eight rounds. There were, I suppose, four more remaining.

Daniel Buckley – Third Class Passenger

There was a great crowd of people. They were all terribly excited. They were all going for the decks as quick as they could. The girls were very excited, and they were crying; and all the boys were trying to console them and saying that it was nothing serious. Then the lifeboats were preparing. There were five lifeboats sent out. I was in the sixth. I was holding the ropes all the time, helping to let down the five lifeboats that went down first, as well as I could.

When the sixth lifeboat was prepared, there was a big crowd of men standing on the deck, passengers and sailors and firemen mixed. And they all jumped in. So I said I would take my chance with them. There were no ladies there at the same time.

I went into the boat. Then two officers came along and said all of the men could come out. And they brought a lot of steerage passengers with them; and they were mixed, every way, ladies and gentlemen. They said all the men could get out and let the ladies in. The men that were in the boat at first fought, and would not get out, but the officers drew their revolvers, and fired shots over our heads, and then the men got out. Six men were left in the boat; I think they were firemen and sailors.

I was crying. There was a woman in the boat, and she had thrown her shawl over me, and she told me to stay in there. I believe she was Mrs Astor.* Then they did not see me, and the boat was lowered down into the water, and we rowed away out from the steamer.

There was a girl from my place, and just when she got down into the lifeboat she thought that the boat was sinking into the water. Her name was Bridget Bradley. She climbed one of the ropes as far as she could and tried to get back into the *Titanic* again, as she thought she would be safer in it than in the lifeboat. She was just getting up when one of the sailors went out to her and pulled her down again.

Frederick Ray – Saloon Steward

I walked leisurely up to the main stairway, saw the two pursers in the purser's office and the clerks busy at the safe, taking things out and putting them in bags. Just then Mr Rothschild left his stateroom and I waited for him – I had waited on him on the *Olympic*. I spoke to him and asked him where his wife was. He said she had gone off in a boat. I said, 'This seems rather serious.' He said, 'I do not think there is any occasion for it.' So we walked leisurely up the stairs until I got to A deck and went through the door.

No 9 boat was just being filled with women and children. I assisted, and saw that lowered away. Then I went along to

---

*Buckley is mistaken, as Mrs Astor was in boat No 4, while he was in boat No 13.

No 11 boat, and saw that loaded with women and children and then that was lowered away. Then I went to No 13 boat. I saw that about half filled with women and children. They said, 'A few of you men get in here.' There were about nine to a dozen men there, passengers and crew.

The boat was not touching the rail, but it was quite close enough to get in without any exertion at all. It may have been a foot. There was not any difficulty in getting into the boat, anyway.

I saw Mr Washington Dodge there, asking where his wife and child were. He said they had gone away in one of the boats. He was standing well back from the boat, and I said, 'You had better get in here, then.' I got behind him and pushed him and I followed. After I got in, there was a rather big woman came along, and we helped her in the boat. She was crying all the time and saying, 'Don't put me in the boat; I don't want to go in the boat; I have never been in an open boat in my life. Don't let me stay in.' I said, 'You have got to go, and you may as well keep quiet.'

After that there was a small child rolled in a blanket thrown into the boat to me, and I caught it. It was just thrown about two or three feet to me, and I caught it, unrolled the blankets, and found that it was a little baby. The woman that brought it along got into the boat afterwards.

The boat was lowered away until we got nearly to the water, when two or three of us noticed a very large discharge of water coming from the ship's side, which I thought was the pumps working. The hole was about two feet wide and about a foot deep; a solid mass of water coming out from the hole. I realised that if the boat was lowered down straight away the boat would be swamped and we should all be thrown into the water. We shouted for the boat to be stopped from being lowered, and they responded promptly and stopped lowering the boat.

We got oars and pushed it off from the side of the ship. It seemed impossible to lower the boat without being swamped. We pushed it out from the side of the ship, and the next I knew we were in the water free from this discharge. I do not think there were any sailors or quartermasters in the boat, because they apparently did not know how to get free from the tackle. They called for knives to cut the boat loose, and somebody gave them a knife and they cut the boat loose. In the meantime we were drifting a little aft and boat No 15 was being lowered immediately upon us, about two feet over our heads, and we all shouted again, and they again replied very promptly and stopped lowering boat No 15.

Edward Wilding – Naval Architect, Harland & Wolff
There is a hook which is thrown out by pulling over the lever amidships in the boat. Both ends are connected up with one lever; and both are released at the same time. There is sufficient power in the lever to draw out that hook while the weight of the boat is still on it. The reason for doing it is to facilitate launching in a seaway. When there is a sea running, a man stands by the lever and watches his chance. It might perhaps be mentioned that that is the invention of a White Star captain for that object.

Paul Mauge – Secretary to the Chef, A La Carte Restaurant
The second or third lifeboat was between two decks, and I jumped directly from the top deck to this lifeboat. It was going to the water, but it was stopped between two decks

when I jumped. About six or ten persons were jumping in it.

Before that, I did ask the chef to jump many times, but the chef was too fat I must say – too big, you know. He could not jump. When I was in the lifeboat, I shouted to him again in French, '*Sautez.*' He said something, but I could not hear because at the same moment a man said to me, 'Shut up,' or something like that. At the same moment another man from the *Titanic* tried to get me off to take my seat.

Berk Pickard – Third Class Passenger

The other passengers started in arguing. One said that it was dangerous and the other said that it was not; one said white and the other said black. No one realised the real danger, not even the stewards. If the stewards knew, they were calm. It was their duty to try to make us believe there was nothing serious. They tried to keep us quiet. They said, 'Nothing serious is the matter.' Perhaps they did not know themselves.

Instead of arguing with those people, I instantly went to the highest spot. I said to myself that if the ship had to sink, I should be one of the last. That was my first idea, which was the best. I went and I found the door. There are always a few steps from this Third Class, with a movable door, and it is marked there Second Class passengers have no right to penetrate there. I found this door open so that I could go into the Second Class, where I did not find any people, only a few men and about two ladies. They had been putting them into lifeboats and, as no women were there, we men sprang in the boat. We had only one woman and another young girl. We were lowered down, and when I was lowered down I saw the whole ship, as big as she was, the right side a little bit sinking, and I was far from imagining that it was the beginning of the end.

When I was going away from the ship, of course I was rather frightened; I was sorry at not being on the ship, and I said to the seaman, 'I would rather be on the ship.' He was laughing at me, and he said, 'Do you not see we are sinking?' I was rather excited, and I said, 'It is fortunate that the sea is nice, but perhaps in five minutes we will be turned over.'

I did not realize the danger, the whole time, even to the last moment. Of course, I would never believe such a thing could happen.

Charles Lightoller – Second Officer

I left the lowering of No 8 to the chief. He came along and, of course, being senior officer, took charge. And so I went then to complete the launching of No 4. Returning forward, down on to A deck, the windows were down. I placed some chairs against the window and formed a step, and standing outside myself, the same order was proceeded with, except that the boat was triced right close into the wire. The list could not have been serious because I was able to stand with one foot on the ship and one foot on the boat. Had the list been serious, the boat would have been too far away for me to stride the distance.

I think the ship righted itself when the order was given to the passengers to go to the starboard side. I am under the impression that a great many went over, and the ship got a righting movement and maintained it. At that height and with that number of passengers, I think it would affect the ship's list.

Next I went to the port collapsible boat, underneath the emergency davits. The sides are made of canvas, and they won't hold many, perhaps 20. They are not as good as a lifeboat; they can merely be stowed in a smaller place, one on top of the other. You can stow at least three of those where you can stow one lifeboat.

The tackles were already rounded up when I got there. We lifted the gunwale of the boat, which opens it up, hooked on the tackles, put it over the side, and loaded up. Mr Wilde was there too at this time.

We had very great difficulty in filling her with women. As far as I remember she was eventually filled, but we experienced considerable difficulty. Two or three times we had to wait, and call out for women. In fact, I think on one, perhaps two, occasions, someone standing close to the boat said, 'Oh, there are no more women,' and with that several men commenced to climb in. Just then, or a moment afterwards, whilst they were still climbing in, someone sang out on the deck, 'Here are a couple more.' Naturally, I judged they were women, and the men got out of the boat again, and we put the women in. I think this happened on two occasions.

No men were allowed in that I know of, but a couple of Filipinos or Chinese got in – they stowed away under the thwarts or something. But for that, there were no men, except the crew I ordered in. I filled her as full of women as I could. I could have put more in that boat and could have put some men in, but I did not feel justified in giving an order for men to get into the boat, as it was the last boat as far as I knew leaving the ship, and I thought it better to get her into the water safely with the number she had in. There were plenty of people about, no doubt men passengers. But I did not want the boat to be rushed.

I can remember distinctly lowering the boat – it was only about ten feet to the sea. A deck was under water, and almost immediately afterwards the water came from the stairway on to the boat deck.

I called for men to go up on the deck of the quarters for the collapsible boat up there. The after end of the boat was underneath the funnel guy. I told them to swing the after end up. There was no time to open her up and cut the lashings adrift. Hemming was the man with me there, and they then swung her round over the edge of the coamings to the upper deck, and then let her down on to the boat deck. That is the last I saw of her for a little while. There was no time to put her on the falls, as the water was then on the boat deck.

I went across to the starboard side of the officers' quarters, on the top of the officers' quarters, to see if I could do anything there. Well, I could not. I saw the first officer working at the falls of the starboard emergency boat, obviously with the intention of overhauling them and hooking on to the collapsible boat on their side. There were a number round there helping.

Bruce Ismay – Managing Director, IMM

I rendered all the assistance I could, putting the women and children in the boats. That was on the boat deck; I do not think I ever left that deck again. I saw Nos 3, 5, 7, and 9 lowered. I should think it took an hour and a half, or perhaps longer than that. All the women that I saw on deck got away in boats. I saw no confusion at all.

Every wooden boat was away. I believe there was another collapsible on the top of the officers' house. She was very fairly full. After all the women and children were in and after all the people that were on deck had got in, I got into the boat as she was being lowered away. There were no passengers on deck. I can only suppose they had gone to the after end of the ship. I presume they went there. I was really not thinking about it.

Charles Lightoller – Second Officer

I draw the conclusion that everyone was notified, by the manner and under the circumstances under which I met them last. It was obvious to me that everything with regard to their duty had been done by the mere fact that shortly before the vessel sank I met a purser, Mr McElroy, Mr Barker, Dr O'Loughlin, and Dr Simpson, and the four assistants. They were just coming from the direction of the bridge. They were evidently just keeping out of everybody's way. They were keeping away from the crowd, so as not to interfere with the loading of the boats. McElroy, if I remember, was walking around with his hands in his pockets. The purser's assistant was coming behind with the ship's bag, to show that all detail work had been attended to. One of them had a roll of papers under his arm, showing that they had been attending to their detail work.

They were perfectly quiet. They came up to me and just shook hands and said, 'Goodbye, old man.' We said goodbye to each other, and that is all there was to it.

All the engineers and many of the firemen were down below and never came on deck at all. They were never seen. Where the others were, I have been unable to fathom. I have tried to find out for my own edification, but I cannot fix it up.

Joseph Boxhall – Fourth Officer

My attention until the time I left the ship was mostly taken up with firing off distress rockets and trying to signal the steamer that was almost ahead of us.

I had sent in the meantime for some rockets, and told the captain that I would send them off. He said, 'Yes, carry on with it.' I was sending rockets off one at a time, at intervals of probably five minutes. I could not say how many – between half a dozen and a dozen. They were the regulation distress signals: you see a luminous tail behind them and then they explode in the air and burst into stars.

Some companies have private night signals for ships passing in the night, signalling to one another. They are coloured stars as a rule. We did not have any time to use any of those things. These distress rockets were not throwing stars; they were throwing balls, I remember, and then they burst. It was the first time I have seen distress rockets sent off, and I could not very well judge what they would be like from a distance, standing as I was underneath them, firing them myself.

I fired them just close to the bows of this emergency boat, because these distress rockets are dangerous things if they explode, and I had to keep people away clear while I fired the rockets. I did not notice who was working at the boat; I was intent on sending out these rockets and did not stop to look.

I talked to Mr Ismay a little while before I left the ship. I had known him by sight for about three years; he has crossed before in some ships I have been in. I had just fired a distress signal and was going to the chart room to put the lanyard back, and Mr Ismay was standing by the wheelhouse door.

He was standing alone at that time. He asked me why I was not getting the boat away. I told him I had no orders to get the boat away. I said the crew were ready, and people were getting in the boat. I went on with my work.

The captain was standing by this emergency boat. He was standing by the wheelhouse door, just abreast of this boat, supervising the boats being loaded. He told me I had to get into that boat and go away. Mr Wilde was superintending the filling. The order was given to lower away when I was told to go in it, and the boat was full. There was one more lifeboat lowered away a few minutes after I left, and then there were no more boats hanging in the davits on the port side.

I was sending the rockets up right to the very last minute when I was sent away in the boat.

Charles Lightoller – Second Officer

You quite understand they are termed rockets, but they are actually distress signals; they do not leave a trail of fire. I just mention that, not to confuse them with the old rockets, which leave a trail of fire. With actual distress signals, a shell bursts at a great height in the air, throwing out a great number of stars. They are principally white, almost white.

I should roughly estimate we fired somewhere about eight at intervals of a few minutes – five or six minutes, or something like that. They were all fired from the starboard side, as far as I know.

There is no ship allowed on the high seas to fire a rocket or anything resembling a rocket unless she requires assistance. I have seen them and known immediately what they were.

Annie Robinson – First Class Stewardess

The band was playing when I went up to A deck to call the other stewardess, and when I left the ship it was still playing.

'It was unmistakably a rocket;
you could make no mistake
about it'

Edward Buley – Able Seaman
There was a ship of some description there when she struck, and she passed right by us. We thought she was coming to us; and if she had come to us, everyone could have boarded her. You could see she was a steamer. She had her steamer lights burning.

She was stationary all night; I am very positive for about three hours she was stationary, and then she made tracks. I should judge she was about three miles away. We could not see anything of her in the morning when it was daylight.

She could not help seeing our rockets. She was close enough to see our lights and to see the ship itself, and also the rockets. She was bound to see them.

Ernest Gill – Donkeyman, SS *Californian*
I was on watch at the time, from eight to twelve. I was coming along the deck to call my mate and looked over the starboard rail and saw a large steamer. It could not have been anything but a passenger boat – she was too large. I could see two rows of lights, which I took to be porthole lights, and several groups of lights, which I took to be saloon and deck lights. I knew it was a passenger boat. She was a good distance off; I should say not more than ten miles, and probably less. I watched her for fully a minute. They could not have helped but see her from the bridge and lookout.

It was now 12 o'clock, and I went to my cabin. I woke my mate, William Thomas. He heard the ice crunching alongside the ship and asked, 'Are we in the ice?' I replied, 'Yes, but it must be clear off to the starboard, for I saw a big vessel going along full speed. She looked as if she might be a big German.' I did not stay long enough to observe which way she was going. I am not a sailor. I do not know anything about the latitude or longitude. My compass is the steam gauge.

I turned in but could not sleep. In half an hour I turned out, thinking to smoke a cigarette. Because of the cargo I could not smoke 'tween decks, so I went on deck again. I had pretty nearly finished my smoke and was looking around, and I saw what I took to be a falling star. It descended and then disappeared. That is how a star does fall. I did not pay any attention to that. A few minutes after, probably five minutes, I threw my cigarette away and looked over, and I could see from the water's edge – what appeared to be the water's edge – a great distance away, well, it was unmistakably a rocket; you could make no mistake about it. Whether it was a distress signal or a signal rocket I could not say, but it was a rocket. It was slightly astern of where I had seen the steamer.

I do not see how they could help seeing it from the bridge. There is a lookout man and a quartermaster, and there is the officer of the watch. I do not see how they could help but see it. I had no business to report it. It was a signal, and other people on the ship, the proper people, would attend to that. It was nothing to do with me.

I stayed for about three or four minutes after that, but it was extremely cold, and I was just dressed in a thin

*flannel suit and I did not care to stay any longer on deck.
I went below.*

Charles Groves – Third Officer, SS *Californian*

*About 11.10pm, ship's time, I made out a steamer coming
up a little bit abaft our starboard beam. At first I just saw
what I took to be one white light, but, of course, when I saw
her first I did not pay particular attention to her, because
I thought it might have been a star rising. The stars were
showing right down to the horizon. It was very difficult at
first to distinguish between the stars and a light, they were
so low down.*

*When I saw her first light, I should think she would
be about 10 or 12 miles, by the look of the light and the
clearness of the night. She got nearer all the time. About
11.25, I made out two white masthead lights.*

*I went down to the lower bridge at about 11.30. I
knocked at Captain Lord's door, and told him there was
a steamer approaching us. He said to me, 'Can you make
anything out of her lights?' I said, 'Yes, she is evidently a
passenger steamer coming up on the starboard quarter.' I
told him that I could see her deck lights and that made me
pass the remark that she was evidently a passenger steamer.
There was absolutely no doubt her being a passenger
steamer, at least in my mind. He said, 'Call her up on the
Morse lamp, and see if you can get any reply.'*

*I went up on the bridge and I rigged the Morse lamp. It
is only a matter of taking a key out of a locker up there and
just putting the plug in. There was no reply whatsoever at
first. Then I saw what I took to be a light answering, and I
sent the word 'What?', meaning to ask what ship she was.*

When I sent 'What?' his light was flickering. I took up the glasses again and I came to the conclusion it could not have been a Morse lamp.

The captain came to the bridge, saw a light flickering, and he said, 'She is answering you.' He said to me, 'That does not look like a passenger steamer.' I said, 'It is, sir. When she stopped her lights seemed to go out, and I suppose they have been put out for the night.' When I remarked about the passenger steamer he said: 'The only passenger steamer near us is the Titanic.'

On the way to my cabin, I stopped at the Marconi house. The operator was asleep. The only thing I remember asking him was, 'What ships have you got, Sparks?' He said, 'Only the Titanic.' I may have said a few more words to him, but I have no recollection. When I left his house I went straight to my cabin and went to bed.

Stanley Lord – Captain, SS *Californian*

When I came off the bridge, at half past ten, I pointed out to the officer that I thought I saw a light coming along. It was a most peculiar light, and we had been making mistakes all along with the stars, thinking they were signals. It was a flat calm, and we could not distinguish where the sky ended and where the water commenced. He said he thought it was a star, and I did not say anything more. I went down below.

I was talking with the engineer about keeping the steam ready, and we saw these signals coming along, and I said, 'There is a steamer passing. Let us go to the wireless and see what the news is.' But on our way down I met the operator coming, and I said, 'Do you know anything?' He said, 'The Titanic.' I said, 'This is not the Titanic; there is no doubt about it.'

She came and lay alongside of us at half past 11 until, I suppose, a quarter past, within four miles of us. We could see everything on her quite distinctly. We signalled her at half past 11 with the Morse lamp. She did not take the slightest notice of it. We signalled her again at ten minutes past 12, half past 12, a quarter to one o'clock. We have a very powerful Morse lamp. I suppose you can see that about ten miles, and she was about four miles off, and she did not take the slightest notice of it.

When the second officer came on the bridge at twelve o'clock, I told him to watch that steamer, that she did not get any closer to us; and I pointed out the ice to him, told him we were surrounded by ice. At 20 minutes to one, I whistled up the speaking tube and asked him if she was getting any nearer. He said, 'No, she is not taking any notice of us.' So, I said, 'I will go and lie down a bit.' At a quarter past he said, 'I think she has fired a rocket.' He said, 'She did not answer the Morse lamp and she has commenced to go away from us.' I said, 'Call her up and let me know at once what her name is.' So he put the whistle back, and apparently he was calling. I could hear him ticking over my head. Then I went to sleep.

I have a faint recollection of the apprentice opening the room door. I said, 'What is it?' He did not answer and I went to sleep again. I believe the boy came down to deliver me the message that this steamer had steamed away from us to the south-west, showing several of these flashes or white rockets.

We never took them to be distress rockets. The second officer, the man in charge of the watch, said most emphatically they were not distress rockets. He said if they had been distress rockets, he would most certainly have come down and called me himself, but he was not a little bit worried about it at all.

James Gibson – Apprentice, SS *Californian*

About 20 minutes past one, the second officer remarked to me that she was slowly steaming away towards the south-west. He said, 'Look at her now; she looks very queer out of the water; her lights look queer.' I looked at her through the glasses after that, and her lights did not seem to be natural. When a vessel rolls at sea her lights do not look the same. She seemed as if she had a heavy list to starboard. Her lights did not seem to look like as they did before when I first saw them. We had been talking about it together. He remarked to me that a ship was not going to fire rockets at sea for nothing. We were talking about it all the time, till five minutes past two, when she disappeared.

I did not think she was exactly in distress. Just that everything was not all right with her. I thought she was a tramp steamer, and I told him so.

I saw three more rockets at about twenty minutes to four. I reported them to the second officer. I saw the first one, and I reported it to the second officer, and we looked out for more to see if we could see any more – and we saw two more.

I was signalling her continuously. The second officer was taking bearings of her all the time. He asked me if there were any colours in the lights, or were they all white. I know now there are only distress rockets used at sea and private signals used near the shore. He told me he had reported it to the captain and the captain had told him to keep calling her up. He said there must be something the matter with her. I only thought the same that he thought: that a ship is not going to fire rockets at sea for nothing, and there must be something the matter with her.

I saw one more vessel during the night previous to getting to the Titanic's position. We saw masthead lights quite distinctly of another steamer between us and the Titanic. That was about quarter past three. One of the officers swore he also saw the port sidelight. I saw the masthead lights myself, but not the sidelight; about two points on the starboard bow.

Stanley Lord – Captain, SS *Californian*

19 and a half miles is a long ways. We could not have seen her Morse code; that is an utter impossibility. It would have been way down on the horizon. It might have been mistaken for a shooting star or anything at all.

'She was going down pretty fast by the bow'

Edward Wheelton – Saloon Steward
I would think, myself, the men took a chance and jumped overboard and swam for it and were picked up by boats. We had very powerful swimmers aboard the ship. Some of the best men I ever saw in the water were on that ship.

Hugh Woolner – First Class Passenger
There was a sort of scramble on the starboard side, and I looked around and I saw two flashes of a pistol in the air. I heard Mr Murdoch shouting out, 'Get out of this, clear out of this,' to a lot of men who were swarming into a boat on that side. It was a collapsible on the starboard side. Mr Steffanson and I went up to help to clear that boat of the men who were climbing in, because there was a bunch of women – I think Italians and foreigners – who were standing on the outside of the crowd, unable to make their way toward the side of the boat.

So we helped the officer to pull these men out, by their legs and anything we could get hold of. They were really flying before Mr Murdoch from inside of the boat at the time. We pulled out five or six each. I think they were probably Third Class passengers. Then they cleared out practically all the men out of that boat, and we lifted in these Italian women, hoisted them up on each side and put them into the boat. They were very limp. They had not much spring in them at all.

When that boat was finally filled up and swung out, I said to Steffanson: 'There is nothing more for us to do. Let us go down on to A deck again.' And we went down again. It was absolutely deserted the whole length, and the electric lights along the ceiling were beginning to turn red, just a glow, a red sort of glow. So I said to Steffanson, 'This is getting rather a tight corner. I do not like being inside these closed windows. Let us go out through the door at the end.' And as we went out through the door the sea came in on to the deck at our feet.

Then we hopped up on to the gunwale preparing to jump out into the sea, because if we had waited a minute longer we should have been boxed in against the ceiling. And as we looked out we saw this collapsible, the last boat on the port side, being lowered right in front of our faces. It was about nine feet out.

It was full up to the bow, and I said to Steffanson: 'There is nobody in the bows. Let us make a jump for it. You go first.' And he jumped out and tumbled in head over heels into the bow. I jumped too, and hit the gunwale with my chest, which had on this life-preserver, and I sort of bounced off the gunwale. I caught the gunwale with my fingers, and slipped off backwards. As my legs dropped down I felt that they were in the sea. I hooked my right heel over the gunwale, and by this time Steffanson was standing up, and he caught hold of me and lifted me in. Then we looked over into the sea and saw a man swimming in the sea just beneath us, and pulled him in.

By that time we were bumping against the side of the ship. She was going down pretty fast by the bow.

Thomas Dillon – Trimmer
When I came up, the last boat was getting lowered. They were singing out, 'Any more women?' and there were two

more on the well deck, and we chased them up on to the boat deck.

Then I went on to the poop deck. There were a great number of people there, steerage passengers. I waited there about 50 minutes. The ship took one final plunge and righted herself again. When she went down, before I left the ship, the aftermost funnel seemed to cant up towards me and to fall up this way.

I did not dive into the water. I went down with the ship, and shoved myself away from her into the water. I was sucked down about two fathoms, and then I seemed to get lifted up to the surface.

Archibald Gracie – First Class Passenger

Soon after that the water came up on the boat deck. We saw it and heard it. I had not noticed in the meantime that we were gradually sinking. I was engaged all the time in working at those davits, trying to work on the falls to let this boat down. Mr Smith and myself thought then that there was no more chance for us there, there were so many people at that particular point, so we decided to go toward the stern, still on the starboard side. As we were going there, to our surprise and consternation, up came from the decks below a mass of humanity, men and women – and we had thought that all the women were already loaded into the boats. The water was then right by us, and we tried to jump, Mr Smith and myself did. We were in a sort of cul-de-sac which was formed by the cabin and the bridge. We were right in this cul-de-sac on the boat deck.

Mr Smith jumped to try to reach the deck. I jumped also. We were unsuccessful. Then the wave came and struck us, and I rose as I would rise in bathing in the surf. I gave a jump with the water, which took me right on the hurricane deck [above the officers' quarters]. Around that was an iron railing, and I grabbed that iron railing and held tight to it. I looked around, and the same wave which saved me engulfed everybody around me. I turned to the right and to the left and looked: Mr Smith was not there, and I could not see any of this vast mass of humanity.

Harold Bride – Assistant Telegraphist

When we had finished with the *Frankfurt*, and we had thoroughly informed the *Carpathia* of our position, Mr Phillips again went out to look and see how things were going outside. He told me the forward well deck was awash. He told me, as far as I remember, that they were putting the women and children in the boats and clearing off. There was a heavy list to port.

I tried to establish a communication with the *Baltic*, and it was not very satisfactory, and I judged myself, from the strength of her signals, that she was too far away to do any good and it was not worth taking any trouble, and I told her we were sinking fast and there was no hope of saving the ship.

The captain kept in communication with us; we either went to him or he came to us. He came in and told us at one time she would not last very long, and he informed us when the engine room was flooded. He told us he thought it was time we put on our lifebelts. Mr Phillips told me that things looked very queer outside. Beyond that I knew nothing. The sooner we were out of it the better.

Just at this moment the captain came into the cabin and

said, 'You can do nothing more; look out for yourselves.' We did not leave the cabin immediately. Mr Phillips resumed the phones and after listening a few seconds jumped up and fairly screamed, 'The —— fool. He says, "What's up, old man?"' I asked, 'Who?' Mr Phillips replied the *Frankfurt*, and at that time it seemed perfectly clear to us that the *Frankfurt*'s operator had taken no notice or misunderstood our first call for help. Mr Phillips expressed his opinion of the *Frankfurt* and then told him to keep out of it, to stand by.

To the best of my recollection he told the *Carpathia* the way we were abandoning the ship, or words to that effect. Mr Phillips called CQD once or twice more, but the power was failing us and I do not think we were getting a spark, as there were no replies. We could hear the water washing over the boat deck, and Mr Phillips said, 'Come, let's clear out.'

On Mr Phillips's request I started to gather up his spare money and put on another coat, and made general preparations for leaving the ship. Someone was taking the lifebelt off Phillips when I left the cabin. I presumed from the appearance of the man that he was a stoker. I forced the man away, and Mr Phillips came and assisted me; I held him and Mr Phillips hit him. I regret to say that we left too hurriedly to take the man in question with us, and without a doubt he sank with the ship in the Marconi cabin as we left him.

There were other people on the deck; they were running around all over the place. Several people looking for lifebelts and looking for refreshments. We had a woman in our cabin who had fainted. We set her down on a chair, which she wanted badly, and were giving her a glass of water, and then her husband took her away again.

We climbed up on top of the Marconi cabin and the

officers' quarters on the port side of the *Titanic*. They were trying to push off a collapsible boat that was up there, and I went to help them. Just as the boat fell I noticed Captain Smith dive from the bridge into the sea. It would be just about five minutes before the boat sank. He had no lifebelt on. Then followed a general scramble down on the boat deck, but no sooner had we got there than the sea washed over. I managed to catch hold of the collapsible and was swept overboard with her.

Harold Cottam – Marconi Officer, SS *Carpathia*

It was 11.55pm New York time [1.45am ship's time] when I received the last message from the Titanic. *He said, 'Come as quickly as possible, old man, the engine room is filling up to the boilers.' That was the last I heard of the* Titanic. *I tried calling at frequent intervals; I did not know that the ship had gone down. The signals were good right away to the end.*

Charles Joughin – Chief Baker

I went down on to B deck. The deck chairs were lying right along, and I started throwing deck chairs through the large ports. It was an idea of my own – I was looking out for something for myself. I should say I threw about fifty chairs out. There was other people on the deck, but I did not see anybody else throwing chairs over.

She had gone a little more to port. I did not notice anything. I did not notice her being much down by the head.

I went to the deck pantry, and while I was in there I thought I would take a drink of water, and while I was getting the drink of water I heard a kind of a crash as if something had buckled. It was like as if the iron was parting, as if part of the ship had buckled. Then I heard a rush overhead – a rush of people overhead on the deck. When I got up on top, I could see them clambering down from those decks. Their idea was to get on to the poop. Of course, I was in the tail end of the rush.

I kept out of the crush as much as I possibly could, and I followed down towards the well of the deck. Just as I got down towards the well, she gave a great list over to port and threw everybody in a bunch except myself. She threw them over. There were many hundreds piled up.

I eventually got on to the starboard side of the poop, and got hold of the outside of the rails. I did not see anybody else besides myself. I was just wondering what next to do. I had tightened my belt and I had transferred some things out of this pocket into my stern pocket. I was just wondering what next to do, when she went.

I do not believe my head went under the water at all. It may have been wetted, but no more. I should say I was in the water for over two hours. I was just paddling and treading water. It was just like a pond. I did not attempt to get anything to hold on to until I reached a collapsible, but that was daylight.

The lifebelts were a new patent, better than the old ones. You slipped it over your head, and it was like a breastplate and a backplate, and you tied two straps. Everybody knew how to put them on, it was so simple. There was no necessity to show. You had to assist it in the water. It is only a case of keeping your head with one of those lifebelts. Just paddling, and you keep afloat indefinitely.

John Collins – Assistant Cook, First Class Galley
We saw the collapsible boat taken off of the saloon deck,

and then the sailors and the firemen that were forward seen the ship's bow in the water and seen that she was intending to sink her bow, and they shouted out for all they were worth we were to go aft, and word came there was a boat getting launched, so we were told to go aft, and we were just turning around and making for the stern end when the wave washed us off the deck. The wave was caused by the suction which took place when the bow went down in the water. It washed the decks clear. There were hundreds on the starboard side; they were all washed off into the water. The child was washed out of my arms, and the wreckage and the people around me kept me down for at least two or three minutes under the water.

Olaus Abelseth – Third Class Passenger

I was standing there, and I asked my brother-in-law if he could swim, and he said no. I asked my cousin if he could swim, and he said no. So we could see the water coming up, the bow of the ship was going down, and there was a kind of an explosion. We could hear the popping and cracking, and the deck raised up and got so steep that the people could not stand on their feet on the deck. So they fell down and slid on the deck into the water right on the ship. Then we hung on to a rope in one of the davits. We were pretty far back at the top deck.

My brother-in-law said to me, 'We had better jump off or the suction will take us down.' I said, 'No. We won't jump yet. We ain't got much show anyhow, so we might as well stay as long as we can.' So he stated again, 'We must jump off.' But I said, 'No, not yet.' So, then, it was only about five feet down to the water when we jumped off. It was not much of a jump. Before that we could see the people were jumping over. There was water coming on to the deck, and they were jumping over, then, out in the water. My brother-in-law took my hand just as we jumped off; and my cousin jumped at the same time.

Edward Brown – First Class Steward

We turned our attention to another collapsible boat that was on top of the officers' house on the same side of the ship. We got two planks on the bow-end of the boat, and we slid it down on to the boat deck. We tried to get it to the davits, and we got it about halfway and then the ship got a list to port, and we had great difficulty. We made it fast by slackening the falls, but we could not haul it away any further.

The captain came past us while we were trying to get this boat away with a megaphone in his hand, and he spoke to us. He said, 'Well, boys, do your best for the women and children, and look out for yourselves.' He walked on the bridge.

The ship took her last plunge a very few seconds after that.

There were four or five women that I could see there waiting to get into this boat if we got it under the davits. The ship was very well down then; the bridge was under water. I found the water come right up to my legs, and I jumped into the collapsible boat then. There was a lot scrambled into it then; when the sea came on to the deck they all scrambled into it. I cut the after fall, and I called out to the man on the forward end of the boat to cut her loose; she would float if we got the falls loose. The boat was practically full, when the sea came into it, and washed them all out. I do not know where the boat went to then. We were washed out of it; that is all I know.

The last I saw of them, the women were in the water struggling.

I do not remember hearing the band stop playing. They were right on the forward boat deck companion, on the very top. They were playing for a long time, but I do not remember hearing them stop.

PART THREE

IN THE BOATS
Monday 15 April 1912

'Then came the dreadful cries'

BOAT NO 6
Arthur Peuchen – First Class Passenger

The quartermaster who was in charge of our boat told us to row as hard as we could to get away from this suction, and just as we got a short distance away this stowaway made his appearance. He was an Italian by birth, I should think, who had a broken wrist or arm, and he was of no use to us to row. He got an oar out, but he could not do much, so we got him to take the oar in.

I think he was stowed away underneath. I should imagine if there was any room for him to get underneath the bow of the boat, he would be there. I imagine that was where he came from. He was not visible when looking at the boat. There were only two men when she was lowered.

As we pulled away from the *Titanic*, there was an officer's call of some kind. A sort of a whistle. We stopped rowing. The quartermaster told us to stop rowing so he could hear it, and this was a call to come back to the boat. So we all thought we ought to go back to the boat. But the quartermaster said, 'No, we are not going back to the boat.' He said, 'It is our lives now, not theirs,' and he insisted upon our rowing farther away.

We commenced to hear signs of the breaking up of the *Titanic*. I kept my eyes watching the lights, as long as possible. I saw her bow pointing down and the stern up; not in a perpendicular position, but considerable. I should think an angle of not as much as 45 degrees. It was intact at that time. We heard a sort of a rumbling sound and the lights were still on at the rumbling sound, then a sort of an explosion, then another. It seemed to be one, two, or three rumbling sounds, then the lights went out. I imagined that the decks had blown up with the pressure; that is my theory of the explosion. I think it was the pressure, that heavy weight shoving that down, the water rushing up, and the air coming between the decks; something had to go.

Then came the dreadful calls and cries. We could not distinguish an exact cry for assistance; it was a moaning and crying. Frightful. It affected all the women in our boat whose husbands were among these. This went on for some time, gradually getting fainter, fainter. At first, it was horrible to listen to. I think we must have been five-eighths of a mile away, I should imagine, when this took place. It was very hard to guess the distance. There were only two of us rowing a very heavy boat with a good many people in it, and I do not think we covered very much ground.

I think the rebellion was made by some of the married women that were leaving their husbands. Some of the women suggested going back. But the quartermaster said it was no use going back there, there was only a lot of stiffs there, which was very unkind, and the women resented it very much. We did not return to the boat.

I did not say anything. I knew I was perfectly powerless. The quartermaster was at the rudder. He was a very talkative man. He had been swearing a great deal, and was very disagreeable. I do not think he was qualified to be a quartermaster. I had one row with him. I asked him to come and row, to assist us in rowing, and let some woman steer the boat, as it was a perfectly calm night. The stars were out. It did not require any skill for steering. He refused to do it, and he told me he was in command of that boat, and I was to row.

He remained at the tiller, and if we wanted to go back while he was in possession of the tiller, I do not think we could have done so. The night was cold and we kept rowing on. Then he imagined he saw a light. I have done a good deal of yachting in my life, I have owned a yacht for six years and have been out on the Lakes, and I could not see these lights. I saw a reflection. He thought it was a boat of some kind. He thought probably it might be a buoy out there of some kind, and he called out to the next boat, which was within hearing, asking if he knew if there was any buoy around there. This struck me as being perfectly absurd, and showed me the man did not know anything about navigating, expecting to see a buoy in the middle of the Atlantic. However, he insisted upon us rowing toward this imaginary light.

We could see those different lifeboats that had lights. They were all over. They were not all staying together at all. Some of them were going east, west, north, and south, it seemed to me, but there was one boat that had a sort of an electric light, and one a sort of a bluish light, as well, which we thought at first was a steamer or something.

The women rowed, very pluckily, too. We got a couple of women rowing aft, on the starboard side of our boat, and I got two women to assist on our side; but of course the woman with me got sick with the heavy work, and she had to give it up. But I believe the others kept on rowing quite pluckily for a considerable time.

I think the quartermaster was at the tiller all the time, with the exception probably of a couple of minutes. I know he asked one of the ladies for some brandy, and he also asked for one of her wraps, which he got.

We could just commence to distinguish light, I think, about near four o'clock. We seemed to be in a nest of icebergs, with some smaller ones. I think you could count five, between a mile and five miles away. Two were large; another was sort of smaller in size. Some were jagged, but very high, and a number of them not so high. They were at least 100 feet high, two of them, and of a width I should think of 300 feet and 400 feet long; somewhat like an island.

Robert Hichens – Quartermaster

I had no trouble with Major Peuchen at all – only once. He was not in the boat more than ten minutes before he wanted to come and take charge of the boat. I told him, 'I am put here in charge of the boat.' I said, 'You go and do what you are told to do.' He did not answer me, but went forward on the starboard bow and sat down, alongside of Seaman Fleet, who was working very hard. He done most of the work himself; Fleet was doing most of the work.

Everybody seemed in a very bad condition in the boat. Everybody was quite upset, and I told them somebody would have to pull; there was no use stopping there alongside of the ship, and the ship gradually going by the head. We were in a dangerous place, so I told them to man the oars, ladies and all. I said, 'All of you do your best.'

I was standing at the tiller. We did hear cries of distress, or I imagined so, for two or three minutes. Some of the men in the boat said it was the cries of one boat hailing the other. The cries I heard lasted about two minutes, and some of them were saying, 'It is one boat aiding the other.' I suppose the reason they said this was not to alarm the women – the ladies in the boat. I was too far away, and I had no compass to go back, to enable me to find where the cries came from.

There was another boat aside of me, the boat the master-at-arms was in, full right up. We all had lights and were showing them to one another. Most all of us. We kept all showing our lights now and then to let them know where we were, too.

Mrs Meyer was rather vexed with me, and I spoke rather straight to her. She accused me of wrapping myself up in the blankets in the boat, using bad language, and drinking all the whisky, which I deny. I was standing to attention, exposed, steering the boat all night, which is a very cold billet. I would rather be pulling the boat than be steering. But I seen no one there to steer, so I thought, being in charge of the boat, it was the best way to steer myself, especially when I seen the ladies get very nervous with the nasty tumble on.

I was very cold, and I was standing up in the boat. I had no hat on. A lady had a flask of whisky or brandy, or something of that description, given her by some gentleman on the ship before she left. She pulled it out and gave me about a tablespoonful, and I drank it. Another lady, who was lying in the bottom of the boat in a rather weak condition, gave me a half wet and half dry blanket to try keep myself a little warm, as I was half frozen.

We got down to the *Carpathia*, and I seen every lady and everybody out of the boat, and I seen them carefully hoisted on board the *Carpathia*, and I was the last man to leave the boat. That is all I can tell you.

Mary Smith – First Class Passenger
There was a small light on the horizon that we were told to

row towards. Some people seemed to think it was a fishing smack or small boat of some description. However, we seemed to get no nearer the longer we rowed, and I am of the opinion it was a star. Many people in our boat said they saw two lights. I could not until I had looked a long time; I think it was the way our eyes focused, and probably the hope for another boat. I do not believe it was anything but a star.

There were 24 people in our boat – they are supposed to hold 50. During the night they looked for water and crackers and a compass, but they found none that night. We were some distance away when the *Titanic* went down. We watched with sorrow, and heard the many cries for help and pitied the captain, because we knew he would have to stay with his ship. The cries we heard I thought were seamen, or possibly steerage, who had overslept, it not occurring to me for a moment that my husband and my friends were not saved.

It was bitterly cold, but I did not seem to mind it particularly. I was trying to locate my husband in all the boats that were near us. The night was beautiful; everything seemed to be with us in that respect, and a very calm sea. The icebergs on the horizon were all watched with interest; some seemed to be as tall as mountains, and reminded me of the pictures I had studied in geography. Then there were flat ones, round ones also.

I am not exactly sure what time, but think it was between five and five thirty when we sighted the *Carpathia*. Our seaman suggested we drift and let them pick us up; however, the women refused and rowed toward it. Our seaman was Hichens, who refused to row, but sat in the end of the boat wrapped in a blanket that one of the women had given him.

I am not of the opinion that he was intoxicated, but a lazy, uncouth man, who had no respect for the ladies, and who was a thorough coward.

We made no attempt to return to the sinking *Titanic*, because we supposed it was thoroughly equipped. Such a thought never entered my head. Nothing of the sort was mentioned in the boat, having left the ship so early, we were innocent of the poor equipment that we now know of.

BOAT NO 2
Joseph Boxhall – Fourth Officer

I pulled around the ship's stern and was intending to go alongside. I reckoned I could take about three more people off the boat with safety. I kept a little distance off the ship, probably a hundred yards or so. I think there was a little suction, while the ship was settling down bodily, as the boat seemed to be drawn closer to the ship. But I do not think there was the suction that the people really thought there was. I was really surprised, myself. By hearsay, it seems to have been a general surprise to everybody that there was so little suction.

I suppose I was about a half a mile away when the *Titanic* sank. We were resting on the oars. I cannot say that I saw her sink. I saw the lights go out, and I looked two or three minutes afterward, and it was 25 minutes past two. So I took it that she sank at about 20 minutes after two.

A little while after the ship's lights went out and the cries subsided, I heard the water rumbling or breaking on the ice. Then I knew that there was a lot of ice about; but I could not see it from the boat. Of course, sound travels quite a long way on the water, and being so close to the water, and it being such a calm night, you would hear the water lapping on those bergs for quite a long, long ways.

It was perfectly clear. You could almost see the stars set. I do not know why we couldn't see the iceberg. I do not know what it was about it; I could not understand.

I have come across a good few icebergs, I suppose. On such a night as that, even if there is no moon, you can very, very often see an iceberg by the water on the sides of it – that is, if there is a little breeze. But when the water is in one of those oily calms, it's much harder to see. If there had been a little ripple on the water, we should have stood a very good chance of seeing that iceberg in time to clear it.

It was like an oily calm when the *Titanic* struck, and for a long, long time after we were in the boats, and you could not see anything at all then.

I did not see anyone in the water. I was looking around for them, keeping my eyes open, but I did not see anyone. If I had, I should have taken them in the boat; I should have taken them in as far as safety would allow. But I did not see anyone in the water.

James Johnson – First Saloon Night Watchman

By the time we came back again and pulled round the stern of the *Titanic*, we must have pulled a mile and a half, I should think, for a good half-hour. We went back and rowed round about 800 yards off, and we heard many cries. There were lots of remarks by the ladies; they said they were sorry and everything. And the officer said to the ladies, 'Do you think we should go back or not?' And the ladies said, 'No.' I think they thought it was dangerous.

When we were all quiet, the officer said, 'Listen,' and

what we heard was the swish of the water against an iceberg. When we looked, there was an iceberg right in front of us.

Joseph Boxhall – Fourth Officer

I had been showing green pyrotechnic lights most of the time. This was a box of green lights that I told the man to put in the boat for anybody that would happen to find them. They made a very brilliant light. I saw several of the boats which had lighted lamps in them, but the usual lifeboat's lights. They are usually held by the man who steers the boat.

I did not see the icebergs until I got within about two or three ship's lengths of the *Carpathia*. Then, as daylight broke, I saw several bergs; they looked quite black. It was just breaking daylight, and the *Carpathia* seemed to have stopped within half a mile of numerous bergs. But after the sun got up they looked white. And field ice; I could see field ice then as far as the eye could see. This is the first time that I have seen field ice on the Grand Banks. I have been running to New York since I was 19 years of age. I have seen icebergs, but have never seen any field ice before.

I do make a distinction between an iceberg and a growler. As I understand, a growler is a low-lying iceberg. They are all submerged; but I mean one lying, it might be, very largely on the surface of the water, but not high. It might be large or it might be small, but it is low lying. The larger it gets, then it gets to be an iceberg. Field ice is a lot of ice all together, not unlike a raft. It is a large expanse of ice covering the water, just a little above the surface.

As far as I understand, they come from the Arctic region. Some people who have been very close to them tell me that they have seen sand and gravel and rocks and things of that kind in them. And earth. I have never been close enough to see that.

Frank Osman – Able Seaman
After I got in the boat, the officer found a bunch of rockets, which was put in the boat by mistake for a box of biscuits. Having them in the boat, the officer fired some off, and the *Carpathia* came to us first and picked us up a half an hour before anybody else.

BOAT NO 5
George Harder – First Class Passenger
We rowed out there some distance from the ship. How far it was, I do not know. It may have been as far as a quarter of a mile, and it may have been one-eighth of a mile. At any rate, we were afraid of the suction. So the passengers said, 'Let us row out a little farther.' So they rowed out farther, perhaps about a half a mile; it may have been three-quarters of a mile. There we waited, and after waiting around a while, this other boat came alongside. They had 29 people in their boat, and we counted the number of people in our boat; and at that time we only counted 36. So we gave them four or five of our people in order to make it even, as we were kind of crowded.

Then we waited out there until the ship went down. Afterwards, we heard a lot of these cries and yells. You could not hear any shouts for help, or anything like that. It was a sort of continuous yelling or moaning. You could not distinguish any sounds. It was more like – what I thought it was – the steerage on rafts, and that they were all hysterical. That is the way it sounded in the distance.

Herbert Pitman – Third Officer

There was a crying, shouting, moaning. It came from the water, after the ship disappeared. We may have been 3 or 400 yards away. As soon as she disappeared, I said, 'Now, men, we will pull toward the wreck.' I said, 'We may be able to pick up a few more.' My boat would have accommodated a few more.

They started to obey my orders. They commenced pulling toward the ship, and the passengers in my boat said it was a mad idea on my part to pull back to the ship, because if I did, we should be swamped with the crowd that was in the water, and it would add another 40 to the list of drowned. So I decided I would not pull back.

There was a continual moan for about an hour – it may have been a shorter time. I cannot very well describe it. Then they died away gradually. I would rather not speak of it. We just simply took our oars in and lay quiet. We may have drifted along. We just simply lay there, in the vicinity of the wreck, doing nothing. We drifted toward daylight, as a little breeze sprang up.

BOAT NO 10
Edward Buley – Able Seaman

It was after the ship went down, when we heard them. When the lights were out. It was terrible cries. We laid to about 250 yards away, not because we could give any assistance, but because the boat I was in was full up, and we had no one to pull the oars.

There were a good few dead. Of course, you could not discern them exactly on account of the wreckage; but we turned over several of them to see if they were alive. It looked as though none of them were drowned. They looked as though they were frozen. The lifebelts they had on were partly out of the water, and their heads were laid back, with their faces on the water, several of them. Their hands were coming up. It looked as though they were frozen altogether.

I never saw any ice until morning. We thought it was a full-rigged ship. We were right in amongst the wreckage, and we thought it was a sailing ship, until the light came on and we saw it was an iceberg.

BOAT NO 4

Emily Ryerson – First Class Passenger

We didn't go back, for people said 'Don't go there' and 'The ship is going down', and nobody seemed to know what was to be done. So we floated by a little, up from the ship. The ship was sinking very rapidly then. We saw two lines of portholes, and then we saw only one. It was very brilliantly lighted and you could see very distinctly.

A great many portholes were open. The water was washing in the portholes, and later some of the square windows seemed to be open. You could see in the cabin and see the water washing in and the gold furniture and decorations. I remember noticing you could look far in; it was brilliantly lighted – which deck, I couldn't tell.

I said to this man in the bow, Perkis, he was smoking a pipe and seemed quite unconcerned, and I said, 'What were your orders?' and he said, 'There is another companionway aft, and we are ordered to go there.' Some of the women were standing up in the boat, and they said, 'Don't go. The ship is going down, and we will be swamped,' and he didn't seem to care which way we went.

Those orders weren't followed out. We saw no gangway, we looked and peered, but it was so black when we got in the water, we couldn't see anything at first. They were throwing things into the water: steamer chairs, and doors, and casks. There seemed to be a mess of things between us and the ship.

Somebody said, 'Row for your lives.' Everybody rowed: Mrs Thayer, and my daughter, and all the women. One or two men were picked up when the ship went down – we picked up seven or eight – and these men were cursing and fighting. I think they were from the crew, not passengers. One died, I think, there.

Samuel Hemming – Lamp-trimmer
I went to the bridge and looked over and saw the water climbing upon the bridge. I went and looked over the starboard side, and everything was black. I could not see any boats. I went over to the port side and saw a boat off the port quarter, so I got up the after boat davits and slid down the fall and swam to the boat. I tried to get hold of the grab line on the bows, and it was too high for me, so I swam along and got hold of one of the grab lines amidships.

I pulled my head above the gunwale, and I said, 'Give us a hand in, Jack.' Foley was in the boat. I saw him standing up in the boat. He said, 'Is that you, Sam?' I said, 'Yes,' and him and the women and children pulled me in the boat.

It was full of women. There were about 40 women and four men. There were children; two young ladies and a little girl. I did not see the babies at all when I got in the boat. I did not see the three babies until later.

After the ship had gone, we pulled back and picked up

seven. Stewards, firemen, seamen, and one or two men, passengers – I could not say exactly which they were. They swam toward the boat, and we went back toward them. We hung around for a bit. We were moving around constantly. We heard the cries, but we did not know what to do.

Walter Perkis – Quartermaster
No 4 was the last big boat on the port side to leave the ship. I took charge of it after I got in. We were about six lengths away from the ship. We picked up eight men, and two died in the boat afterwards; one was a fireman and one was a steward. After we had picked up the men, I could not hear any more cries anywhere. Everything was over. I waited then until daylight, or just before daylight, when we saw the lights of the *Carpathia*.

Every man knew his station and took it. They conducted themselves the same as they would if it were an ordinary everyday occurrence.

Andrew Cunningham – Bedroom Steward
I waited on the ship until all the boats had gone, and then I took to the water. I went in about two o'clock, about half an hour before she sank. I swam clear about three-quarters of a mile of the ship, because I was afraid of the suction. I had a mate with me. We saw the ship go down, then we struck out to look for a boat.

We called to No 4 boat, and they picked us up. I think his was the nearest boat to the scene of the accident, because he picked up most of the lot. There were only about eight or nine men in it. The majority of them were picked up out of the water. I think there was another fireman in the bottom of the boat; and besides that there was my mate, who died just after he was pulled in.

As soon as I got into the boat, I took an oar, and we rowed away from the scene of the wreck until morning, until we sighted the *Carpathia*. Of course, we took the two dead men on board with us.

Thomas Dillon – Trimmer

I was swimming for about 20 minutes after the ship went down. I saw about 1,000 people in the water. When I was picked up, I was unconscious, and I was not properly right when I came to. Lyons was lying on top of me, a seaman, and a passenger lying on top of me dead.

BOAT NO 1

George Symons – Lookout

After we left the ship, I gave the order to pull away. We pulled away I should say about 200 yards, and I told them to lay on their oars, and just a little while after that, after I saw that the ship was doomed, I gave the order to pull a little further and so escape the suction. Being the master of the situation, I used my own discretion. I said nothing to anybody about the ship being doomed in my opinion. A little while after that we pulled a little way and lay on the oars again.

The other boats were around us by that time, and some were pulling further away from us. I stood and watched it till I heard two sharp explosions in the ship. What they were I could not say. Then she suddenly took a heavy cant, and her bow went down clear. Her forecastle head was well under water then. Her foremost lights had all disappeared. You could see her starboard sidelight, which was still burning, was not so very far from the water, and her stern was well up in the air. You could not see her keel; you could just see the propellers.

The next thing I saw was her poop. As she went down like that so her poop righted itself and I thought to myself, 'The poop is going to float.' It righted itself without the bow; in my estimation she must have broken in half. I should think myself it was abaft the after expansion plate. It could not have been more than two or three minutes after that that her poop went up as straight as anything; there was a sound like steady thunder as you hear on an ordinary night at a distance, and soon she disappeared from view.

I thought at the time, being master of the situation, it was not safe in any case to go back at that time. Not at that time; not as soon as the ship disappeared. I was only going by the cries. You could hear them; you could hear a decent few, it sounded like. But I thought at the time, by using my own discretion, that it was not safe in any way to have gone back to that ship as she disappeared.

I determined by my own wish, as I was master of the situation, to go back when I thought that most of the danger was over. I used my own discretion. I was not afraid of anything; I was only afraid of endangering the lives of the people I had in the boat. We had room, say, for another eight or a dozen more in the boat, but I was afraid of the swarming. Of the swarming of the people – swamping the boat.

I never had a thought in my head of cowardice. I do not admit it was cowardly.

We continued rowing for the light. It was bearing

roughly on our port beam when we were rowing away from the ship. I thought my own self she was gradually going away from us. After we rowed a little way, we stopped and laid on our oars. Then I gave the order to pull back, and told the men in the boat we would pull back to the other boats. I was going my way back then as near as I possibly could to the scene of the disaster. I strained my ears to hear whether I could hear anybody, any person whatever making a cry. I heard no one.

I could not say that they were all drowned, because there were some picked up in a boat out of the water before daylight, according to the other story. Of course, I cannot say about other people.

Lady Lucy Duff Gordon – First Class Passenger

The moment we touched the water, the men began rowing. As far as I can remember, the order was to row quickly away from the boat for about 200 yards. After the *Titanic* sank, I never heard a cry. Before she sank, there were terrible cries. But my impression was that, after she sank, there was absolute silence. Well, perhaps I may have heard it, but I was terribly sick, and I could not swear to it.

Sir Cosmo Duff Gordon – First Class Passenger

The moment the *Titanic* sank, of course everything stopped. There was a dead silence. Then we did hear cries – until the men started rowing again, which was very soon, immediately, almost. I do not know which way they were rowing, but I think they began to row away immediately; in my opinion it was to stop the sound.

I heard no suggestion of going back. I do not think it

would have been possible, for one thing. I do not know whether it would have been safe. I do not know which way we should have gone. I had been watching the *Titanic*, of course, to the last moment, and after that, one did not know where it had been. As soon as the *Titanic* had gone down, one lost all idea of where she had been.

It is difficult to say what occurred to me. I was minding my wife, and we were rather in an abnormal condition. There were many things to think about, but of course it quite well occurred to one that people in the water could be saved by a boat. It might have been possible, but it would have been very difficult to get back, the distance we were, and in the darkness, to find anything. I was not thinking about it. At that time I was attending to my wife. We had had rather a serious evening.

Charles Hendrickson – Leading Fireman

There were terrible cries some distance off, about 200 yards away. Certainly, we all heard them. I proposed going back, and they would not hear of it. None of them would not go back. None of the passengers or anybody else. It was after the ship had gone then. I spoke to everyone there; I shouted out in the boat, to anyone who was listening. There was plenty of room for another dozen.

Sir Duff Gordon and his wife and this other lady passenger objected. They said it would be too dangerous to go back, we might get swamped. Sir Duff Gordon and his wife as well, that was all. I never heard anyone else. Symons never said anything. The crew never said anything.

I never said any more. The coxswain was in charge of the boat; he should know what to do best. It would not do for everybody to be in charge of a boat that is in her. When a man gets in a boat, the coxswain takes charge and does everything.

George Symons – Lookout

I never heard anybody of any description, passengers or crew, say anything as regards going back. I expected fully for someone to say something about it. That seemed reasonable. Had there been anything said, I was almost sure to have heard it. We were all doing our work. They were saying nothing. I heard no conversation whatever. The only conversation that I caught once was Sir Cosmo Duff Gordon trying to cheer Lady Duff Gordon up. That was the only conversation – some words he spoke to her, and that was nearly at the break of daylight. If there was any other conversation it was unknown to me. I never heard nothing. I used my own discretion.

Sir Cosmo Duff Gordon – First Class Passenger

There was a man sitting next to me, and of course in the dark I could see nothing of him. I never did see him, and I do not know yet who he is. I suppose it would be some time when they rested on their oars, 20 minutes or half an hour after the *Titanic* had sunk, this man said to me, 'I suppose you have lost everything,' and I said, 'Of course.' He said, 'But you can get some more,' and I said, 'Yes.' 'Well,' he said, 'we have lost all our kit and the company won't give us any more, and what is more our pay stops from tonight. All they will do is to send us back to London.' So I said to them, 'You fellows need not worry about that. I will give you a fiver each to start a new kit.' That is the whole of that

£5 note story. I said it to one of them, and I do not know yet which.

Robert Pusey – Fireman

After the *Titanic* was a wreck, after everything was quiet, Lady Gordon said to Miss Franks, 'There is your beautiful nightdress gone,' and I said, 'Never mind about your nightdress, madam, as long as you have got your life.' I said we had lost our kits and that our pay was stopped from the time she was a wreck. Then I heard someone forward at the fore end of me say, 'We will give you a little to start a new kit.' That was all I heard. It was about three o'clock in the morning, because we were rowing for the light when this was said. We were rowing for this light half an hour or more.

Henry Stengel – First Class Passenger

Between Sir Duff Gordon and myself we decided which way to go. We followed a light that was to the bow of the boat, which looked like in the dead of winter, when the windows are frosted with a light coming through them. It was in a haze. Most of the boats rowed toward that light, and after the green lights began to burn, I suggested it was better to turn around and go toward the green lights, because I presumed there was an officer of the ship in that boat, and he evidently knew his business.

In one of those boats there was an old sailor, and he afterwards explained that he took the end of a rope and dipped it in oil and lit that. That was a flare light that every now and then would show.

It was toward morning that we turned, and by that time another man and myself thought we saw a rocket explode. I said, 'I think I saw a rocket,' and another one said, 'I think I saw a rocket,' and one of the stokers, I think it was, said, 'I see two lights. I believe that is a vessel.' Then, after that, when another green light was burned, there was a flash light from a boat, and I said, 'Now, I am pretty positive that is a boat, because that is an answer to the green signal,' and one of the stokers said, 'The green light is the company's colour.' That is what he said. Whether he was right or not, I do not know.

When we saw that flash light, it was like powder was set off. I said, 'Now, let us give it to her and let us steer in between the green light – where we saw the green light – and that boat,' and that being a very light boat, we left the other boats quite a way behind. I felt somewhat enthused to see the boat, and I began to jolly them along to pull. I said, 'Keep pulling.' We kept pulling, and I thought we were the first boat aboard, but I found that the boat that had the green lights burning was ahead of us. We were the second boat aboard.

The icebergs were all around. As soon as we were afloat, you could see icebergs all around, because we thought they were sailing vessels at first, and began pulling this way, and then turning around and going the other way. They were in sight all along the horizon. It was quite a ways, but you could see the outline in the dusk. There was one of them, particularly, that I noticed, a very large one, which looked something like the Rock of Gibraltar; it was high at one point, and another point came up at the other end, about the same shape as the Rock of Gibraltar. It was not quite as large as the *Titanic* but it was an enormous iceberg. At such a distance I should judge it was 250 feet high at the highest point.

Edward Wilding – Naval Architect, Harland & Wolff

I do not believe the ship split in two. I have tried to make an approximate calculation, and I feel quite sure it did not happen. I made a rough calculation as to the probable stress arising when the ship foundered as she got her stern out of the water. I can only do it very roughly, of course. It showed the stress in the ship was probably not greater than she would encounter in a severe Atlantic storm. The ship was made to go through an Atlantic storm, and therefore would be capable of meeting that stress.

BOAT NO 8

George Hogg – Lookout

As soon as I unhooked her, I mustered her people to see how many I had. I must have had 42. When I shoved away, I asked a lady if she could steer, and she said she could. I said: 'You may sit here and do this for me, and I will take the stroke oar.'

I was ordered to pull away from the ship for safety, for the time being. I pulled a little way from the ship, about a quarter of a mile. I went alongside another boat, and they transferred some of the passengers to my boat. I think they transferred four ladies and a baby and one gentleman. We were about 47. One lady said I should not take any more in that boat. I said: 'I will take all I can get.'

As soon as she went down, I went to try to assist them in picking up anybody if I could. I pulled around in search of other people before I could pull to the wreck. One man said, 'We have done our best. There are no more people around. We have pulled all around.' I said, 'Very good. We will get away now.' I laid off, then, until I saw the lights of the *Carpathia*. If we had had more boats, I dare say that we could have got away with a lot more.

It was bitter cold. Not a ripple on the water; the sea was as smooth as glass.

I saw the lights of the *Carpathia*. I said, 'It is all right, now, ladies. Do not grieve. We are picked up. Now, gentlemen, see what you can do in pulling these oars for this light.' It was practically daylight then. Then the passengers could see for themselves that there was a ship there. I pulled up and went alongside, and I assisted in putting a bowline around all the ladies, to haul them up aboard. After I saw all aboard the boat, me and my friend went aboard, and I put some blankets around myself and went to sleep.

Everything was done, as far as I can see. Everybody did their best, ladies and gentlemen and sailormen.

Alfred Crawford – Bedroom Steward
The captain gave me orders to ship the rowlocks and to pull for a light. It was the light of a vessel in the distance. There were two lights, not farther than ten miles away. They were stationary masthead lights, one on the fore and one on the main. Everybody saw them – all the ladies in the boat. I am sure it was a steamer, because a sailing ship would not have two masthead lights. The captain told us to row for the light and to land the people there and come back to the ship.

We all took an oar and pulled away from the ship. A lady – I have found out since it was the Countess of Rothes – took the tiller. Four men took the oars, and pulled away. We pulled until daybreak, but we could not catch the ship. When day broke we saw another steamer coming up which proved to be the *Carpathia*; and then we turned around and came back. We were the farthest boat away.

Ella White – First Class Passenger

Before we cut loose from the ship, two of the seamen with us – the men, I should say; I do not call them seamen, I think they were dining-room stewards – before we were cut loose from the ship, they took out cigarettes and lighted them. On an occasion like that! All of those men escaped under the pretence of being oarsmen. The man who rowed me took his oar and rowed all over the boat, in every direction. I said to him, 'Why don't you put the oar in the oarlock?' He said, 'Do you put it in that hole?' I said, 'Certainly.' He said, 'I never had an oar in my hand before.' I spoke to the other man, and he said, 'I have never had an oar in my hand before, but I think I can row.' Those were the men that we were put to sea with at night – with all these magnificent fellows left on board, who would have been such a protection to us. Those were the kind of men with whom we were put out to sea that night.

There were 22 women and four men on the boat. There was one there who was supposed to be a seaman, up at the end of our boat, who gave the orders. I do not know the names of any of those men. But he seemed to know something about it.

Our head seaman would give an order, and those men who knew nothing about the handling of a boat would say, 'If you don't stop talking through that hole in your face there will be one less in the boat.' We were in the hands of men of that kind. I settled two or three fights between them, and quieted them down. Imagine getting right out there and taking out a pipe and filling it and standing there smoking, with the women rowing, which was most dangerous, as we had woollen rugs all around us.

The women all rowed, every one of them. Miss Swift, from Brooklyn, rowed every mile, from the steamer to the *Carpathia*. Miss Young rowed every minute also, except when she was throwing up, which she did six or seven times. Countess Rothe stood at the tiller. Where would we have been if it had not been for our women, with such men as that put in charge of the boat?

We simply rowed away. We had the order, on leaving the ship, to do that. The officer who put us in the boat gave strict orders to the men to make for the light opposite and land the passengers and get back just as soon as possible. That was the light that everybody saw in the distance. I saw it distinctly. It was a boat of some kind. It was ten miles away, but we could see it distinctly. There was no doubt but that it was a boat. But we rowed and rowed and rowed, and then we all suggested that it was simply impossible for us to get to it; that we never could get to it, and the thing to do was to go back and see what we could do for the others. We only had 22 in our boat.

Then we turned and went back, and lingered around there for a long time, trying to locate the other boats, but we could not locate them except by hearing them. The only way they could locate us was by my electric lamp. The lamp on the boat was absolutely worth nothing. They tinkered with it all along, but they could not get it in shape. I had an electric cane – a cane with an electric light in it – and that was the only light we had. We sat there for a long time, and we saw the ship go down, distinctly.

In my opinion, the ship when it went down was broken in two. I think very probably it broke in two. I heard four distinct explosions, which we supposed were the boilers. Of course, we did not know anything about it.

It was something dreadful. They speak of the bravery of the men, but I do not think there was any particular bravery, because none of the men thought it was going down. Nobody ever thought the ship was going down. If they had thought the ship was going down, they would not have frivoled as they did about it. Some of them said, 'When you come back you will need a pass,' and, 'You cannot get on tomorrow morning without a pass.' They never would have said these things if anybody had had any idea that the ship was going to sink.

Just to think that on a beautiful starlit night – you could see the stars reflected in the water – with all those Marconi warnings, that they would allow such an accident to happen, with such a terrible loss of life and property. I never saw a finer body of men in my life than the men passengers on this trip – athletes and men of sense – and if they had been permitted to enter these lifeboats with their families the boats would have been appropriately manned and many more lives saved, instead of allowing the stewards to get in the boats and save their lives, under the pretence that they could row, when they knew nothing whatever about it.

It is simply unbearable, I think.

George Hogg – Lookout

I think all the women ought to have a gold medal on their breasts. They were American women that I had in mind; they were all Americans. I took the oar all the time, myself, and one lady steered. Then I got another lady to steer, and she gave me a hand on the oar, to keep herself warm. God bless them. I will always raise my hat to a woman, after what I saw.

BOAT NO 14
Harold Lowe – Fifth Officer

I lay off from the *Titanic*, as near as I could roughly estimate, about 150 yards, because I wanted to be close enough in order to pick up anybody that came by. We unshipped our oars, and I made the five boats fast together and we hung on like that for I should say an hour and a half; somewhere under two hours.

I did not return immediately. I had to wait until the yells and shrieks had subsided, because it would have been suicide to go back there until the people had thinned out. How could you detach them? Could not a man hold his weight on the side without help from me? There are lifelines round the lifeboat too, and they could get hold of those and hang on the rail. It would have been useless to try it, because a drowning man clings at anything.

It would not have been wise or safe for me to have gone there before, because the whole lot of us would have been swamped and then nobody would have been saved. What are you going to do with a boat of 65 where 1,600 people are drowning?

I made the attempt, as soon as any man could do so, and I am not scared of saying it. I did not hang back or anything else. Before going to the scene of the wreck, I was just on the margin. If anybody had struggled out of the mass, I was there to pick them up; but it was useless for me to go into the mass. It would have been suicide.

When I deemed it safe, I transferred all my passengers –
somewhere about 53 passengers – I equally distributed them
between my other four boats so as to have an empty boat
to go back. Then I asked for volunteers to go with me, and
I went off and I rowed off to the wreckage. It was rather
awkward to get in amongst it, because you could not row,
because of the bodies. You had to push your way through. It
was pretty well dark, and we could not see the people.

I picked up four, four alive. But one died, and that was
a Mr Hoyt, of New York. It took all the boat's crew to pull
this gentleman into the boat, because he was an enormous
man, and I suppose he had been soaked fairly well with
water. When we picked him up he was bleeding from the
mouth and from the nose. We did get him on board and I
propped him up at the stern of the boat. We let go his collar,
took his collar off, and loosened his shirt so as to give him
every chance to breathe, but unfortunately he died. I suppose
he was too far gone when we picked him up. But the other
three survived.

I then left the wreck. I went right around and, strange to
say, I did not see a single female body, not one, around the
wreckage. I left my crowd of boats somewhere, I should say,
about between half past three and four in the morning, and
after I had been around it was just breaking day, and I am
quite satisfied that I had a real good look around, and that
there was nothing left.

I could see the *Carpathia* coming up, and the thought then
flashed through my mind, 'Perhaps the ship has not seen us
in the semi-gloom.' I thought, 'Well, I am the fastest boat of
the lot,' as I was sailing, you see. I was going through the
water very nicely, going at about four, five knots, maybe – it

may have been a little more; it may have been six. Anyhow, I was bowling along very nicely in the direction of the *Carpathia*, and I thought, 'I am the fastest boat, and I think if I go toward her, for fear of her leaving us to our doom.' That is what I was scared about, and you will understand that day was dawning more and more as the time came on.

By and by, I noticed a collapsible boat, and it looked rather sorry, so I thought, 'Well, I will go down and pick her up and make sure of her.' So I went about and sailed down to this collapsible, and took her in tow.

I had taken this first collapsible in tow, and I noticed that there was another collapsible in a worse plight. I was just thinking and wondering whether it would be better for me to cut this one adrift and let her go, and for me to travel faster to the sinking one, but I thought, 'No, I think I can manage it.' So I cracked on a bit, and I got down there just in time and took off about 20 men and one lady out of this sinking collapsible. They were all up to their ankles in water when I took them off. Another three minutes and they would have been down.

I left three bodies on it; three male bodies. I think they had lifebelts on. The people on the raft told me they had been dead some time. I said, 'Are you sure they are dead?' They said, 'Absolutely sure.' I made the men turn those bodies over before I took them into my boat. I said, 'Before you come on board here you turn those bodies over and make sure they are dead,' and they did so. I may have been a bit hard-hearted, I cannot say, but I thought to myself, 'I am not here to worry about bodies; I am here for life, to save life, and not to bother about bodies,' and I left them.

Joseph Scarrott – Able Seaman

She was sinking by the head. Very slow it appeared to be. As the water seemed to get above the bridge, she increased her rate of going down. Head first. She was right up on end then. You could see her propeller right clear, and you could see part of her keel. She seemed to go with a rush then. You could hear the breaking up of things in the ship, and then followed four explosions. To the best of my recollection that is the number of the explosions.

We rowed in company with the four other boats, under the orders of Mr Lowe, to see if we could pick up anybody from the wreckage. There was not so much wreckage as you would expect from a big ship like that. We did not see many people in the water when we got right over the top of the ship. There did not appear to be many at all. Later on, we heard cries – rather a great deal.

Mr Lowe ordered four of the boats to tie together by the painters. He told the men that were in charge of them, the seamen there, what the object was. He said, 'If you are tied together and keep all together, if there is any passing steamer they will see a large object like that on the water quicker than they would a small one.'

During the time that was going on, we heard cries coming from another direction. Mr Lowe decided to transfer the passengers that we had, and then make up the full crew and go in the direction of those cries and see if we could save anybody else. The boats were made fast and the passengers were transferred, and we went away and went among the wreckage. When we got to where the cries were, we were amongst hundreds of dead bodies floating in lifebelts.

It was still dark, and the wreckage and bodies seemed to

be all hanging in one cluster. When we got up to it, we got one man in the stern of the boat – a passenger it was – and he died shortly after. One of the stewards that was in the boat tried means to restore life to the man; he loosed him and worked his limbs about and rubbed him; but it was of no avail at all, because the man never recovered.

We got two others then, as we pushed our way towards the wreckage, and as we got towards the centre we saw one man there. I have since found out he was a storekeeper. He was on top of a large piece of wreckage which had come from some part of the ship. It looked like a staircase. He was kneeling there as if he was praying, and at the same time he was calling for help. When we saw him, we were a short distance away from him, and the wreckage were that thick – and I am sorry to say there were more bodies than there was wreckage – it took us a good half hour to get that distance to that man, to get through the bodies.

We could not row the boat; we had to push them out of the way and force our boat up to this man. But we did not get close enough to get him right off – only just within the reach of an oar. We put out an oar on the fore part of the boat, and he got hold of it, and he managed to hold on, and we got him into the boat. Those three survived.

We made sail and sailed back to take our other boats in tow that could not manage themselves at all. We made sail then, but just as we were getting clear of the wreckage we sighted the *Carpathia*'s lights.

Harold Lowe – Fifth Officer

I have seen icebergs, down south, off Cape Horn and down that way. I cannot say that I have seen them in the South

Atlantic. That is the only one I saw until daybreak on the Monday morning, after the accident. I saw quite a few of them then. I did not count them, but I should say there were anywhere up to 20. They were all around. I should say that the largest one was about 100 feet high above water – all within a radius of, at the outside, six miles. The nearest would be three miles.

They must have been in the *Titanic*'s way if they were all along the horizon.

They were anything from 20 feet up to 100 feet in height. That is, above water. There is one-eighth of an iceberg supposed to be above water, and seven-eighths below water. There are only two places for them to come from; that is from the north pole and the south pole, from the polar regions. That is what I learned at school. I suppose it is right. I think it will turn out to be about that if you test it.

Frank Morris – First Class Bath Steward
Our officer did the finest action he could have done.

BOAT NO 12
Frederick Clench – Able Seaman
After the ship sank, there were awful cries, and yelling and shouting, and that. Of course I told the women in the boats to keep quiet, and consoled them a bit. I told them it was men in the boats shouting out to the others, to keep them from getting away from one another. I saw no one in the water whatsoever, whether alive or dead, and we never seen no wreckage around us.

We remained there, I should say, up until about four o'clock. It was just after we got the women from Mr Lowe's boat, and he said he was going around the wreckage to see if he could find anybody. I should say we had close to 60, then; we were pretty well full up. He told us to lie on our oars and keep together until he came back to us.

While Mr Lowe was gone I heard shouts. I looked around, and I saw a boat in the way that appeared to be like a funnel. We started to back away then. We thought it was the top of the funnel. I put my head over the gunwale and looked along the water's edge and saw some men on a raft. Then I heard two whistles blown. I sang out 'Aye, aye. I am coming over,' and we pulled over and found it was a raft – not a raft, exactly, but an overturned boat – and Mr Lightoller was there on that boat, and I believe the wireless operator was on there, too. We took them on board the boat and we shared the amount of the room that was there.

Mr Lightoller took charge of us and sighted the *Carpathia*'s lights. Then we started heading for that. We had to row a tidy distance to the *Carpathia*, because there was boats ahead of us, and we had a boat in tow with us, besides all the people we had aboard.

COLLAPSIBLE D
Hugh Woolner – First Class Passenger

I could not really see a thing when the lights went out. It was all brilliantly lighted at the stem end, and suddenly the lights went out, and your eyes were so unaccustomed to the darkness, you could see nothing, and you could only hear sounds. There was nobody in sight. Not a soul. We were right up close, and it was like the side of a house and we could see nothing at all.

She seemed to me to stop for about 30 seconds at one

place before she took the final plunge, because I watched one particular porthole, and the water did not rise there for at least half a minute, and then she suddenly slid under with her propellers under the water.

For quite a considerable time we simply rowed out into the sea. We heard other boats around about us, and when the eyes got accustomed to the darkness we could see a certain amount. There was a lantern on board, but there was no oil in it. Then some officer came along and said, 'I want all these boats tied up by their painters, head and tail, so as to make a more conspicuous mark,' and we did that.

Then we drifted about for a long time. We had a water breaker, I think they call it, but there was no water in it. A sailor offered some biscuits, which I was using for feeding a small child who had waked up and was crying. It was one of those little children for whose parents everybody was looking. I should think it was about 15, as nearly as I can judge. It looked like a French child; but it kept shouting for its doll, and I could not make out what it said before that. It kept saying it over and over again.

Then dawn began to break very slowly, and we could see more. There were a great many icebergs. They were of different colours as the sun struck them. Some looked white and some looked blue, and some sort of mauve, and others were dark grey. There was one double-toothed one that looked to be of good size.

I saw a faint line, what looked like a faint line along the horizon. From the boat it looked like a brilliant white line along the horizon. But when we got on the *Carpathia*, we saw it was a huge floe which stretched out I do not know how far, but we were several hours steaming along it. It seemed to be stationary; but there were lumps on it, sort of lumps like haystacks or little mountains.

The *Carpathia* seemed to come up very slowly and then she stopped. Then we looked out and we saw that there was a boat alongside her, and then we realised that she was waiting for us to come up to her instead of her coming to us, as we hoped. Then, just at that time, when we began to row toward the *Carpathia*, Mr Lowe came down with his boat under sail, again, and hailed us and said, 'Are you a collapsible?' We answered, 'Yes.' He said 'How are you?' I said, 'We have about all we want.' He said, 'Would you like a tow?' We answered, 'Yes, we would.' So he took our painter and towed us away to the *Carpathia*.

There were several other children in the boat. We handed them into a bag, and they were pulled up the *Carpathia*'s side.

John Hardy – Chief Second Class Steward
They were all strangers to me. There were a number of Third Class passengers, that were Syrians, in the bottom of the boat, chattering the whole night in their strange language. We were some of the last.

We picked up the husband of a wife that we had taken off another boat. The gentleman took to the water, and climbed in the boat when we were afloat. I remember that quite distinctly. I know the gentleman – but I do not know his name – because he sat there, wringing wet, alongside of me, helping me row. He was an American gentleman.

COLLAPSIBLE C
Bruce Ismay – Managing Director, IMM
I do not know how far we were away. I was sitting with my

back to the ship. I did not wish to see her go down. I only looked around once. She was very much down by the head; her starboard light was just about level with the water. I never looked around again. I was rowing all the time I was in the boat. We were pulling away.

We saw a light a long way from us, which, I think, was a little bit on our starboard side. We thought we gained on her, and then she seemed to draw away from us again when daylight came. I do not think it was a steamer at all; I think it was a sailing ship we saw. I am sure it was not the *Californian*. This light was on the starboard side of the *Titanic*. I understand the *Californian* – or the ship that was supposed to be the *Californian* – was seen on the port side. The only light I saw was the one we rowed for. I saw no other light.

We found four Chinamen stowed away under the thwarts after we got away. I think they were Filipinos, perhaps. There were four of them. I believe one was a cook, another was the butcher, and another was the quartermaster.

There was very little wind, up to a certain hour in the morning, when the wind did get up. We gave it up because the wind got up; a little sea got up and we were making no progress at all.

COLLAPSIBLE A
Edward Brown – First Class Steward

When I got in the water, I was in a whirlpool going round. I came up to the top. There was what I took to be an explosion – a great noise, a great report. There was no wreckage, but a lot of people in the water. And well I know it, because they tore my clothing away from me with struggling in the water.

With the first report of that explosion, I saw the after part of the ship giving a bit of a tremble, that the bow had fallen off. The part right before the forward funnel was practically under water then. There were lights burning then.

I saw a black object and swam towards it. I never swam in my life; but I kept myself up with the lifebelt, and I made my way the best I could towards it. It seemed a very long time; it seemed a lifetime to me. The lifebelt saved me.

It was a good while after daylight I was picked up by the lifeboat. It was submerged with the weight of men on it. I should say there were 16 or 17 on it, all men. They were mixed up; there were some stewards, some firemen, and the rest passengers. The women were picked up after I got aboard of it.

There was nobody pulling then, because the boat was under sail when I got into it. The officer asked for volunteers to row. There were three oars put out on the starboard side of the boat, and I took one on the port side.

My feet had burst my boots, and my hands were all swollen up.

Olaus Abelseth – Third Class Passenger

When we came into the water, I think it was from the suction – or anyway we went under, and I swallowed some water. I got a rope tangled around me, and I let loose of my brother-in-law's hand to get away from the rope. I thought then, 'I am a goner.' That is what I thought when I got tangled up in this rope. But I came on top again, and I was trying to swim, and there was a man – lots of them were floating around – and he got me on the neck like and pressed me under, trying to get on top of me. I said to him, 'Let go.' Of course, he did not pay any attention to that, but I got away from him. Then there was another man, and he hung on to me for a while, but he let go. Then I swam, I could not say how long, but it must have been about 15 or 20 minutes. It could not have been over that. Then I saw something dark ahead of me. I did not know what it was, but I swam toward that, and it was one of those collapsible boats.

When we jumped off of the ship, we had life-preservers on. There was no suction from the ship at all. I was lying still, and I thought, 'I will try to see if I can float on the lifebelt without help from swimming,' and I floated easily on the lifebelt.

When I got on this raft or collapsible boat, they did not try to push me off and they did not do anything for me to get on. All they said when I got on there was, 'Don't capsize the boat.' So I hung on to the raft for a little while before I got on.

Some of them were trying to get up on their feet. They were sitting down or lying down on the raft. Some of them fell into the water again. Some of them were frozen; and there were two dead, that they threw overboard.

I got on this raft or collapsible boat and raised up, and then I was continually moving my arms and swinging them around to keep warm. There was one lady aboard this raft, and she got saved. I do not know her name.* There were also two Swedes, and a First Class passenger, and he had just his underwear on. I asked him if he was married, and he said he had a wife and a child. There was also a fireman named Thompson on the same raft. He had burned one of

---

* Rhoda Abbott was the only woman on Collapsible A.

his hands. Also there was a young boy, with a name that sounded like 'volunteer'.

The next morning we could see some of the lifeboats. One of the boats had a sail up, and he came pretty close, and then we said, 'One, two, three.' We said that quite often. We did not talk very much, except that we would say, 'One, two, three,' and scream together for help.

The boat was not capsized, but there was water on the top. We were standing on the deck; the canvas was not raised up. We tried to raise the canvas up but we could not get it up. We stood all night in about 12 or 14 inches of water on this thing, and our feet were in the water all the time. I could not say exactly how long we were there, but I know it was more than four hours on this raft.

It was broad daylight when the *Carpathia* came. There were several boats there then. Then this boat sailed down to us and took us aboard, and took us in. I helped row into the *Carpathia*. There must have been ten or twelve on board. They got saved off this raft.

There was one man from New Jersey that I came in company with from London. I do not know what his name was. I tried to keep this man alive; but I could not make it. It was just at the break of day, and he was lying down, and he seemed to be kind of unconscious; he was not really dead, and I took him by the shoulder and raised him up, so that he was sitting up on this deck.

He was just sitting down right on the deck. I said to him, 'We can see a ship now. Brace up.' And I took one of his hands and raised it up, and I took him by the shoulder and shook him, and he said, 'Who are you?' He said, 'Let me be. Who are you?' I held him up like that for a while, but I got tired and cold, and I took a little piece of a small board – a lot of which were floating around there – and laid it under his head on the edge of the boat to keep his head from the water. But it was not more than about half an hour or so when he died.

We saw three big icebergs. They were quite a ways off.

Riversdale French – Surgeon, SS *Oceanic*
I went on the second visit to the boat. We found three bodies, a fur rug, a ring, and a lady's comb. They were three men. One evidently was a passenger, and two probably members of the crew. The passenger's body was in evening clothes, and we found his name. By the light of what I know now, I know those bodies had died of exposure.

COLLAPSIBLE B

Charles Lightoller – Second Officer

The ship seemed to take a bit of a dive, and I just walked into the water. I was swimming out towards the head of the ship, the crow's nest. I could see the crow's nest. The water was intensely cold, and one's natural instinct was to try to get out of the water. I do not know whether I swam to the foremast with that idea, but of course I soon realised it was rather foolish, so I turned to swim across clear of the ship to starboard. The next thing I knew I was up against the blower on the fore part of the funnel. The water was rushing down this blower, through a grating, right down into the stokehold. The water rushing down held me against the blower a little while. After a while – it seemed a good long while, though I do not suppose it was many moments – there seemed to be a rush of air from down below, and I was blown away from it.

I was in the sea between half an hour and an hour. With a lifejacket on, there is no necessity to swim; you can paddle, it holds you high in the water. But you cannot swim, because you cannot get your breast deep down in the water. I have heard since that the gymnasium instructor refused to put one on for that reason; he could swim far better and get clear of people and things without it.

I found myself alongside of the collapsible boat, which I had previously launched on the port side, the one I had thrown on to the boat deck. It was still shut up, bottom side up. I just held on to something, a piece of rope or something, and was there for a little while, and then the forward funnel fell down. It fell within three or four inches of the boat. It lifted the boat bodily, and threw her about 20 feet clear of the ship.

Edward Wilding – Naval Architect, Harland & Wolff
The funnels are carried from the casings in the way of the comparatively light upper decks – that is, the boat deck and A deck. When these decks became submerged and the water got inside the house, the water would rise outside much faster than inside, and the excessive pressure on the comparatively light casings which are not made to take a pressure of that kind would cause the casing to collapse; would take the seating from under the funnel and bring the funnel down.

Charles Lightoller – Second Officer
After the funnel fell, some little time elapsed. I do not know exactly what came or went, but the next thing I remember I was alongside this collapsible boat again, and there were about half a dozen people standing on it. I climbed on it,

and then turned my attention to the ship. The third if not the second funnel was still visible – certainly the third funnel was still visible. The stern was then clear of the water. Even at that time I think the propellers were clear of the water. She did eventually attain the absolutely perpendicular.

The ship did not and could not have broken in two, and the stern did not settle on the water. I am perfectly certain of that. I was watching her keenly the whole time.

After she reached an angle of 50 or 60 degrees, or something about that, there was this rumbling sound, which I attributed to the boilers leaving their beds and crushing down on or through the bulkheads. The ship at that time was becoming more perpendicular, until finally she attained the absolute perpendicular, and then went slowly down. She went down very slowly until the end, and then the after part of the second cabin deck went down much quicker.

The only thing that I should attribute to explosions was when I was, in the first place, sucked to the blower, and, in the second place, shortly before the forward funnel falling, there was an up-rush of certainly warm water. But whether it was caused by an explosion or what, I could not say. It may have been the cold water reaching the boilers – if boilers do explode under those circumstances, which is quite an open question. Some say they do and a great many capable men certainly say they do not explode. If her boilers did not explode, it was not from that and must have been the rush of imprisoned air. The heat would be caused merely through its coming from the stokehold.

Edward Wilding – Naval Architect, Harland & Wolff
I should think it was very unlikely that the boilers exploded.

There are very few cases, I believe, of boilers examined in ships after they have been flooded which have exploded. Of course, when sea water reaches a hot boiler there is a great cloud of steam which might give a certain impression of explosion. The boilers might have moved when the bow was down; I do not think the machinery did. The fact that the electric lights remained burning up to the moment almost that she disappeared indicates that one boiler room, most probably No 2, was still supplying steam to the emergency dynamos.

Charles Lightoller – Second Officer

As far as I remember, I was standing or kneeling on the upside-down lifeboat. There were several people in the water round about us who struggled towards the boat and swarmed towards it and got on to it during the night occasionally. Of course, we could not paddle that boat about; it was absolutely water-logged. Six others got on during the night, and there were nearly 28 or 30 people on this raft in the morning.

The swell got up almost immediately after I was in the water. I had not been on the upturned boat more than half an hour or so before a slight swell was distinctly noticeable. In the morning there was quite a breeze and we maintained our equilibrium with the greatest difficulty when the rough sea came towards us.

We saw then there were several icebergs scattered about. I should say the nearest must have been at least ten miles away. That is a pretty rough estimate. I cannot say with any degree of accuracy now what the nearest was, it may have been less. They ranged from a matter of 50 or 60 feet to perhaps 200 or 300 feet. There was no pack ice that we saw then.

Two lifeboats approached us. I had my whistle in my pocket. I whistled by way of showing it was an officer that was calling, and I asked them if they could take some of us on board. I said if they could manage to take half a dozen – because we were sinking then – it would lighten us up so that we could continue afloat.

We all got into one of the boats, I do not know the number. This being the lighter one of the two, I chose it. Standing in the stern, I counted 65 heads, including those taken off that boat. I could not myself see anyone who sat in the bottom of the boat. I judge there were at least 75 in the boat. Bride was on board, the Marconi operator, of course; that is the boat that Phillips was on. There were two or three died during the night.

It was one of the later boats to be taken on board the *Carpathia*, and therefore would be one of those that was turned adrift. It was the last boat to get to the *Carpathia*, as a matter of fact, I think.

Harold Bride – Assistant Telegraphist

I was upside down, on the under-side of the collapsible, lying on my back. After I had been there two or three seconds, I cleared myself and swam away from it. I do not know why. I swam away from the *Titanic*. I was in the water, I should estimate, nearly three-quarters of an hour. It may have been more. It seemed a lifetime to me. I was swimming when she went down – I estimate I was within 150 feet of her – and I felt practically no suction at all.

I joined the raft again later on, three-quarters of an hour

to an hour I should estimate, and I climbed on top of it. I was the last man they invited on board, and there was a big crowd on top when I got on. I should judge they were all employees, all part of the boat's crews. They had all been in the water some time or other. We did not have much to say to each other.

I called to Phillips several times, but got no response, and learned later from several sources that he was on this boat and expired even before we were picked off by the other [life]boat. I am told fright and exposure was the cause of his death.

Charles Joughin – Chief Baker

Just as it was breaking daylight, I saw what I thought was some wreckage, and I started to swim towards it slowly. When I got near enough, I found it was a collapsible not properly upturned but on its side, with an officer and I should say about 20 or 25 men standing on the top of it.

They were standing on the side, holding one another's shoulders. There was no room for any more. I tried to get on it, but I was pushed off it, and I what you call hung around it. I eventually got round to the opposite side, and a cook that was on the collapsible recognised me, and held out his hand and held me – a chap named Maynard. My lifebelt helped me, and I held on the side of the boat.

We were hanging on to this collapsible, and eventually a lifeboat came in sight. They got within about 50 yards and they sung out that they could only take ten. So I said to this Maynard, 'Let go my hand,' and I swam to meet it, so that I would be one of the ten. I climbed in, and then she went alongside the collapsible afterwards, but I did not notice how many she took. Mr Lightoller left the collapsible and then took charge of the boat till we reached the *Carpathia*.

I was all right, barring my feet – they were swelled. I walked up the ladder on my knees.

Archibald Gracie – First Class Passenger

I was taken down with the ship, and hanging on to that railing, but I soon let go. I felt myself whirled around, swam under water, fearful that the hot water that came up from the boilers might boil me up – and the second officer told me that he had the same feeling – swam it seemed to me with unusual strength, and succeeded finally in reaching the surface and in getting a good distance away from the ship.

How far, I could not say, because I could not see the ship. When I came up to the surface, there was no ship there. The ship would then have been behind me, and all around me was wreckage. I saw what seemed to be bodies all around.

I noticed no suction, and I did not go down so far as that it would affect my nose or my ears. My great concern was to keep my breath, which I was able to do, and being able to do that was what I think saved me. I did not notice any coldness of the water at that time. I was too much preoccupied in getting away.

There was a sort of gulp, as if something had occurred behind me, and I suppose that was where the water was closing up, where the ship had gone down; but the surface of the water was perfectly still, and there were, I say, this wreckage, and these bodies, and there were the horrible sounds of drowning people and people gasping for breath.

While collecting the wreckage together, I got on a big wooden crate, some sort of wooden crate, or wood of that sort. I saw an upturned boat, and I struck out for that boat, and there I saw what I supposed were members of the crew on this upset boat. I grabbed the arm of one of them and pulled myself up on this boat.

I was among the first. I suppose the boat was then about half full – there must have been between 15 and 20 people on board. Officer Lightoller was on that same boat. There was one man in front, with an oar, and another man in the stern with what I think was a piece of a board, propelling the boat along. Then we loaded the raft with as many as it would contain, until she became under water, until we could take no more, because the water was up to our waists.

Our concern now was to get out of the wreckage and to get away from the swimmers in the water before they tried to get on the boat, and all of us would be lost.

We were taken through the wreckage and away from the screams of the drowning people, and we were on the lookout then in every direction for lights and ships to come to our rescue, hallooing all the time, 'Boat ahoy,' or 'Ship ahoy,' our spirits kept up all the time by what we thought were steamship lights and boat lights. But I think most of those lights we saw were the lights of the lifeboats of the *Titanic*, particularly one that was steering ahead of us, and making lights every little while. I do not know what kind of light they had, but it was a green light that was every little while conspicuous from some lifeboats directly ahead of us.

And then right to the port side we finally did see the lights of a ship, and that was finally the *Carpathia*. The Marconi man who was on the raft said he thought this was the *Carpathia*, because he had conversed with the operator on the *Carpathia*. That was the nearest ship, he thought, to us at the time.

We had to keep the equilibrium of the boat all night long, from half past two. I say half past two; I might say from 2.22, because my watch, when I looked at it afterwards on the *Carpathia*, had stopped, and the time indicated was 2.22. So that would indicate the time between the collision and the time that I went down with the ship.

We stood upon this collapsible boat in the early morn, just before dawn, so that we might be seen the better, and also, it was not quite so cold, although our feet were in the water. Then, as the sun came up, a welcome sight was the four lifeboats of the *Titanic* on our starboard side. Lightoller blew his whistle and ordered them to come over and take us off of our upset boat. 'Aye, aye, sir,' they replied, and immediately turned toward us, and two boats came right up close and then began the difficult task of a transfer.

We were transferred successfully from the raft. The complement of the lifeboat I was on was filled up to 65. There were a considerable number of women; possibly half the number were women.

The second officer stayed until the last, lifting up the body of one of the crew and putting it right down by me, where I chafed his temples and his wrists to see whether there was any life in him. Then rigor mortis set in and I thought the man was dead, and there was no more use trying to resuscitate him.

There was a splendid Frenchwoman, who was very kind to us, who loaned us one of her blankets to put over our heads – that is, four of us. One poor Englishman, who was the only other passenger besides Mr Thayer and myself who was saved on this raft – he was bald, and for that reason he needed this protection, which was very grateful to him. It was very grateful to me, too. The people on the *Carpathia* received us with open arms, and provided us with hot comforts, and acted as ministering angels.

THE *CALIFORNIAN*
Cyril Evans – Marconi Officer, SS *Californian*

At about 3.30am New York time [5.20am ship's time] the chief officer came into my room and woke me up. He said, 'Wireless, there is a ship that has been firing rockets in the night. Please see if there is anything the matter.'

I jumped out of bed, slipped on a pair of trousers and a pair of slippers. My bunk is in the same room as the apparatus. I went at once to my key and started my motor and gave 'CQ' – that means all stations, someone answer – and gave my own code signal. About a second later I was answered by the Frankfurt, *'DKD, DFT'. The DFT is the* Frankfurt's *call.*

He said, 'Do you know the Titanic *has sunk during the night, collided with an iceberg?' I said, 'No. Please give me the latest position.' He gave me the position. I put the position down on a slip of paper, and then I said, 'Thanks, old man,' to the German operator. Then the* Virginian *started to call me up. I answered him, and told him to go. He said, 'Do you know the* Titanic *had sunk?' I said, 'Yes, the* Frankfurt *has just told me.' I sent them a service message, and said, 'Please send me official message regarding* Titanic, *giving position.'*

The message from the Frankfurt *was not an official message; that was only a conversation. But a few minutes after that I got an official message from the* Virginian. *The position I got from the* Virginian *and the position I got from the* Frankfurt *were both the same. I sent that up to the skipper. I did not have time to date the message. I dated my own copy of the message, but I did not get the name of the ship on either, or the date, or who it was addressed to, in my hurry.*

I was trying to get the Carpathia. *He told me he was about 30 or 40 miles off from the scene of the disaster. I remember that. I forget how it happened, but he said, 'We are 30 or 40 miles off. We are steaming as fast as we can.' This was after I had taken the message up, and we were under way. I said, 'We are steaming full speed, now.'*

Stanley Lord – Captain, SS Californian
I was conversing with the chief officer about the probability of pushing through the ice. I was undecided whether to go through it or to turn round and go back. We decided to go on, so I told him to put the engines on and stand by. He did so. Then he said, 'Will you go down to look at this steamer to the southward?' I asked him, 'Why, what is the matter with it?' He said, 'He might have lost his rudder.' But I said, 'Why? He has not got any signals up.' 'No, but the second officer in his watch said he fired several rockets.' I said, 'Go and call the wireless operator.'

The chief officer came back after 15 to 20 minutes and said, 'The operator reports a ship sunk.' I said, 'Go back and wait until you find out what it is. Get some more about it.' So he went back, and I suppose ten minutes afterwards he came back and said, 'The Titanic *is sunk, and hit an iceberg.'*

I said, 'Go back again and find the position as quickly as possible.' So he went back, and he came back and said, 'We have a position here, but it seems a bit doubtful.' I said, 'You must get me a better position. We do not want to go on a wild goose chase.' So in the meantime, I marked off the position from the course given me by the Frankfurt in the message just from one operator to another. I marked that off and headed the ship down there.

As we were trying to get official news from the Frankfurt, the Virginian chipped in, and he gave me this message, which confirmed the position.

I should think it was 30 miles at the least to the wreckage. There was a dense ice-field running north and south after the style of a T, and the T was dividing the position where the Titanic was supposed to have sunk and where we were. I suppose for the two or three miles all the way down to where she was, it was studded with bergs and loose ice. I ran along bearing north-east, and then I cut straight through the ice at full speed.

PART FOUR

RESCUE
Monday 15 April 1912

'Considering the size of the disaster, there was very little wreckage. It seemed more like an old fishing boat had sunk'

Arthur Rostron – Captain, SS *Carpathia*

At 20 minutes to three, I saw the green flare, which is the White Star Company's night signal, and, knowing I must be at least 20 miles away, I thought it was the ship herself still. It was showing just for a few seconds, and I passed the remark that she must still be afloat. Before this, I had got the wireless message that the engine room was filling, so I felt it was a case of all up.

At a quarter to three I saw what we knew was an iceberg by the light from a star – I saw a streak of light right on the iceberg. From then on till four o'clock, I passed icebergs on every side and had to alter our course several times to clear the bergs. At four o'clock, I considered I was practically up to the position, and I stopped. In the meantime I had been firing rockets and the company's signals every time we saw this green light.

A few minutes later, I saw the green light again, and I was going to pick the boat up on the port bow, but just as it showed the green light I saw an iceberg right ahead of me. It was very close, so I had to port my helm hard a-starboard and put her head round quick and pick up the boat on the starboard side. Then I saw the light on my starboard side. It was getting close. I went full speed astern. I went a little bit past the boat before I could get the way off the ship, and I came back again, because they sang out from the boat that they had only one seaman, and could not handle her. I brought the ship back to the boat. At ten minutes past four we got alongside.

By the time we had the first boat's people, it was breaking day, and then I could see the remaining boats all around within an area of about four miles. I also saw icebergs all around me. There were about 20 icebergs that would be anywhere from about 150 to 200 feet high and numerous smaller bergs; also numerous what we call 'growlers'. They were anywhere from 10 to 12 feet high and 10 to 15 feet long above the water. There were dozens and dozens of them all over the place.

It was quite daylight before we saw the ice-field. We were then about four or five miles from a huge ice-field extending as far as we could see, NW to SE.

There were several ladies in the boats. They were slightly injured about the arms and things of that kind, of course – although I must say, from the very start, all these people behaved magnificently. As each boat came alongside everyone was calm, and they kept perfectly still in their boats. They were quiet and orderly, and each person came up the ladder, or was pulled up, in turn as they were told off. Everyone we saw in the boats was wearing a lifebelt. There was no confusion whatever among the passengers. They behaved magnificently, every one of them.

As they came aboard, they were, of course, attended to. My instructions had already been given to that effect.

We took three dead men from the boats, and they were brought on board. They had died of exposure. Another man was brought up – I think he was one of the crew – who died that morning about ten o'clock. One of my own officers and the Titanic's officers identified the bodies, as far as possible, and took everything from them that could be of the slightest clue or use. Nothing was left but their clothes. There was very little taken, of course. The four bodies were buried at sea later that afternoon.

We got 13 lifeboats alongside, two emergency boats, two Berthon boats. There was one lifeboat which we saw was abandoned, and one of the Berthon boats was not launched from the ship but was bottom up in the wreckage. That made 20 altogether.* Several of the boats could have accommodated a good many more people, and two or three boats were rather crowded, I thought.

While they were getting all the people aboard from the boats, I got the spare men and some of my officers, and swung my boats inboard again, and landed them on their blocks and secured them. I then swung the davits out again, disconnected the falls again, and got up the Titanic's boats.

I have only been in one or two of the boats, but they were all marked 'Titanic', as they came up. They were all brand new, as far as I could see. I saw both water and biscuits in the boats, not all, of course, but one or two where the men were working about when we secured them. And all of the boats had the bread tanks, that I know for certain. And they also had water breakers.

The position given me by the Titanic was absolutely correct and he was absolutely on her track, bound for New York. I forget the true course now, but he had passed what we call the corner on the great circle. It is some years

---

*Rostron is miscounting. The missing boat is probably Collapsible A, picked up a month later by the *Oceanic* with three bodies on board.

since I was in the North Atlantic trade; I have been in the Mediterranean trade, and I have forgotten the exact course. But he was on the southerly route for western-bound steamers, on his proper track, where he ought to have been at this time of year.

Bruce Ismay – Managing Director, IMM

I think that I boarded the ship *Carpathia* at a quarter to six or a quarter past six. I happened to see a clock somewhere on the ship when I got on her.

When I got on board the ship, I stood up with my back against the bulkhead, and somebody came up to me and said, 'Will you not go into the saloon and get some soup, or something to drink?' I said, 'No, I really do not want anything at all.' He said, 'Do go and get something.' I said, 'No. If you will leave me alone I will be very much happier here.' I said, 'If you will get me in some room where I can be quiet, I wish you would.' He said, 'Please go in the saloon and get something hot.' I said, 'I would rather not.' Then he took me and put me into a room. I did not know whose the room was, at all. This man proved to be the doctor of the *Carpathia*. I was in that room until I left the ship. I was never outside the door of that room. During the whole of the time I was in this room, I never had anything of a solid nature, at all; I lived on soup. I did not want very much of anything.

I had a suit of pyjamas on, a pair of slippers, a suit of clothes and an overcoat.

On Monday morning, very shortly after I got on board the *Carpathia*, the captain came down to me and said, 'Don't you think, sir, you had better send a message to New

York, telling them about this accident?' I said, 'Yes.' I wrote it out on a slip of paper, and I turned to the commander of the *Carpathia* and I said, 'Captain, do you think that is all I can tell them?' He said, 'Yes.' Then he took it away from the room.

This is the message I sent on the fifteenth of April at about eight o'clock. It was received by Mr Franklin on the seventeenth of April:

```
Deeply regret advise you Titanic sank
this morning after collision iceberg,
resulting serious loss life. Full
particulars later. Signed Bruce Ismay
```

Joseph Boxhall – Fourth Officer

One of the first things that Captain Rostron said after I met him was: 'What a splendid position that was you gave us.'

I was on the bridge for several minutes, about a quarter of an hour, shortly after we got the boats on board. We were steaming around the scene of the disaster. I saw one floating body of a man. It had a life-preserver on, and it was quite dead. We could see by the way the body was lying. This body looked as if the man had fallen asleep lying on his side, with his face over his arm. That is the only body I saw, dead or alive.

After we got on board the *Carpathia* I met one or two American passengers. I recall that Colonel Astor and his wife were aboard. I saw him walking on the top deck – one of the officers told me who he was. I never saw his wife at all.

It was well on in the forenoon when the captain set the course to New York.

Arthur Rostron – Captain, SS *Carpathia*
At 8.30 all the people were on board. I asked for the purser, and told him that I wanted to hold a service, a short prayer of thankfulness for those rescued and a short burial service for those who were lost. I consulted with Mr Ismay. I ran down for a moment and told them that I wished to do this, and Mr Ismay left everything in my hands. I then got an episcopal clergyman, one of our passengers, and asked him if he would do this for me, which he did, willingly.

While they were holding the service, I was on the bridge, of course, and I manoeuvred around the scene of the wreckage. We were then very close to where the Titanic *must have gone down, as there was a lot of wreckage – hardly wreckage but small pieces of broken-up stuff, nothing in the way of anything large; a few deck chairs and pieces of cork from lifebelts, a few lifebelts, and things of that description, all very small stuff indeed.*

We only saw one body. It was floating, with a life-preserver on. It was male and appeared to me to be one of the crew; he was only about 100 yards from the ship. We could see him quite distinctly, and saw that he was absolutely dead. He was lying on his side, and his head was awash. Of course he could not possibly have been alive and remain in that position. I did not take him aboard. For one reason, the Titanic's *passengers then were knocking about the deck and I did not want to cause any unnecessary excitement or any more hysteria among them, so I steamed past, trying to get them not to see it.*

At eight o'clock the Leyland Line steamer Californian *hove up, and we exchanged messages. I gave them the notes by semaphore about the* Titanic *going down, and that I had* got all the passengers from the boats; but we were then not quite sure whether we could account for all the boats. I told them: 'Think one boat still unaccounted for.' He then asked me if he should search around, and I said, 'Yes, please.'

The next day I got a message from the Californian saying: 'Have searched position carefully up to noon and found nothing and seen no bodies.'

James Moore – Captain, SS Mount Temple

At 3.25am I stopped the engines, and then went slowly to avoid the ice, because it was too dark to proceed full speed on account of the ice. I reached the Titanic's position, or very close to it, at 4.30 in the morning. I saw a large ice pack right to the east of me; at least five miles wide and 20 miles long, perhaps more than that.

I searched around to see if there was a clear place we could go through, because I feared the ice was too heavy for me to push through, and I realised that the Titanic could not have been through it. I steered away to the south-south-east true, because I thought the ice appeared thinner down there. When I found the ice was too heavy, I stopped there and turned around, and searched for a passage, and I could not see any passage whatever. I had a man pulled up to the masthead in a bowline, right to the foretopmast head, and I had the chief officer at the mainmast head, and he could not see any line through the ice at all that I could go through.

Of course, I had no idea then that the Titanic had sunk. I had not the slightest idea of that.

On the way back again, at about six o'clock in the morning, I sighted the Carpathia on the other side of this great ice pack, and there is where I understand he picked up *the boats. So this great pack of ice was between us and the Titanic's position. It was not until I received word from the Carpathia that she had picked up the boats and the Titanic had sunk that I gave up hopes of seeing her. I stayed there until nine o'clock, and was cruising around all that time. I saw nothing whatever in the way of wreckage.*

I saw the Californian cruising around there; she was there shortly after me. She was to the north of the Carpathia and steaming to the westward.

Stanley Lord – Captain, SS *Californian*
I don't know what time we got there. I think he was taking the last boat up when I got there. I saw several empty boats, some floating planks, a few deck chairs and cushions, a few lifebelts floating around; but considering the size of the disaster, there was very little wreckage. It seemed more like an old fishing boat had sunk.

I talked to the Carpathia until nine o'clock. Then he left. Then we went full speed in circles over a radius – that is, I took a big circle and then came around and around and got back to the boats again, where I had left them. At 11.20 we proceeded on our course.

Arthur Peuchen – First Class Passenger
I felt sure that an explosion had taken place in the boat, because in passing the wreck the next morning – I was standing forward, looking to see if I could see any dead bodies, or any of my friends – and to my surprise I saw the barber's pole floating. The barber's pole was on the C deck, my recollection is, and that must have been a tremendous explosion to allow this pole to have broken from its

fastenings and drift with the wood.

I was surprised, when we steamed through this wreckage, that we did not see any bodies in the water. That is something that astonished me very much. The wreckage was something like two islands, and was strewn along. I was interested to see if I could see any bodies, and I was surprised to think that with all these deaths that had taken place we could not see one body. I understand a life-preserver is supposed to keep up a person, whether dead or alive.

There was a very large quantity of floating cork. I am at a loss to understand where it came from. There were a great many chairs in the water, all the steamer chairs were floating, and pieces of wreckage – but there was a particularly large quantity of cork.

I think two or three of the boats were allowed to drift. One, I think, had some dead bodies in it. I saw at least two boats drifting away. I was afraid they could not take care of more. I saw dead bodies in one of the boats that came up, lying in the bow. I do not know whether that was set adrift or not.

I would not say we were in the immediate vicinity of the scene of the disaster, because there was a breeze started up at daybreak, and the wreckage would naturally float away from where she went down, somewhat. It might be that it had floated away, probably a mile or half a mile; probably not more than that, considering that the wind only sprang up at daybreak. The wind was blowing, I imagine, from the north at that time.

James Moore – Captain, SS *Mount Temple*
The time I heard there were so many people left on board

I said, 'Then it is just possible those bodies might never be recovered,' because there were so many decks, and if these people had been underneath those decks, the ship going down would cause the pressure to be very great. That pressure would have pressed them up under those decks and it is just a matter that they would never be released, because as they got lower down there would be such tremendous pressure that, even supposing the ship listed in any way, it was not possible for these bodies to withstand the pressure.

It may be too that the ice has covered the spot where the Titanic *sank*, and that has kept those bodies under.

Edward Wilding – Naval Architect, Harland & Wolff
There were nine Harland & Wolff staff on board altogether; one of our managing directors and eight others. None were saved.

'It was very remarkable, and the whole thing was providential, as regards our being able to get there'

Mary Smith – First Class Passenger

The sea had started to get fairly rough by the time we were taken on the *Carpathia*, and we were quite cold and glad for the shelter and protection. I have every praise for the *Carpathia*'s captain and its crew, as well as the passengers aboard. They were kindness itself to each and every one of us, regardless of which position we occupied on boat. One lady very kindly gave me her berth, and I was as comfortable as can be expected under the circumstances until we arrived in New York. The ship's doctors were particularly nice to us. I know many women who slept on the floor in the smoking room while Mr Ismay occupied the best room on the *Carpathia*, being in the centre of the boat, with every attention, and a sign on the door saying, 'Please do not knock.' There were other men who were miraculously saved, and barely injured, sleeping on the engine room floor, and such places as that, as the ship was very crowded.

The discipline coming into New York was excellent. We were carefully looked after in every way, with the exception of a Marconigram I sent from the *Carpathia* on Monday morning, April 15, to my friends. Knowing of their anxiety, I borrowed money from a gentleman and took this Marconigram myself and asked the operator to send it for me, and he promised he would. However, it was not received. Had it been sent, it would have spared my family, as well as Mr Smith's, the terrible anxiety which they went through for four days. This is the only complaint I have to make against the *Carpathia*. They did tell me they were near enough to land to send it, but would send it through other steamers, as they were cabling the list of the rescued that way. He also said it was not necessary to pay him, because the White Star Line was responsible. I insisted, however, because I thought that probably the money might have some weight with them, as the whole thing seemed to have been a monied accident.

Daniel Buckley – Third Class Passenger
One of the firemen that was working on the *Titanic* told me, when I got on board the *Carpathia* and he was speaking to me, that he did not think it was any iceberg; that it was only that they wanted to make a record, and they ran too much steam and the boilers bursted. That is what he said.

Charles Lightoller – Second Officer
I may say that at that time Mr Ismay did not seem to me to be in a mental condition to finally decide anything. I tried my utmost to rouse Mr Ismay, for he was obsessed with the idea, and kept repeating, that he ought to have gone down with the ship, because he found that women had gone down. I told him there was no such reason. I told him a very great deal. I tried to get that idea out of his head, but he was taken with it, and I know the doctor tried, too. But we had difficulty in arousing Mr Ismay, purely owing to that wholly and solely, that women had gone down in the boat and he had not.

Harold Cottam – Marconi Officer, SS *Carpathia*
*I informed the Baltic of the whole catastrophe about half
past ten in the morning, the morning after the wreck. She
was steaming in the direction of the wreck. I told her the
distress signal received the previous night, and told her that
we had been to the wreck and picked up as many passengers
as we could find in the small boats, and were returning to
New York. I believe I did mention something about Halifax,
simply because the captain was bound for Halifax first, and
then he changed his mind and was bound for New York. I
may have sent the same to the other ships. There were three
or four ships in the vicinity: the* Virginian, *the* Californian,
and the Baltic. *I may have sent the same message to the
three, I can not be certain.*

Arthur Rostron – Captain, SS *Carpathia*
*The first and principal reason for going to New York was
that we had all these women aboard, and I knew they were
hysterical and in a bad state. I knew very well, also, that
people on land would want all the news possible. I knew
very well, further, that if I went to Halifax, we could get
them there all right, but I did not know how many of these
people were half dead, how many were injured, or how
many were really sick, or anything like that. I knew, also,
that if we went to Halifax, we would have the possibility
of coming across more ice, and I knew very well what
the effect of that would be on people who had had the
experience these people had had. I knew what that would
be, the whole time we were in the vicinity of ice. I took
that into consideration. I knew very well that if we went
to Halifax it would be a case of railway journey for these*

passengers, as I knew they would have to go to New York, and there would be all the miseries of that.

Furthermore, I did not know what the condition of the weather might be, or what accommodation I could give them in Halifax, and that was a great consideration – one of the greatest considerations that made me turn back.

I had very little opportunity of being amongst the passengers or any of them. To tell you the truth, I was on the bridge or about my duties most of the time. I had, however, one or two conversations with the passengers on Tuesday afternoon. I heard then that all the people on the Titanic, *as far as they could see, had all been supplied with lifebelts. That was the only time I had anything to do with the people.*

Sir Cosmo Duff Gordon – First Class Passenger

When I got on the *Carpathia*, there was a little hitch in getting one of the men up the ladder. Hendrickson brought my coat, which I had thrown in the bottom of the boat, up after me, and I asked him to get the men's names.

I went to see the captain one afternoon and told him I had promised the crew of my boat a £5 note each. He said, 'It is quite unnecessary.' I laughed and said, 'I promised it; so I have got to give it them.'

George Symons – Lookout

I only know I heard that they took my name, and I understood from the other fireman they were to send a wire to our parents. It was a great surprise to me when I received a cheque for £5. It was a day or two before we arrived in New York.

I was took in several photographs on the *Carpathia*. It's quite nice to know you are so big. I wrote my name on Lady Duff Gordon's lifebelt at her request. We were asked to put our names on it, and we did it.

Charles Hendrickson – Leading Fireman

I received an order for £5 from Duff Gordon on the *Carpathia*. The others received the same. I think it was the day before we docked in New York we got that. Mr Duff Gordon sent for us, and we all went up together on the promenade deck of the *Carpathia*. He promised us this present in the early hours of the morning, before we were picked up from the lifeboat, he said he would do something for us. He said, 'I am going to make a little present to the members of the boat's crew,' but we did not know what it was. After we got on board the *Carpathia*, he said, 'See me later on, I am too busy now.'

Henry Stengel – First Class Passenger

There was another quite large bulletin posted by the captain which said there had been rumours aboard brought to him that the press was using the wires, and the captain made it very emphatic, and said, 'I wish to state emphatically that there have not been but 20 words sent to the press,' and that the wires were at the service of the survivors of the *Titanic*. That was signed by, I think, the purser.

I contacted home, and through the efforts I made to help the people aboard the boat there, they said, 'We appreciate what you are doing, and your two messages have gone.' I think the first message was sent on Monday, just stating, 'Both aboard the *Carpathia*; both safe aboard the *Carpathia*.' It was addressed to the firm of Stengel and Rothschild, Newark, NJ. That message was received.

I sent another message after that, asking to have two automobiles to meet me at the *Carpathia* pier; that I expected to bring some survivors home with me. I expected to bring several ladies, one from Fond du Lac, one from Green Bay, one from North Dakota, and another lady from West Orange. But as we left the boat they all found their friends, and I had no use for the two machines after that.

Harold Cottam – Marconi Officer, SS *Carpathia*

I do not remember when I went on, but I did not come off for a couple of days after I got on. I was never off. I believe it was Tuesday night when I fell off to sleep, and I had about three hours' sleep. I don't remember the days at all, being up all the time. I know I only had about eight or ten hours' sleep from the time we left the scene of the wreck until we arrived at New York.

Mr Bride came on Wednesday afternoon and carried on with the work while I was not there. His services were entirely voluntary. He could not walk or stand from injuries received at the time of the wreck. Bride had the phones right up to docking and right after docking. I was in the station having my dinner.

I can not say the apparatus was in good condition, because the weather was not good. The atmosphere was in a static condition. There was rain about all the time. It was wet, foul weather. It caused a leak through the insulators when they were wet. I did repeat everything; I never send a telegram without repeating it. If there is a lot of static

*about, of course you would – when there is atmospheric
disturbance; when there is stormy weather about.*

Harold Bride – Assistant Telegraphist

After a short stay in the hospital of the *Carpathia*, I was asked
to assist Mr Cottam, the operator, who seemed fairly worn
out with work. The list of survivors, Mr Cottam told me, had
been sent to the *Minnewaska* and the *Olympic*. There were
hundreds of telegrams from survivors waiting to go as soon as
we could get communication with shore stations.

When we established communication with the various
coast stations, all of which had heavy traffic for us, in some
cases running into hundreds of messages, we told them
we would only accept service and urgent messages, as we
knew the remainder would be press and messages inquiring
after someone on the *Titanic*. It is easy to see we might
have spent hours receiving messages inquiring after some
survivor, while we had messages waiting from that survivor
for transmission.

I was at the wireless apparatus from Tuesday night to
the time of docking. Mr Cottam spent a great majority of
the time in the actual transmission, and I was preparing
the messages for him for transmission, and myself I did a
certain amount.

Arthur Rostron – Captain, SS *Carpathia*

*From the very commencement, I took charge of the whole
thing and issued orders that every message sent would be
sent under my authority, and no message was to be sent
unless authorised by me. My orders were: first of all, the
two official messages. The two official messages were to the*

Cunard Company and the White Star Company, as regards the accident, telling them that I had got an approximate number of passengers aboard and was returning to New York. That was to the White Star Company, and the other one was to our company telling them that I was proceeding to New York unless otherwise ordered, and considered New York the best, for many considerations.

After those two messages were sent, I sent a press message to the Associated Press, practically in the same words as I had sent to the companies, over my signature. Those were the three first messages that were sent. After these messages were sent, we began sending in the names of the First Class passengers. This was by the Olympic *on Monday evening. We got the first, and I think all the Second Class passengers off by the* Olympic. *Then we lost touch.*

Cottam, the Marconi operator, was constantly at his instrument, the whole time. He is a young man, I should think about 25 years old, employed by the Marconi Company.

There was absolutely no censorship whatever. I controlled the whole thing, through my orders. I placed official messages first. After they had gone, and the first press message, then the names of the passengers. After the names of the passengers and crew had been sent, my orders were to send all private messages from the Titanic's *passengers first in the order in which they were given in to the purser; no preference to any message.*

Harold Bride – Assistant Telegraphist

News was not withheld by Mr Cottam or myself with the idea of making money, but because, as far as I know, the captain of the *Carpathia* was advising Mr Cottam to get off the survivors' traffic first. Quite 75 per cent of this we got off.

Harold Cottam – Marconi Officer, SS *Carpathia*
There was no information at all – I did not get any news ashore at all. The captain said, 'Do not deal with anything otherwise than official traffic and passengers' messages.' That was the captain's orders. I cannot go beyond the captain's orders.

I was working for the shipping company, handling official messages all the time. I had a good many messages from Mr Ismay, and I had other Cunard messages; and when I was not busy with those, I was on passenger traffic.

I could not cope with the work at all. I sent more than 500 messages, about half official and half passenger. All the passengers' names had to go, and the survivors' names. I did not get the survivors' messages all off. I had not sufficient time; I could not do an impossibility. When I docked in New York, there was one wireless station that had between 150 and 200 messages for me that I had not time to take on the way along.

Bruce Ismay – Managing Director, IMM
There was absolutely no embargo; and I asked for no preferential treatment for any messages that I sent. I do not know that any was given.

Harold Cottam – Marconi Officer, SS *Carpathia*
I had a message from the company asking me to meet Mr Marconi in the Strand Hotel, and I was preparing to get

ashore as she touched. We were getting into the dock when the message came. Bride was writing it down, and I looked over as he was taking it. I do not remember anything about it. I was running about the ship at the time. The meeting was within less than an hour of docking.

I didn't talk during all the voyage, from the catastrophe up to the time of arriving in New York. I did not say anything; I sent out nothing. Because I had the passengers' messages and official traffic to get off before I could provide newspapers with news. That was not the most important thing to do. The captain told me to ignore all stations other than those I was in communication with and could benefit by.

Harold Bride – Assistant Telegraphist

On arrival in New York, Mr Marconi came on board with a reporter of the *New York Times*. Also Mr Sammis [chief engineer at Marconi] was present, and I received $500 for my story, which both Mr Marconi and Mr Sammis authorised me to tell.

I stayed with relatives and awaited orders from the Marconi Company, who have been most considerate and kind, buying me much needed clothes and looking after me generally.

I am glad to say I can now walk around, the sprain in my left foot being much better, though my right foot remains numbed from the exposure and cold, but causes me no pain or inconvenience whatever. I greatly appreciate the cable the company so kindly sent me and thank them for the same.

Lady Lucy Duff Gordon – First Class Passenger

After we arrived in New York, we had dinner with several

friends. Mr Merritt, the editor of the *Sunday American**, who is a great friend of ours, was there. After he had left us about half an hour he telephoned to me, and he said, 'Mr Hearst has just rung me up, and must have your story of the *Titanic* wreck for tomorrow morning's newspaper.' He said, 'May I tell your story as I have heard it?' I said, 'Yes,' and he tells me afterwards that he telephoned to their head office all he knew about it, and then a clever reporter put all that into words and it appeared next morning in the *New York American*. It was published all over – everywhere. It is rather inventive, and the last little bit is absolutely a story. My signature was a forgery. Absolutely.

Arthur Rostron – Captain, SS *Carpathia*

I had previously to this sent a wireless to the White Star Line asking them to send a couple of tugboats down to quarantine to take these lifeboats away, as I would not be able to come into dock with those boats up in the davits or on the forecastle head. There were none there, and so I was worrying about these. It was a dirty night, coming up the river last night, and I was worrying about what I was going to do with the boats. I had the boats lowered half way to the water, to avoid any waste of time. When we got right off the dock, I asked them to send some tugboats out to take the boats away, as I could not dock until they were gotten out of the way. After that I do not know anything about them.

It was reported to me that 705 was the number of survivors, and we took three dead bodies from one of the boats. Not

---

*Merritt was in fact the city correspondent of the *Sunday American*, which was owned by William Randolph Hearst.

counting the 705, there was another man, a passenger we took up from the boat, who died two or three hours after we got him on board. We landed in New York 705.*

Charles Lightoller – Second Officer

It is very difficult indeed to come to any conclusion. Of course, we know now the extraordinary combination of circumstances that existed at that time which you would not meet again once in 100 years; that they should all have existed just on that particular night shows, of course, that everything was against us.

In the first place, there was no moon. I daresay it had been the last quarter or the first quarter. Then there was no wind, not the slightest breath of air. And most particular of all in my estimation is the fact, a most extraordinary circumstance, that there was not any swell. Had there been the slightest degree of swell I have no doubt that berg would have been seen in plenty of time to clear it.

The moon we knew of, the wind we knew of, but the absence of swell we did not know of. You naturally conclude that you do not meet with a sea like it was, like a table top or a floor, a most extraordinary circumstance, and I guarantee that 99 men out of 100 could never call to mind actual proof of there having been such an absolutely smooth sea.

Arthur Rostron – Captain, SS *Carpathia*

The whole thing was absolutely providential. I will tell you this, that the wireless operator was in his cabin, at the time, not on official business at all, but just simply listening as he

---

*The actual number of survivors landed at New York was 711.

was undressing. He was unlacing his boots at the time. He had this apparatus on his ear, and the message came. That was the whole thing. In ten minutes, maybe he would have been in bed, and we would not have heard the messages.

It was very remarkable, and, as I say, the whole thing was providential, as regards our being able to get there.

Charles Lightoller – Second Officer

There is no doubt we might make some improvements, which shipbuilders are trying to do all the time, and the White Star, as far as I know them, in particular. We have instructions, particularly to the commander and officers. As far as our side of it is concerned – the officers on deck – every suggestion we have to offer is met with every consideration, and is deeply considered. Anything that tends toward the improvement of the ship, or members of the ship, is immediately carried out.

PART FIVE

EXTRACTS FROM THE INQUIRY VERDICTS

WAS THE *TITANIC* GOING TOO FAST?

The US Inquiry

The speed of the *Titanic* was gradually increased after leaving Queenstown. The first day's run was 464 miles, the second day's run was 519 miles, the third day's run was 546 miles. Just prior to the collision the ship was making her maximum speed of the voyage – not less than 21 knots, or 24½ miles per hour.

The British Inquiry

The entire passage had been made at high speed, though not at the ship's maximum, and this speed was never reduced until the collision was unavoidable. Yet the evidence establishes quite clearly that Captain Smith, Mr Murdoch, Mr Lightoller and Mr Moody all knew on the Sunday evening that the vessel was entering a region where ice might be expected.

Why, then, did the Master persevere in his course and maintain his speed? The answer is to be found in the evidence. It was shown that for many years past, indeed, for a quarter of a century or more, the practice of liners using this track when in the vicinity of ice at night had been in clear weather to keep the course, to maintain the speed and to trust to a sharp lookout to enable them to avoid the danger. This practice, it was said, had been justified by experience, no casualties having resulted from it.

I accept* the evidence as to the practice and as to the immunity from casualties which is said to have accompanied

---

*Lord Mersey, Wreck Commissioner, appointed by the British Government to investigate the *Titanic* disaster.

it. But the event has proved the practice to be bad. Its root is probably to be found in competition and in the desire of the public for quick passages rather than in the judgement of navigators. But unfortunately experience appeared to justify it.

In these circumstances I am not able to blame Captain Smith. He had not the experience which his own misfortune has afforded to those whom he has left behind, and he was doing only that which other skilled men would have done in the same position.

It was suggested at the bar that he was yielding to influences which ought not to have affected him; that the presence of Mr Ismay on board and the knowledge which he perhaps had of a conversation between Mr Ismay and the chief engineer at Queenstown about the speed of the ship and the consumption of coal probably induced him to neglect precautions which he would otherwise have taken. But I do not believe this. The evidence shows that he was not trying to make any record passage or indeed any exceptionally quick passage. He was not trying to please anybody, but was exercising his own discretion in the way he thought best. He made a mistake, a very grievous mistake, but one in which, in face of the practice and of past experience, negligence cannot be said to have had any part; and in the absence of negligence it is, in my opinion, impossible to fix Captain Smith with blame.

WERE THERE ENOUGH LIFEBOATS?

The US Inquiry
The *Titanic* was fitted with 16 sets of double-acting boat davits of modern type, capable of handling two or three

boats per set of davits. The davits were thus capable of handling 48 boats, whereas the ship carried but 16 lifeboats and four collapsibles, fulfilling all the requirements of the British Board of Trade. The total lifeboat capacity was 1,176. There was ample lifebelt equipment for all. Including the crew, the *Titanic* sailed with 2,223 persons aboard, of 1,517 were lost and 706 were saved.

It will be noted in this connection that 60 per cent of the First Class passengers were saved, 42 per cent of the Second Class passengers were saved, 25 per cent of the Third Class passengers were saved, and 24 per cent of the crew were saved.

The British Inquiry

Under the Merchant Shipping Act, 1894, a table showing the minimum number of boats to be placed under davits, and their minimum cubic contents, was issued by the Board of Trade. This table was based on the gross tonnage of the vessels to which it was to apply, and not upon the numbers carried, and it provided that the number of boats and their capacity should increase as the tonnage increased. The table, however, stopped short at the point where the gross tonnage of the vessels reached '10,000 and upwards'. As to all such vessels, whatever their size might be, the minimum number of boats under davits was fixed by the table at 16, with a total minimum capacity of 5,500 cubic feet.

After 1894, steamers were built of a much larger tonnage than 10,000, the increase culminating in the *Titanic*, with a gross tonnage of 46,328. As the vessels built increased in size, so one would have thought the necessity for increased lifeboat accommodation would grow; but the Rules and Table remained stationary, and nothing was done to them by way of change. Thus it will be seen that the boats carried by this class of vessel are also quite inadequate as an effectual means of saving life should a disaster happen to a ship with her full complement of passengers on board.

It cannot be that the provision for boat accommodation made in 1894 for vessels of 10,000 tons and upwards remained sufficient to 1910, when vessels of 45,000 tons were being built.

The gross tonnage of a vessel is not, in my opinion, a satisfactory basis on which to calculate the provision of boat accommodation. Hitherto, I believe, it has been accepted as the best basis by all nations. But there seems much more to be said in favour of making the number of lives carried the basis and for providing boat or raft accommodation for all on board. When naval architects have devised practical means for rendering ships unsinkable, the question of boat accommodation may have to be reconsidered, but until that time arrives boat accommodation should, where practicable, be carried for all on board.

This suggestion may be thought by some to be extravagant. It has never been enforced in the mercantile marine of Great Britain, nor, as far as I know, in that of any foreign nation. But it appears, nevertheless, to be admitted by all that it is possible, without undue inconvenience or undue interference with commerce, to increase, considerably in many cases, the accommodation hitherto carried, and it seems, therefore, reasonable that the law should require an increase to be made. As far as foreign-going passenger and emigrant steamships are concerned, I am of opinion that, unless justification be shown for deviating from this course, such ships should carry boats or rafts for all on board.

WERE THIRD CLASS PASSENGERS
PREVENTED FROM REACHING
THE LIFEBOATS?

The US Inquiry
The testimony is definite that, except in isolated instances, there was no panic. In loading boats no distinction was made between First, Second, and Third Class passengers, although the proportion of lost is larger among Third Class passengers than in either of the other classes. Women and children, without discrimination, were given preference.

The British Inquiry
It had been suggested that the Third Class passengers had been unfairly treated; that their access to the boat deck had been impeded, and that when at last they reached that deck, the First and Second Class passengers were given precedence in getting places in the boats. There appears to have been no truth in these suggestions. It is no doubt true that the proportion of Third Class passengers saved falls far short of the proportion of the First and Second Class, but this is accounted for by the greater reluctance of the Third Class passengers to leave the ship, by their unwillingness to part with their baggage, by the difficulty in getting them up from their quarters, which were at the extreme ends of the ship, and by other similar causes.

The interests of the relatives of some of the Third Class passengers who had perished were in the hands of Mr Harbinson, who attended the inquiry on their behalf. He said at the end of his address to the Court: 'I wish to say distinctly that no evidence has been given in the course of this case which would substantiate a charge that any attempt was made to keep back the Third Class passengers... I desire further to say that there is no evidence that when they did reach the boat deck there was any discrimination practised either by the officers or the sailors in putting them into the boats.'

I am satisfied that the explanation of the excessive proportion of Third Class passengers lost is not to be found in the suggestion that the Third Class passengers were in any way unfairly treated. They were not unfairly treated.

WHY WEREN'T THE BOATS FILLED PROPERLY?

The US Inquiry

The vessel was provided with lifeboats, as above stated, for 1,176 persons, while but 706 were saved. Only a few of the ship's lifeboats were fully loaded, while others were partially filled. Some were loaded at the boat deck, and some at the A deck, and these were successfully lowered to the water. The twentieth boat was washed overboard when the forward part of the ship was submerged, and in its overturned conditions served as a life raft for about 30 people.

The lack of preparation during loading was most noticeable. There was no system adopted for loading the boats; there was no direction whatever as to the number of passengers to be carried by each boat, and no uniformity in loading them. On one side only women and children were put in the boats, while on the other side there was almost equal proportion of men and women put into the boats, the women and children being given the preference in all cases. The failure to utilise all lifeboats to their recognised capacity for safety unquestionably resulted in the needless sacrifice of several hundred lives which might otherwise have been saved.

The British Inquiry

The real difficulty in dealing with the question of the boats is to find the explanation of so many of them leaving the ship with comparatively few persons in them. No 1 certainly left with only 12; this was an emergency boat with a carrying capacity of 40. No 7 left with only 27, and No 6 with only 28; these were lifeboats with a carrying capacity of 65 each; and several of the others, according to the evidence and certainly according to the truth, must have left only partly filled.

Many explanations are forthcoming, one being that the passengers were unwilling to leave the ship. When the earlier boats left, and before the *Titanic* had begun materially to settle down, there was a drop of 65 feet from the boat deck to the water, and the women feared to get into the boats. Many people thought that the risk in the ship was less than the risk in the boats.

At one time, the Master appears to have had the intention of putting the people into the boats from the gangway doors in the side of the ship. This was possibly with a view to allay the fears of the passengers, for the water could be reached from these doors by means of ladders, and the lowering of some of the earlier boats when only partly filled may be accounted for in this way. There is no doubt that the Master did order some of the partly filled boats to row to a position under one of the doors with the object taking in passengers at that point. It appears, however, that these doors were never opened.

Another explanation is that some women refused to leave their husbands. It is said further that the officers engaged in putting the people into the boats feared that the boats might buckle if they were filled; but this proved to be an unfounded apprehension, for one or more boats were completely filled and then successfully lowered to the water.

These explanations are perhaps sufficient to account for so many of the lifeboats leaving without a full boat load; but I think, nevertheless, that if the boats had been kept a little longer before being lowered, or if the after gangway doors had been opened, more passengers might have been induced to enter the boats. And if women could not be induced to enter the boats, the boats ought to then to have been filled up with men. It is difficult to account for so many of the lifeboats being sent from the sinking ship, in a smooth sea, far from full. These boats left behind them many hundreds of lives to perish.

I do not, however, desire these observations to be read as casting any reflection on the officers of the ship or on the crew who were working on the boat deck. They all worked admirably, but I think that if there had been better organisation the results would have been more satisfactory.

WHY WEREN'T MORE PEOPLE RESCUED FROM THE WATER BY THE LIFEBOATS?

The US Inquiry

After lowering, several of the boats rowed many hours in the direction of the lights supposed to have been displayed by the *Californian*. Other boats lay on their oars in the vicinity of the sinking ship, with few survivors being rescued from the water.

Your committee* believes that under proper discipline the survivors could have been concentrated into fewer boats after reaching the water, and we think that it would have been possible to have saved many lives if those in charge of the boats had returned promptly to the scene of the disaster.

The British Inquiry

I heard much evidence as to the conduct of the boats after the *Titanic* sank and when there must have been many struggling people in the water, and I regret to say that in my opinion some, at all events, of the boats failed to attempt to save lives when they might have done so, and might have done so successfully. This was particularly the case of boat No 1.** It may reasonably have been thought that the risk of making the attempt was too great; but it seems to me that if the attempt had been made by some of these boats, it might have been the means of saving a few more lives.

WERE THE LIFEBOATS PROPERLY EQUIPPED?

The British Inquiry

In ordinary circumstances all these boats (with the exception of Nos 1 and 2) were kept covered up, and contained only a portion of their equipment, such as oars, masts and sails,

---

*The Committee on Commerce headed by Senator Smith, which was directed by the US Government to investigate the tragedy.

**The boat Sir Cosmo and Lady Duff Gordon were on board.

and water; some of the remaining portion, such as lamps, compasses and biscuits being stowed in the ship in some convenient place, ready for use when required. Much examination was directed at the hearing to show that some boats left the ship without a lamp and others without a compass and so on, but in the circumstances of confusion and excitement which existed at the time of the disaster, this seems to me to be excusable.

The 14 lifeboats, two emergency boats, and C and D collapsible boats were sent away in a seaworthy condition, but some of them were possibly undermanned. The evidence on this point was unsatisfactory. The total number of crew taken on board the *Carpathia* exceeded the number which would be required for manning the boats. The collapsible boats A and B appeared to have floated off the ship at the time she foundered. The necessary equipment and provisions for the boats were carried in the ship, but some of the boats, nevertheless, left without having their full equipment in them.

WAS THERE A LIFEBOAT DRILL AND/OR BOAT MUSTER LIST?

The US Inquiry

Many of the crew did not join the ship until a few hours before sailing, and the only drill while the vessel lay at Southampton or on the voyage consisted in lowering two lifeboats on the starboard side into the water, which boats were again hoisted to the boat deck within a half hour. No boat list designating the stations of members of the crew was posted until several days after sailing from Southampton, boatmen being left in ignorance of their proper stations until the following Friday morning.

The British Inquiry

There had been no proper boat drill nor a muster. It was explained that great difficulty frequently exists in getting firemen to take part in a boat drill. They regard it as no part of their work. There seem to be no statutory requirements as to boat drills or musters. Each member of the crew had a boat assigned to him in printed lists which were posted up in convenient places for the men to see; but it appeared that in some cases the men had not looked at these lists and did not know their respective boats.

WHY WERE SO FEW BODIES FOUND?

The US Inquiry

The committee directs attention to the fact that Captain Rostron, of the *Carpathia*, although four hours in the vicinity of the accident, saw only one body, and that Captain Lord, of the *Californian*, who remained three hours in the vicinity of the wreckage, saw none. The failure of the captain of the *Carpathia*, of the captain of the *Californian*, and of the captain of the *Mount Temple* to find bodies floating in that vicinity in the early morning of the day following can only be accounted for on the theory that those who went down with the ship either did not rise to the surface or were carried away or hidden by the extensive ice floe which during the night came down over the spot where the ship disappeared, while those bodies which have been found remote from the place where the ship went down were probably carried away from the scene by the currents or by the movement of the ice.

DID SIR COSMO BRIBE THE CREW?

The British Inquiry
The very gross charge against Sir Cosmo Duff Gordon that, having got into No 1 boat, he bribed the men in it to row away from the drowning people is unfounded. I have said that the members of the crew in that boat might have made some attempt to save the people in the water, and that such an attempt would probably have been successful; but I do not believe that the men were deterred from making the attempt by any act of Sir Cosmo Duff Gordon's. At the same time I think that if he had encouraged to the men to return to the position where the *Titanic* had foundered they would probably have made an effort to do so and could have saved some lives.

DID MR ISMAY LEAVE THE SHIP TOO SOON?

The British Inquiry
As to the attack on Mr Bruce Ismay, it resolved itself into the suggestion that, occupying the position of Managing Director of the Steamship Company, some moral duty was imposed upon him to wait on board until the vessel foundered. I do not agree. Mr Ismay, after rendering assistance to many passengers, found C collapsible, the last boat on the starboard side, actually being lowered. No other people were there at the time. There was room for him and he jumped in. Had he not jumped in, he would merely have

added one more life, namely, his own, to the number of those lost.

DID BRIDE AND COTTAM BEHAVE IMPROPERLY?

The US Inquiry

The committee does not believe that the wireless operator on the *Carpathia* showed proper vigilance in handling the important work confided to his care after the accident. Information concerning an accident at sea had been used by a wireless operator prior to this accident for his own advantage. That such procedure had been permitted by the Marconi Company may have had its effect on this occasion. The disposition of officials of the Marconi Company to permit this practice and the fact of that company's representatives making the arrangements for the sale of the experiences of the operators of the *Titanic* and *Carpathia* subjects the participants to criticism, and the practice should be prohibited. The committee are pleased to note that Mr Marconi approves of such prohibition.

WERE THE LOOKOUTS NEGLIGENT?

The British Inquiry

The men in the crow's nest were warned at 9.30pm to keep a sharp lookout for ice; the officer of the watch was then aware that he had reached the reported ice region, and so also was the officer who relieved him at 10pm. Without implying that those actually on duty were not keeping a good lookout, in view of the night being moonless, there being no wind and perhaps very little swell, and especially in view of the high speed at which the vessel was running, it is not considered that the lookout was sufficient. An extra lookout should, under the circumstances, have been placed at the stemhead, and a sharp lookout should have been kept from both sides of the bridge by an officer.

WAS THE *CALIFORNIAN* NEGLIGENT?

The US Inquiry

16 witnesses from the *Titanic*, including officers, an experienced seaman, and passengers of sound judgement, testified seeing the light of a ship in the distance, and some of the lifeboats were directed to pull for that light, to leave the passengers and return to the side of the *Titanic* [to pick up more passengers]. The *Titanic* fired distress rockets and attempted to signal by electric lamp and Morse code to this vessel.

At about the same time the officers of the *Californian* admit seeing rockets in the general direction of the *Titanic* and say that they immediately displayed a powerful Morse lamp, which could be easily seen a distance of ten miles off. Several of the crew of the *Californian* testify that the side lights of a large vessel going at full speed were plainly visible from the lower deck of the *Californian* at 11.30pm, ship's time, just before the accident. There's no evidence that any rockets were fired by any vessel between the *Titanic* and the *Californian*, although every eye on the *Titanic* was searching the horizon for possible assistance.

The committee is forced to the inevitable conclusion that the *Californian*, controlled by the same company, was nearer the *Titanic* than the 19 miles reported by her captain, and that her officers and crew saw the distress signals of the *Titanic* and failed to respond to them in accordance with the dictates of humanity, international usage, and the requirements of the law. The only reply to the distress signals was a counter signal from a large white light, which was flashed for nearly two hours from the mast of the *Californian*. In our opinion such conduct, whether arising from indifference or gross carelessness, is most reprehensible, and places upon the commander of the *Californian* a grave responsibility.

Had assistance been promptly proffered, or had the wireless operator of the *Californian* remained a few minutes longer at his post on Sunday evening, that ship might have had the proud distinction of rescuing the lives of the passengers and crew of the *Titanic*.

The British Inquiry

The circumstances revealed during the inquiry convince me that the ship seen by the *Californian* was the *Titanic*, and if so, according to Captain Lord, the two vessels were about five miles apart at the time of the disaster. The evidence from the *Titanic* corroborates this estimate, but I am advised that the distance was probably greater, though not more than eight to ten miles. The ice by which the *Californian* was surrounded was loose ice extending for a distance of not more than two or three miles in the direction of the *Titanic*. The night was clear and the sea was smooth. When she first saw the rockets, the *Californian* could have pushed through the ice to the open water without any serious risk and so have come to the assistance of the *Titanic*. Had she done so she might have saved many, if not all, of the lives that were lost.

DID THE OFFICERS, CREW AND PASSENGERS BEHAVE CORRECTLY?

The US Inquiry

The ice positions said to have been reported to the *Titanic* just preceding the accident located ice on both sides of the *Titanic* or the lane which the *Titanic* was following, and in her immediate vicinity. No general discussion took place among the officers; no conference was called to consider these warnings; no heed was given to them. The speed was not relaxed, the lookout was not increased, and the only vigilance displayed by the officer of the watch was by instructions to the lookout to keep 'a sharp lookout for ice'.

It should be said, however, the testimony shows Captain Smith remarked to officer Lightoller, who was the officer doing duty on the bridge until ten o'clock ship's time, or 8.27 New York time, 'if it was in a slight degree hazy there would be no doubt we should have to go very slowly', and 'if in the slightest degree doubtful, let me know'. The evidence is that it was exceptionally clear. There was no haze, and the ship's speed was not reduced.

The British Inquiry

The evidence satisfies me that the officers did their work very well and without any thought of themselves. Captain Smith, the Master, Mr Wilde, the chief officer, Mr Murdoch, the first officer, and Mr Moody, the sixth officer, all went down with the ship while performing their duties. The others, with the exception of Mr Lightoller, took charge of boats and thus were saved. Mr Lightoller was swept off the deck as the vessel went down and was subsequently picked up.

The discipline both among passengers and crew during the lowering of the boats was good, but the organisation should have been better, and if it had been it is possible that more lives would have been saved.

Subject to these few adverse comments, I have nothing but praise for both passengers and crew. All the witnesses speak well of their behaviour. It is to be remembered that the night was dark, the noise of the escaping steam was terrifying, the peril, though perhaps not generally recognised, was imminent and great, and many passengers who were unable to speak or to understand English were being collected together and hurried into the boats.

During the inquiry, there was a tendency in the evidence to exaggerate the numbers in each boat, to exaggerate the proportion of women to men, and to diminish the number of crew. I do not attribute this to any wish on the part of the witnesses to mislead the Court, but to a natural desire to make the best case for themselves and their ship. The seamen who gave evidence were too frequently encouraged when under examination in the witness box to understate the number of crew in the boats. The number of crew actually saved was 189, giving an average of ten per boat.

WAS THE MESSAGE FROM THE *BALTIC* PROPERLY DEALT WITH?

The British Inquiry
Mr Ismay was on board the *Titanic*, and it appears that the Master handed the *Baltic*'s message to him almost immediately after it was received. This no doubt was in order that he might know that ice was to be expected. Mr

Ismay showed this message to two ladies, and it is therefore probable that many persons on board became aware of its contents. This message ought in my opinion to have been put on the board in the chart room as soon as it was received. It remained, however, in Mr Ismay's possession until 7.15pm, when the Master asked him to return it. It was then that it was first posted in the chart room.

This was considerably before the time at which the vessel reached the position recorded in the message. Nevertheless, I think it was irregular for the Master to part with the document, and improper for Mr Ismay to retain it, but the incident had, in my opinion, no connection with or influence upon the manner in which the vessel was navigated by the Master.

WAS THE MESSAGE FROM THE *AMERIKA* PROPERLY DEALT WITH?

The British Inquiry

Being a message affecting navigation, the message from the *Amerika* should in the ordinary course have been taken to the bridge. So far as can be ascertained, it was never heard of by anyone on board the *Titanic* outside the Marconi room. There were two Marconi operators in the Marconi room, namely, Phillips, who perished, and Bride, who survived and gave evidence. Bride did not receive the *Amerika* message nor did Phillips mention it to him, though the two had much conversation together after it had been received. I am of opinion that when this message reached the Marconi room it was put aside by Phillips to wait until the *Titanic* would be within call of Cape Race, and that it was never handed to any officer of the *Titanic*.

WAS THE MESSAGE FROM THE *MESABA* PROPERLY DEALT WITH?

The British Inquiry

The message from the *Mesaba* clearly indicated the presence of ice in the immediate vicinity of the *Titanic*, and if it had reached the bridge would perhaps have affected the navigation of the vessel. Unfortunately, it does not appear to have been delivered to the Master or to any of the officers. The Marconi operator was very busy from eight o'clock onward transmitting messages via Cape Race for passengers on board the *Titanic*, and the probability is that he failed to grasp the significance and importance of the message, and put it aside until he should be less busy. It was never acknowledged by Captain Smith, and I am satisfied that it was not received by him.

WAS THE *TITANIC* ON THE CORRECT COURSE?

The British Inquiry

It is quite incorrect to assume that icebergs had never before been encountered or field ice observed so far south, at the particular time of year when the *Titanic* disaster occurred; but it is true to say that the field ice was certainly at that time further south than it has been seen for many years.

The outward- and homeward-bound southern tracks were decided on as the outcome of many years' experience of the normal movement of ice. They were reasonably safe tracks for the time of year, provided, of course, that great caution and vigilance when crossing the ice region were observed.

Captain Smith was not fettered by any orders to remain on the track should information as to position of ice make it in his opinion undesirable to adhere to it. The fact, however, of lane routes having been laid down for the common safety of all, would necessarily influence him to keep on (or very near) the accepted route, unless circumstances as indicated above should induce him to deviate largely from it.

DID THE DELAY IN 'TURNING THE CORNER' AFFECT WHAT HAPPENED?

The British Inquiry

At 5.50pm the *Titanic*'s course was changed to bring her on a westerly course for New York. In ordinary circumstances, this change in her course should have been made about half an hour earlier, but she seems on this occasion to have continued for about ten miles longer on her south-westerly course before turning, with the result that she found herself, after altering course at 5.50pm, about four or five miles south of the customary route on a course S 86° W true.

Her course, as thus set, would bring her at the time of the collision to a point about two miles to the southward of the customary route and four miles south and considerably to the westward of the indicated position of the *Baltic*'s ice. Her position at the time of the collision would also be well to the southward of the indicated position of the ice mentioned in the *Caronia* message. This change of course was so insignificant that in my opinion it cannot have been made in consequence of information as to ice.

WHY DIDN'T THE WATERPROOF BULKHEADS KEEP HER AFLOAT?

The British Inquiry

I am advised that the *Titanic* as constructed could not have remained afloat long with such damage as she received.* Her bulkheads were spaced to enable her to remain afloat with any two compartments in communication with the sea. She had a sufficient margin of safety with any two of the compartments flooded which were actually damaged. In fact any three of the four forward compartments could have been flooded by the damage received without sinking the ship to the top of her bulkheads.

WHY WEREN'T THE WATERTIGHT DOORS KEPT SHUT?

The British Inquiry

There does not appear to have been any appreciable effect upon the sinking of the ship caused by either shutting or not shutting the doors. Evidence was given showing that after the watertight doors in the engine and boiler rooms had been all closed, except those forward of No 4 group of boilers, they were opened again, and there is no evidence to show that they were again closed.

It is probable, however, that the life of the ship would have been lengthened somewhat if these doors had been left open, for the water would have flowed through them to the after part of the ship, and the rate of flow of the water

---

*The hull was damaged for 300 feet and across five compartments.

into the ship would have been for a time reduced as the bow might have been kept up a little by the water which flowed aft.

There does not appear to have been any difficulty in working the watertight doors. They appear to have been shut in good time after the collision. It is thus seen that the efficiency of the automatic arrangements for the closing of the watertight doors, which was questioned during the inquiry, had no important bearing on the question of hastening the sinking of the ship.

WERE THE BILGE PUMPS ACTIVATED?

The British Inquiry
The engineers were applying the pumps when Barrett, leading stoker, left No 5 boiler room, but even if they had succeeded in getting all the pumps in the ship to work they could not have saved the ship or prolonged her life to any appreciable extent.

DID SUCTION HAVE ANY EFFECT?

The British Inquiry
The committee deems it of sufficient importance to call attention to the fact that as the ship disappeared under the water there was no apparent suction or unusual disturbance of the surface of the water. Testimony is abundant that while she was going down there was not sufficient suction to be manifest to any of the witnesses who were in the water or on the overturned collapsible boat or on the floating debris, or to the occupants of the lifeboats in the vicinity of the vessel,

or to prevent those in the water, whether equipped with lifebelts or not, from easily swimming away from the ship's side while she was sinking.

The Biographies

The biographies below include all the *Titanic* survivors quoted in this book, as well as other inquiry witnesses directly involved in the rescue operation. The lives of certain key figures who perished in the disaster (such as Captain Smith and wireless operator Jack Phillips) are also covered.

Olaus Abelseth, 26, Third Class Passenger

Abelseth was one of 31 Norwegian passengers on the *Titanic*. Born in Norway in 1886, he worked as a fisherman and casual labourer until he emigrated to America with his brother Hans in 1902/03. In 1908 he set up his own homestead in South Dakota. He visited his family in 1911, and was on his way back to America when the *Titanic* sank. After testifying at the US Inquiry, he travelled through Canada, Indianapolis and Montana. He married Anna Grinde, eight years his senior, in 1915, and the couple had four children together. Anna was 100 years old when she died in 1978; Abelseth followed her two years later.

Frederick Barrett, 28, Leading Fireman

A former coal miner from Stoke-on-Trent, Barrett is said to have gone to sea after discovering his wife was being unfaithful. He initially found work as a stoker, before working his way up to leading fireman. Before joining the *Titanic*, he was on board the *New York*. Although little is known about his whereabouts after the disaster, his character played a prominent role in the 1997 *Titanic* musical on Broadway. Unlike the real Barrett, who survived the sinking and gave evidence at the US Inquiry, however, the fictional Barrett goes down with the ship.

Helen Bishop (née Walton), 19, First Class Passenger

Helen and Dickinson Bishop were heading home after a four-month honeymoon, taking in Egypt, Algiers, Italy and France, and delayed their return to travel on the *Titanic*. Both of them escaped unharmed but, eight months later, Helen gave birth to a baby boy who died soon after birth. Bishop survived a near-fatal car crash in 1913, but was taken ill after a trip to the West Indies in 1916 and died at a friend's house near Chicago, just two months after separating from her husband.

Joseph Boxhall, 28, Fourth Officer

Boxhall came from a family with a strong nautical tradition and joined his first ship, a square-rigged barque, when he was 15. He joined the White Star Line in 1907, and served on several of the company's ships, including the liner *Oceanic*, before boarding the *Titanic*. After returning to England, he joined the Royal Navy Reserve and was promoted to lieutenant, serving on a commando boat in Gibraltar during the war. After the end of hostilities, he rejoined the White Star Line, serving initially as second officer on the *Olympic*. Although reluctant to talk about his role in the disaster, he was technical consultant on the *Titanic* film *A Night to Remember* in 1958. He died in 1967, and, following his instructions, his ashes were scattered at sea at 41° 46' N, 50° 14' W, the position he had calculated *Titanic* sank.

Harold Bride, 22, Assistant Telegraphist
Radio was in its infancy when Bride decided he wanted to become a wireless operator. He trained with the Marconi Company in 1910 and 1911 and served on several ships before joining the *Titanic*. He was a key figure at both inquiries, and went on to serve as wireless operator on the steamship *Mona's Isle* during World War I. After the war, he married Lucy Downie and, partly to escape the notoriety of being a *Titanic* survivor, the couple moved to Scotland, where Bride became a travelling salesman. They had three children.

Edward Brown, 34, First Class Steward
Brown was born in Holyhead in 1878. He served on several White Star Line ships before joining the *Titanic* in Belfast.

Daniel Buckley, 21, Third Class Passenger
Buckley was among a group of friends who joined the *Titanic* at Queenstown, planning to start a new life in the New Land. His reasons for going to America were straightforward: 'I wanted to come over here to make some money.' After surviving the sinking, he found work in a hotel in New York. In 1917, he joined the 69th regiment, the so-called 'Irish Brigade', and served at the Western Front, where he was shot by a sniper while rescuing injured soldiers. His remains were buried in Ireland in 1919.

Edward Buley, 27, Able Seaman
Buley had been in the Royal Navy for 13 years, including serving on HMS *Dreadnought* as a gunner, before joining the White Star Line. The *Titanic* was his first trip in the

merchant service. Although he survived her sinking, he was not so lucky when his ship, HMS *Partridge*, was attacked while escorting a convoy from Scotland to Norway in 1917, and he became one of 92 casualties on board.

George Cavell, 22, Trimmer

Cavell had served 18 months with the White Star Line before joining the *Titanic*. His job was to feed coal from the bunkers to the firemen, who controlled the fires which heated the boilers that supplied steam to the ship's engines. It was the dirtiest job on the ship – and one of the worst paid. After the disaster, Cavell carried on working for the company and, according to his daughter-in-law Dorothy, quoted by BBC Hampshire, 'lived to a grand old age'.

Norman Chambers, 27, First Class Passenger

Chambers was a mechanical engineer from New York, where he worked for a tool company on East 44th Street. He and his wife Bertha survived the sinking and remained together until she died in 1958. Chambers remarried, and died of a heart attack while on holiday in Portugal in 1966.

Frederick Clench, 34, Able Seaman

Frederick and his younger brother George Clench were both Able Seamen who were initially assigned to the *Titanic*'s sistership the *Olympic*, but at the last minute transferred to the *Titanic*. Frederick survived, but George died in the disaster.

John Collins, 17, Assistant Cook, First Class Galley

One of the youngest members of the *Titanic* crew, Collins

was born in Belfast in 1894 and worked at the Ulster Reform Club before joining the ship. He eventually married and returned to Belfast, where he died of syphilis in 1941.

Harold Cottam, 22, Marconi Officer, SS *Carpathia*

At the age of 17, Cottam became the youngest person to graduate at the British School of Telegraphy – a record that is still unbeaten to this day. So young was he that he had to wait five years before he could fulfil his ambition and go to sea. He worked at a number of stations, on land and at sea, and befriended both Jack Phillips and Harold Bride, before joining the Carpathia *in 1912. After the accident, Cottam continued to work as a wireless operator on board a variety of ships. He married Elsie Shepperson in 1922 and retired from the sea to help raise their four children. He died in 1984 at the age of 93.*

Alfred Crawford, 41, Bedroom Steward

According to his evidence at the US Inquiry, Crawford had been 'going to sea' since 1881 and had worked with the White Star Line for six years before joining the *Titanic*. He gave his age at the inquiry as 41, while he told his employees he was 36 – suggesting that he started 'going to sea' at the age of either ten or five – although even the former seems improbably young.

Andrew Cunningham, 38, Bedroom Steward

Born in Edinburgh, Cunningham joined the *Titanic* at Belfast. His previous post had been on another White Star Line ship, the *Oceanic*.

Thomas Dillon, 34, Trimmer
Born in Liverpool in 1878, Dillon served on the *Oceanic* before joining the *Titanic*. He died suddenly in 1939, and was buried in his native Liverpool.

Sir Cosmo Duff Gordon, 49, First Class Passenger
A keen sportsman, Sir Cosmo represented Britain in two Olympic Games, winning silver in the team fencing event in 1906. He was co-founder of the London Fencing League, and a keen wrestler. In 1900, he married Lucy Sutherland, founder of the Lucile fashion chain, and herself a divorcee. The couple boarded the *Titanic* using the pseudonym 'Mr & Mrs Morgan', probably to avoid publicity. The events of the *Titanic* cast a shadow over Sir Cosmo's life and he tried to keep out of the public eye thereafter. He died in London in 1931, aged 68.

Lady Lucy Duff Gordon (née Sutherland), 48, First Class Passenger
One of the most colourful characters on the *Titanic*, Lady Lucy ran a successful fashion label known originally as Maison Lucile, and later Lucile Ltd. As well as promoting less restrictive lingerie and lower necklines for women, she is credited with training the first professional models and introducing the concept of the catwalk. Famous clients included Mary Pickford and the Duchess of York (later Queen Mary). By 1912, Lady Lucy had left the company she set up but continued trading under the name of Lucile. She published her memoirs, *Discretions and Indiscretions*, in 1932, and died of breast cancer three years later, aged 71.

Henry Etches, 40, Bedroom Steward

Although living in Southampton, Etches joined the ship in Belfast. He is said to have survived another sinking after the *Titanic*: that of her sister ship *Britannic*. With the advent of war, the *Britannic* was turned into a hospital ship in 1915 and was sunk off the Greek island of Kea the following year.

Frank Evans, 27, Able Seaman

According to his evidence at the US Inquiry, Evans served on more than 15 ships during his 'nine years and six months' in the Royal Navy. In common with many of the crew, he transferred from the *Oceanic* to the *Titanic* for her maiden voyage. He later worked for the famous Southampton yacht builders Camper & Nicholsons. He died in 1974, aged 86.

Frederick Fleet, 24, Lookout

Raised as an orphan, Fleet escaped to sea at the age of 16, training first as a deck boy and eventually qualifying as Able Seaman. He worked as a lookout on the *Olympic* for four years before joining the *Titanic*. After the disaster, he spent another 24 years at sea, before retiring to land in the mid-1930s. He later worked for Harland & Wolff and the Union-Castle Line, but ended his days selling newspapers on the street in Southampton. He slipped into depression following the death of his wife in 1965, and two weeks later hanged himself. He was buried in a pauper's grave, which remained unmarked until 1993, when the Titanic Historic Society paid for a headstone to be erected.

Archibald Gracie, 53, First Class Passenger

Gracie came from a wealthy New York family. A colonel

in the 7th Regiment, he was active in the New York real estate business and dabbled in military history. Gracie was profoundly affected by his experiences on the *Titanic* and spent the months after landing in New York contacting other survivors while researching a book about the disaster. His manuscript was at the printers when he died the following year, apparently still haunted by his memories of that night. *The Truth About the Titanic* was published in 1913, shortly after his death, and is still in print.

George Harder, 25, First Class Passenger
Harder was at the start of a successful career in manufacturing when he and his wife Dorothy boarded the *Titanic* on their way home from honeymoon. They were one of only three honeymoon couples, out of 13 on board the ship, to both survive the sinking. Dorothy died of kidney failure in 1926, but George remarried and went on to become chairman of a large foundry. He died in 1956.

John Hardy, 36, Chief Second Class Steward
Hardy had served 12 of his 14 years at sea with the White Star Line, including six years as chief Second Class steward, when he joined the *Titanic* in Belfast. He later emigrated to America and worked for the United States Lines for 20 years, retiring in 1940. He died in Maplewood, New Jersey, in 1953.

John Hart, 32, Third Class Steward
Born in London in 1880, Hart fought in the Boer War before signing up as crew on the White Star Line ship the *New York*. After the disaster, he worked briefly on another White

Star ship, the *Oceanic*, before moving to Rhodesia with his wife and two children. There, both children drowned and his wife died soon after. He moved back to England and was married again in Devon, where he lived until his death in 1954.

Samuel Hemming, 43, Lamp-trimmer

Hemming had been to sea since the age of 15 and had served five years with the White Star Line before he signed up on the *Titanic*. He married Elizabeth Browning in 1903, and the couple had several children. A Southampton resident, he died there in 1928, aged 59.

Charles Hendrickson, 29, Leading Fireman

Hendrickson was another crew transferred from the *Oceanic*, and another to come from Southampton. He played a controversial role during the British Inquiry by claiming that Sir Duff Gordon and his wife Lady Lucy had discouraged the crew on Lifeboat No 1 from going back to rescue more survivors. His defiant stand duly earned him a place in the 1997 movie of the event.

Robert Hichens, 29, Quartermaster

The son of a Cornish fisherman, Hichens served on numerous ships before joining the *Titanic*, sailing as far afield as India and the Baltic – but he had never crossed the Atlantic before. He married Florence Mortimer in 1906, and by the time the *Titanic* left Southampton, she was pregnant with the couple's third daughter. After the disaster, Hichens carried on working on ships, travelling to South Africa and the Far East, and the couple had another three children. Hichens fell on hard times in the 1930s, and in 1933 was imprisoned for the attempted murder of a man, after a business deal went sour. He was released from prison in 1937, and three years later Florence died of a brain tumour. Hichens eventually found work as Third Mate on the *English Trader* in 1940, but died of 'heart disease' on the ship a few months later. His body was buried at sea off Aberdeen, Scotland.

George Hogg, Lookout

Hogg had worked as a 'sailorman' for 13 years before the *Titanic*, serving variously as Quartermaster, Mate, Boatswain's Mate and Lookout. He was married, and died in Southampton in 1946.

Bruce Ismay, 49, Managing Director, International Mercantile Marine

The son of a prominent shipowner, Ismay was sent to Harrow before embarking on a four-year apprenticeship at his father's company, the Oceanic Steam Navigation Company (OSNC). After a year travelling the world, he settled in New York where he became the agent for the White Star Line, a subsidiary of OSNC. In 1888, he married Julia Florence Schieffelin, and the couple went on to have five children, one of whom died in infancy. The family moved to England in 1891, and when his father died in 1899 Ismay took over the family business. After protracted negotiations, OSNC merged with International Mercantile Marine, funded by JP Morgan, and Ismay was subsequently appointed its managing director. His status in the company made him an easy target for the press after the *Titanic* sank, and Ismay never recovered his social standing. He retired as director in 1916, and divided his time between Conamarra, Ireland, and London. In later life, he suffered from diabetes and died of a cerebral thrombosis in London in 1937.

James Johnson, 41, First Saloon Night Watchman
Although he gave his address when he joined the *Titanic* as 'the Sailor's Home, Southampton', Johnson told the British Inquiry he lived in Liverpool. His previous position was aboard the *Olympic*.

Charles Joughin, 32, Chief Baker
Starting his nautical career at the tender age of 11, Joughin already had more than 20 years' experience under his belt when he boarded the *Titanic*. After surviving the disaster, he emigrated to Paterson, New Jersey, and served on ships run by the American Export Lines and later World War II troop carriers. He was married twice, and had a daughter, Agnes, by his first wife, born in his native Liverpool. He died in Paterson in 1956.

Reginald Lee, 41, Lookout
As one of the lookouts when the *Titanic* struck the iceberg, Lee was the focus of considerable scrutiny at both inquiries. He had more than 15 years' experience at sea, and was lookout on the *Olympic* before he joined the *Titanic*. He also had a history of alcoholism, and had already been discharged from the Royal Navy on that account. His habit may also have lead to the breakdown of his marriage. After the British Inquiry, he served briefly on the *Kenilworth Castle*, but died of pneumonia the following year. Unlike many other *Titanic* survivors, there is no mention of the ship on his grave.

Charles Lightoller, 38, Second Officer

From the age of 13, Lightoller served a four-year apprenticeship on sailing ships, during which he was shipwrecked once, dismasted twice, and also survived a cyclone. He then spent three years on steam ships on the West African coast, at the end of which he almost died of malaria. He left the sea after this and tried his hand first prospecting for gold at the Yukon, then as a cowboy in Alberta, before working his passage back to England on a cattle boat. He joined the White Star Line in 1900, and served under Captain Smith several times before joining the *Titanic*. Lightoller took part in the ship's sea trials as First Officer but was demoted to Second Officer after a shuffle in the ranks. His colourful career continued after the *Titanic*, first on the *Oceanic* which, as HMS *Oceanic*, ran aground off the Shetland Isles, and then as commander of HMS *Falcon*, which sank after colliding with a fellow escort ship in fog. He earned himself a Distinguished Service Cross (DSC), however, by attacking a zeppelin with a ship's gun, and added a 'bar' to his medal by ramming a German U-boat in a later ship. During World War II, Commander Lightoller rescued 130 soldiers from the beaches at Dunkirk on his yacht *Sundowner*. He retired in 1946, and ran a boatyard on the Thames building boats for the London River Police until his death in 1952.

Elizabeth Lines (née James), 50, First Class passenger

Born in Burlington, New Jersey, Lines lived in Paris with her husband Ernest, president of the New York Insurance Company. She and her daughter Mary were returning to America to attend her son's graduation at Dartmouth. She was not questioned during the inquiries, but later gave highly contentious evidence during a lawsuit against the Oceanic Steam Navigation Company (owners of the White Star Line) suggesting that Ismay had encouraged Captain Smith to increase the *Titanic*'s speed despite the danger of ice. Her evidence is included here as it was given under oath and, like the inquiry accounts, can be regarded as official evidence. She died in Salem, Massachusetts, in 1942.

Stanley Lord, 35, Captain, SS *Californian*

Lord started his sailing career at the age of 13, and gained his Master's certificate at the precocious age of 23. He joined the West India and Pacific Steam Navigation Company in 1897, and achieved his first command when he was just 28. He skippered three ships, the Antillian, *the* Louisianian *and the* William Cliff, *before assuming command of the* Californian *in 1911. Although he was never prosecuted for negligence, both inquiries found heavily against him and he was forced to resign his post. Despite the damage to his reputation, he managed to find work at sea until his retirement due to poor eyesight in 1928. He denied any wrongdoing right up until his death in 1962, aged 82.*

Harold Lowe, 28, Fifth Officer

Lowe 'ran away to sea' when he was 14 and served on seven schooners and various square-rigged ships before transferring to steam. He worked for five years on the West African coast, and joined the White Star Line in 1911. The *Titanic* was his first transatlantic crossing. His actions during the disaster were widely praised, and he was welcomed back home to Wales as a hero. He married Ellen

Whitehouse the following year, and the couple had two children. He joined the Royal Naval Reserve during Word War I, but never achieved command of a ship. He died in 1944, aged 61.

Paul Mauge, 25, Secretary to the Chef, A La Carte Restaurant

The *Titanic* was Mauge's first employment at sea. Born in Paris in 1887, he had a London address when he boarded the ship. After the disaster, he married twice, and moved to Montreal, Canada, with his second wife Madeline. He died there in 1971.

Frank Morris, 28, First Class Bath Steward

Born in London, Morris boarded the *Titanic* in Belfast. He was one of several crew who had previously served under Captain Smith on the *Olympic*.

William Murdoch, 39, First Officer

Murdoch came from a notable Scottish seafaring family and followed the family tradition by going straight from school to start his nautical career. He served mainly on sailing ships, travelling to South America and the Far East, and gained his Master's certificate at the age of 23. He joined the White Star Line in 1900, serving on the *Arabic*, the *Adriatic*, the *Oceanic* and the *Olympic*, before joining the *Titanic*. Originally signed up as Chief Officer, he was demoted to First Officer following a shuffle in the ranks. Murdoch was depicted shooting himself in the 1997 movie *Titanic*, although most of the evidence suggests he died performing his duty. His body was never recovered.

Alfred Olliver, 27, Quartermaster

Born on the island of Jersey in 1884, Olliver had worked on ships for 11 years, including seven years in the Royal Navy, before he signed up to the *Titanic*. His brother-in-law Walter Perkis was also Quartermaster on the ship. After the disaster, Olliver is said to have carried on working for the White Star Line, but never went to sea again. He died on Jersey in 1934.

Frank Osman, 38, Able Seaman

Osman first went to sea at the age of 14. He served 11 years with the Royal Navy before joining the White Star Line. His previous post was on the *Oceanic*.

Walter Perkis, 37, Quartermaster

Born on the Isle of Wight, Perkis started working on ships from the age of 16. He had previously served as Quartermaster, Able Seaman and Lookout, but on this trip he and his brother-in-law Alfred Olliver were both signed on as quartermasters. After the disaster, he rejoined his old ship the *Olympic*. He died in Southampton in 1954, aged 79.

Arthur Peuchen, First Class Passenger

Born to a wealthy Anglo-Prussian family in Montreal in 1859, Peuchen had a privileged upbringing. Aged 22, he enlisted with the Queen's Own Rifles in Toronto, and moved swiftly up the ranks, becoming Major by 1904. He was president of the Standard Chemical Company and helped developed a method to make acetone from wood. He travelled widely with his work, and the *Titanic* was his 40th transatlantic crossing. His was ridiculed following his testimony at the US Inquiry and labelled a coward. He fought in World War I, but never recovered his social standing and, after a series of bad investments, lost much of his money in the 1920s. He died in Toronto in 1929, aged 69.

John 'Jack' Phillips, 25, Senior Wireless Operator
Phillips learned the art of telegraphy at the Post Office in Godalming, a small town in Surrey where his parents ran a draper's shop. He joined the Marconi Company in 1906, and got his first assignment on the White Star Line ship *Teutonic*. He worked on various vessels until 1908, when he went to work at the Marconi station near Clifden, Ireland. He returned to sea in 1911 on the *Adriatic*, followed by the *Oceanic* and the *Titanic*. He celebrated his 25th birthday the day after the ship left Southampton, but died during the disaster. His body was never recovered.

Herbert Pitman, 34, Third Officer
Despite being born to a farming family in the middle of Somerset, Pitman dreamed of the sea and joined the Merchant Navy at the age of 18. He served on sailing ships for three years before joining steamships travelling to Australia and Japan. In 1906, he qualified as a Master Mariner and transferred to the White Star Line, working on several ships before eventually joining the *Titanic* in Belfast. After she was lost, he continued working for the White Star Line, eventually transferring to the pursers' section due to failing eyesight. He married New Zealander Mildred 'Mimi' Kalman in 1922, who predeceased him. In 1946, he was awarded an MBE for 'long and meritorious service at sea'.

Pitman retired in Pitcombe, Somerset, close to the village where he was born. He died in 1962, aged 84.

Benoit 'Berk' Pickard, 32, Third Class passenger
Born in Warsaw as Berk Trembisky, Pickard was a Jewish leatherworker who adopted a French name while living in France. When he boarded the *Titanic*, he was heading to San Francisco. Reports suggest he may have died there in May 1941.

Robert Pusey, 24, Fireman
Before joining the *Titanic* in Southampton, Pusey's previous post had been on the American Lines ship the *St Paul*. He was one of more than 170 firemen on the *Titanic*.

Frederick Ray, 33, Saloon Steward
Born in London in 1879, by 1912 Ray was married and living in Reading, Berkshire. He later gave up working at sea and became a poultry famer. He died in 1977, aged 97.

George Rheims, 36, First Class Passenger
Born in Paris in 1879, Rheims was travelling to New York with his brother-in-law Joseph Loring. Only Rheims made it to America. He died in Paris in 1962.

Annie Robinson, 40, First Class Stewardess
Born in Bedford, UK, Robinson had more reason than most to fear ice. According to *Titanic* legend, she was on board the *Lake Champlain* when it struck an iceberg in 1907. Although she survived both that incident and the *Titanic* disaster, she was clearly traumatised by the experience and

two years later, while travelling from Liverpool to Boston on the passenger ship *Devonian*, jumped over the side. According to a contemporary report, the ship had slowed down due to fog, and Robinson, 'labouring under mental aberration', became so convinced another disaster was about to take place that she abandoned ship.

Arthur Rostron, 42, Captain, SS *Carpathia*

Born in Bolton in 1869, Rostron went to sea at the age of 13. After two years training with the Royal Navy, he worked for nearly ten years on sailing ships before joining his first steam ship in 1894. He joined the Cunard Line the following year, and stayed with them for the next 17 years. He took command of the Carpathia *in January 1912, three months before the* Titanic *tragedy. His decisive action during the incident earned him a Congressional Medal of Honour from the American government. Rostron subsequently took command of the* Mauretania, *one of the most loved Cunard ships, and was responsible for breaking several transatlantic records. He was knighted in 1926 and made commodore of the Cunard Line two years later. He retired to Southampton in 1931 and wrote his autobiography,* Home from the Sea. *He died of pneumonia in 1940.*

George Rowe, 32, Quartermaster

Born in the naval town of Gosport, Rowe served 14 years in the Royal Navy before joining the merchant service in 1910. He initially joined the *Titanic* in Belfast as Lookout, but was switched to Quartermaster in Southampton. After giving evidence at the inquiries, he rejoined his previous ship the *Oceanic* and served on the hospital ship *Plassy* during

World War I. He later joined the shipbuilders Thornycroft in Southampton, where he worked until he was in his 80s, and was responsible for, among other things, fitting stabilisers to the *Queen Mary* and the *Queen Elizabeth*. He died in 1974.

Emily Ryerson (née Borie), 48, First Class Passenger

Ryerson was holidaying in Europe with her husband and three of their five children, when she learned of their oldest son's death in a car crash back in the USA. They boarded the *Titanic* at Cherbourg with their maid, headed for Cooperstown, NY. Although not questioned during the inquiries, she later gave evidence at a lawsuit against the Oceanic Steam Navigation Company (owners of the White Star Line). Her evidence is included here as it was given under oath and, like the inquiry accounts, can be regarded as official evidence. After World War I, she became head of the American Fund for French Wounded and the Society for Fatherless Children in France and received the Croix de Guerre from the French Government. She later accompanied President Hoover on a good-will tour of South America. In 1927, she was remarried to Forsythe Sherfesse, a financial adviser to the Chinese Government. Travelling to the end, Ryerson died of a heart attack in Montevideo, Uruguay, in 1939.

Joseph Scarrott, 33, Able Seaman

Born in Plymouth in 1878, Scarrott lived in Portsmouth from the age of three. He married Annie Till, and the couple had a child who died in infancy. Before joining the *Titanic*, he worked on several White Star Line ships, but transferred from the Castle Line ship *Kildonan Castle*. He later remarried and moved to Southend-on-Sea, where he is said to have worked on the pier. He died in 1938, aged 60.

Frederick Scott, 28, Greaser
Scott joined the *Titanic* at Southampton and was one of 33 greasers employed on the ship. Their job was to ensure all mechanical equipment was properly lubricated.

Edward Smith, 62, Captain
The son of a potter, Smith's first job, at the age of 13, was operating a steam hammer at a steel foundry in Etruria, Stoke-on-Trent, far away from the sea. In 1869, however, he signed up for an apprenticeship on the American-built sailing ship the *Senator Weber*, commanded by his half-brother Joseph Hancock. He joined the White Star Line in 1880, and received his first command in 1887 aboard the *Republic*. Married to Eleanor Pennington in 1887, the couple had a daughter, their only child, in 1898. Smith was captain of the *Majestic* for nine years from 1895 and, as a member of the Royal Naval Reserve, served in the Boer War. He was known as a safe pair of hands, and was entrusted with many of the White Star Line's new ships on their maiden voyages. It wasn't all plain sailing, however. The year before taking command of the *Titanic*, he had two collisions while in command of the *Olympic* and, while leaving Southampton on the *Titanic*, had a close shave with another ship. Smith was exonerated by the British Inquiry, and a statue was erected in his memory in Lichfield in 1914. His body was never recovered.

Mary Smith (née Hughes), 18, First Class Passenger
Lucien and Mary Smith had been married for just eight weeks

and were returning from their honeymoon when they boarded the *Titanic* in Southampton. He was 24, she was just 18. Eight months after the disaster, Smith gave birth to a baby boy, whom she named Lucien P. Smith II after his deceased father. Less than a year later, she married Robert Daniel, another *Titanic* survivor, who was rescued in the same boat as Smith and Mrs Astor.

Henry Stengel, 54, First Class Passenger
The son of a 'pioneering' leather manufacturer, Stengel set up the firm Stengel & Rothschild with Abraham Rothschild in Newark. He and his wife Annie boarded the *Titanic* at Cherbourg. After arriving in New York, she told reporters: 'The nearest thing I've ever known to heaven on earth was meeting my husband again on the deck of the *Carpathia*.' Two years after surviving the *Titanic*, Stengel died of pneumonia – the same illness that would kill his wife 42 years later.

George Symons, 24, Lookout
Born in Weymouth in 1888, Symons had served on ships since the age of 15. His previous post was on board the *Olympic*.

William Ward, 36, Saloon Steward
Ward had had 20 years' experience at sea when he joined the *Titanic* in Southampton. He was one of more than 300 stewards on the ship.

Joseph Wheat, 29, Assistant Second Steward
Born in Rock Ferry, in Merseyside, Wheat joined the *Titanic* in Belfast for the delivery trip to Southampton. In common

with many of the ship's crew, he had previously served on the *Olympic*.

Edward Wheelton, 28/29, Saloon Steward
Born in Liverpool in either 1883 or 1884 (there are conflicting sources), Wheelton was another transfer from the *Olympic*. He claimed to have worked for six years as First Class Steward with the White Star Line.

Ella White (née Holmes), 55, First Class Passenger
A resident of New York, White boarded the ship with her maid and her manservant at Cherbourg. She later explained her living arrangements to the US Inquiry as follows: 'My home really is Briarcliffe Lodge, Briarcliffe Manor, NY. That is my summer house. When I am in New York, I am always here at the Waldorf-Astoria.' By 1942, however, it seems she had forsaken the Waldorf-Astoria in favour of the Plaza, which is where she died.

James Widgery, 37, Bath Steward
Born in Bristol, Widgery boarded the *Titanic* at Southampton. His previous post had been on board the *St Paul*.

Henry Wilde, 39, Chief Officer
Born in 1872, Wilde was an apprentice and then Third Mate on sailing ships until he served on his first steamship in 1895. He joined the White Star Line in 1897, and served on several ships before becoming First Officer on the *Olympic* in 1911. He replaced Murdoch as Chief Officer of the *Titanic* in a reshuffle of the ranks. He married and had six children, but in December 1910 his wife and their newly born twins died

– possibly of scarlet fever. The other four children survived. Wilde had misgivings about the *Titanic* and, before leaving Queenstown, wrote a letter to his sister saying: 'I still don't like this ship... I have a queer feeling about it.' His body was never recovered.

Hugh Woolner, First Class Passenger

Son of the British sculptor Thomas Woolner, Hugh Woolner graduated from Cambridge University in 1888. He joined the London Stock Exchange in 1892, and three years later set up his own brokerage firm, Woolner & Co. Just before his 32nd birthday, he married Mary Simpson, an American woman, and the couple had a daughter soon after. Mary died of a suspected brain aneurysm in 1906. After a series of mishaps, including several court cases, Woolner's company went bankrupt in 1907, and he tried to build a new life for himself in America. In March 1912, his mother died and he had to rush home for her funeral, booking his return journey on the *Titanic*. After surviving the sinking, he was married a few months later to another Mary, the daughter of fellow stockbroker Luke Ionides, with whom he would go on to have six children. Woolner died of respiratory failure in 1925 at a relative's home in Budapest, aged 58.